THE JEWISH PEOPLE

HISTORY • RELIGION • LITERATURE

THE JEWISH PEOPLE

HISTORY • RELIGION • LITERATURE

Advisory Editor
Jacob B. Agus

Editorial Board
Louis Jacob
Jacob Petuchowski
Seymour Siegel

THE JEWISH PEOPLE

HISTORY • RELIGION • LITERATURE

THE JEWISH PEOPLE

HISTORY • RELIGION • LITERATURE

PHARISAIC JUDAISM
IN TRANSITION

BEN ZION BOKSER

ARNO PRESS
A New York Times Company
NEW YORK • 1973

Reprint Edition 1973 by Arno Press Inc.

Reprinted from a copy in
  The University of Illinois Library

THE JEWISH PEOPLE: History, Religion, Literature
ISBN for complete set: 0-405-05250-2
See last pages of this volume for titles.

Manufactured in the United States of America

———◆———

Library of Congress Cataloging in Publication Data

Bokser, Ben Zion, 1907-
    Pharisaic Judaism in transition.

    (The Jewish people: history, religion, literature)
    Reprint of the ed. published by Bloch Pub. Co.,
New York.
    Thesis—Columbia University, 1935.
    Bibliography: p.
    1. Eliezer ben Hyracanus. 2. Judaism—History—
Talmudic period. 3. Pharisees. I. Title.
II. Series.
BM755.E55B6 1973   296.6'1'0924 [B]
ISBN 0-405-05255-3   73-2189

PHARISAIC JUDAISM IN TRANSITION

R. Eliezer the Great and Jewish Reconstruction After the War with Rome

By

BEN ZION BOKSER, Ph.D.

Submitted in partial fulfillment of the requirements for the degree of Doctor of Philosophy, in the Faculty of Political Science, Columbia University

NEW YORK
BLOCH PUBLISHING COMPANY
1 9 3 5

Printed in the United States of America

Posy-Shoulson Press, 19 W. 21st St., New York, N. Y.

VITA

The author of this dissertation was born on July 4, 1907, at Luboml, in Poland. He came to this country in August, 1920. He has received his education at the Talmudical Academy High School, the College of the City of New York (B. A., 1928), and Columbia University (M. A., 1930). In 1931 he was ordained Rabbi, *with distinction,* at the Jewish Theological Seminary of America. He is a member of *Phi Beta Kappa,* Gamma Chapter

FOREWORD

THE interrelations between social and religious history occupy a prominent place in recent discussions on the history of religion. In the field of Judaism, however, little progress has been made since the publication of Max Weber's stimulating studies on the sociology of the Old Testament religion. The fundamental transformations brought about by the Pharisaic and talmudic reformulations of the ancient Israelitic creed and ritual have been the subject of still fewer searching sociological analyses.

Dr. Bokser's investigation into the social motivations of the teachings of Rabbi Eliezer ben Hyrcanus appears, therefore, as a welcome contribution to the study of post-Biblical Judaism. Rabbi Eliezer's historical position at the crossroads of Pharisaism after the second fall of Jerusalem; his unflinching adherence to the achievements of the Pharisaic evolution up to his own time; his equally staunch resistance to all innovations thereafter; the reason for this conservative attitude which was largely dictated by his status as landowner and aristocrat—are all minutely outlined here on the basis of the vast and scattered source material. After a careful analysis of the numerous utterances of the "great" rabbi—many of them incidental and not a few dubious—as well as the captivating legends which loving folk imagination had spun around the tragic personality of this upright, unbending defender of orthodoxy, the author has succeeded in reconstructing the major phases of his unusual career and in reinterpreting his theological, social and legal doctrines. One may sometimes disagree with Dr. Bokser's explanation of a particular statement through R. Eliezer's social biases, where personal elements, temporary moods or other factors of an "accidental" nature appear mainly responsible. Here and there one may differ in the evaluation of the underlying, very complex trends themselves. But one will find with gratification that on the whole the author has been reticent in the use of generalizations and judicious in his decisions between conflicting alternatives.

Apart from the novel general approach, this study offers a number of stimulating detailed observations pertaining to the peculiar differences between the dominant majority of the Jewish scholars of that day and the vanishing minority as represented by Rabbi Eliezer. Especially the thought-provoking discussion of the legal methods employed by Rabbi Eliezer and his colleagues deserves further monographic treatment. It is to be hoped that the author will pursue this line of research also with respect to the other tannaitic as well as amoraic schools of jurisprudence.

SALO W. BARON

PREFACE

THE value of the critical study of a figure like R. Eliezer, in relation to his social milieu, was originally pointed out to me by my teacher, Professor Louis Finkelstein, of the Jewish Theological Seminary. The actual preparation of the work I carried through under the immediate supervision of Professor Salo W. Baron, of Columbia University. To Professor Baron and to Professor Louis Ginzberg of the Seminary, I acknowledge my great indebtedness for the assistance which they have given me. Professor Baron suggested the correlation of the developments in Pharisaic Judaism with Hellenistic religion generally and helped me with the organization of the material and the interpretation of both sources and events. Professor Ginzberg, under whom I studied Talmudic literature and times at the Seminary, gave of his valuable time to read the manuscript and, out of his incomparable knowledge, made numerous suggestions, leading me in many instances to a revision in the text. Many valuable suggestions were also offered me by Professor Alexander Marx and Professor Louis Finkelstein, of the Seminary. Dr. Michael Higger was ever ready to discuss with me the many complicated problems of Talmudic research. To Rabbis Irwin Hyman, Gershon Levi, Morris Adler, Max Gelb, and to Mr. Emanuel Polack, Miss Vera Peters, and other friends, I am deeply grateful for technical assistance. These expressions of indebtedness in no way involve a transfer of responsibility.

BEN ZION BOKSER

TABLE OF CONTENTS

Chapter VI

Chapter I

THE PHARISAIC SOLUTION

The conclusion of the disastrous war with Rome in 70 C.E. proved as momentous for the development of the Jewish religion as it was for the future of the Jewish people. For it was as a result of this war that Pharisaism, in its more progressive manifestations, was finally able to achieve complete mastery over Jewish life. In a certain sense this was inevitable. Of all the 'philosophies' that had been at play in Jewish life, Pharisaism alone had survival value amidst the new conditions which that disaster had called into being.

In addition to Sadduceeism, Parisaism, and Essenism, Palestine before the war also saw the development of zealotism and Christianity. Zealotism with its policy of armed opposition to Rome had become discredited by the tragic conclusion of the war. Certainly the remnant of Jews surviving the war could not find in zealotism a program with which to begin the reconstruction of the sadly shaken Jewish national life. It is quite obvious that Christianity could not offer such a program either. The Jews had been trained to hope that the coming of the Messiah would usher in for them a period of national glory, a golden age of blessedness and peace. They could not see a realization of that hope in the career of one who was crucified by the Romans and after whose coming they had reached the very nadir of national humiliation. Moreover, Christianity, certainly in its Hellenistic representations, had by this time proceeded a long way toward detachment from its Jewish base; it had rejected the Law and repudiated Jewish nationalism. Even the Judeo-Christian community deserted the nation in the hour of crisis, fleeing at the outbreak of the war to the safe retreat of Pella, beyond

1

the Jordan. Such a "Judaism" might have appealed to many of the proselytes and semi-proselytes whom it offered the moral elements of Judaism without the austere demands of the Law and the unwelcome obligations of Jewish nationalism. Couched in the theology of Paul, it could appeal to pagans who knew the savior gods of the mystery religions. It could not, however, have any profound appeal for the great masses of Jews of native stock. They had been taught to regard the Law not as a burden, but as a privilege, a mark of God's favor to Israel. They undoubtedly resented above all the great slur to the nationhood of Israel which, in the face of the contemporary challenge, assumed for them even more precious significance. They could not but find the theology of Paul strange and essentially inharmonious with the monotheism which they had learnt to accept.

It is also clear that they could not look for salvation through Essenism. In its austere discipline of life, its communism of property, its general repudiation of wedlock, the confinement of its membership to men, and the limitations of the economic activity of its adherents to handicrafts, Essenism furnished a technique for renouncing the world. Such a 'philosophy' might have appealed to the few, but the great need of the hour for the masses was not for a technique whereby the world might be renounced but for a techniue whereby it might be faced, mastered, and overcome.

Nor did Sadduceeism have much to offer. At a time when men craved for nearness to God, the Sadducees denied the existence of mediating forces, thereby making God remote and inaccessible. They denied the resurrection of the dead and retribution in the hereafter, which, in the face of a present so dark, unhappy and full of injustice, could not but have destroyed for many all meaning and purpose in life. Furthermore, the Sadducees had placed the emphasis of their system of piety on the Temple services, and these were now discontinued.

Sadduceeism also suffered because of its social orientation. Identified throughout its history with the attitude of the ruling classes, the wealthy landowners, the nobility, the high priestly families, it was always opposed by the masses of the people. This opposition could only have become more acute as a result of the war. For the war was more than a rebellion against the political tyranny of Rome; it was also a social upheaval on the part of the hard pressed peasantry, the impoverished proletariat and the discontented lower rank members of the priesthood against the ruling classes, both lay and sacerdotal. Finally, the very dislocation of Jewish life brought about by the war called for far-reaching adjustments in law and custom. This certainly could not have been accomplished through the Sadducees, the champions of a rigid and literal adherence to the ancient Law and the enemies of change.

Pharisaism, on the other hand, was eminently suited to satisfy all these needs of the hour. Pharisaic Judaism had long been moving away from the national unit and the territorial state in the direction of individualism and universalism—the only bases on which a reconstruction of Jewish life was now possible. The God of the Pharisees, conceived of in the most exalted and universal terms, could guide Israel everywhere, in Palestine and out of it. The Pharisaic doctrine of providence held out the comforting assurance that in spite of the national disaster, God was still master of events, and that He would in the end move all things for Israel's ultimate good. Furthermore, the Pharisees also admitted to their conceptions of God the popular notions of an extensive angelology, which helped to make God near and accessible. Included in this angelology were also the forces of evil which tended to absolve God of some of the evil and tragedy in the world, so recently experienced to the full by the Jewish people. Pharisaic eschatology, too, with its beliefs in retribution after death, the Messianic age at the end of time, the world judgment and the resurrection of the dead, offered a very real compensation for the contemporary unhappiness and injustice.

Moreover, the loss of political autonomy and the destruction of the Temple broke no essential links in Judaism, as the Pharisees conceived it. They had developed, in addition to their theology, a ritual of personal observances, such as prayer with its institution of the synagogue, the Sabbath and the Holidays, which alone constituted for them a criterion of Jewishness. Accepting these, even a born pagan could be considered a good Jew, and the successes actually achieved by Jewish propaganda among the pagans, as well as the flourishing state of the Jewish communities scattered throughout the far-flung diaspora, testified to the adequacy of a Jewish life based on a piety of belief and observance. Indeed, an important sector of Pharisaism, the Damascan sect, had repudiated the Temple altogether, because of its domination by the Sadducean priesthood. The greater number of the Pharisees retained in their conception of Jewish piety a place for the Temple with its cult of sacrifices, because it was ordained in the Torah, and it served as a useful symbol of Jewish unity and solidarity throughout the world. But their emphasis on personal observance moved them to modify the Temple service itself, so as to restrict the sphere of priestly supremacy and increase the extent of lay participation.

Pharisaism was, of course, also helped by its social orientation. Identified with the interests and aspirations of the urban elements, the middle and lower classes, the Pharisees had always enjoyed the confidence of the great masses of the people. It is true that, because of their persistent pacifism, they seem to have lost this popular confidence at the outbreak of the war. Yet the disastrous conclusion of the war fully vindicated their position. Finally, the Pharisees were at an advantage because, through the oral law, they had worked out a technique of reconciling development and change with loyalty to tradition, which enabled them to undertake the far reaching adjustments of Jewish life which the new conditions demanded.

Pharisaism was also placed in a more favorable position because the followers of the competing 'philosopies' had, in many instances, been eliminated by the events of the war. The zealots, who bore the brunt of most of the fighting in the war, were largely exterminated by the Romans. We have already mentioned that the Nazarene community, detached from the national cause, withdrew to Pella beyond the Jordan, even before the sack of Jerusalem. Many of the Essenes seem to have joined the zealots in the course of the war, suffering with them the same fate. The Sadducees, the lay and sacerdotal aristocracy, had been the principal targets of zealot fury, and many of them lost their lives as a result. What was left of them, it would seem, migrated northward and settled, principally in Lydda, content to live their own life, without offering any serious competition to the Pharisees for national leadership.

But before Pharisaism could actually achieve complete ascendency in Jewish life, it had to go through some very important adjustments. If it was to become an adequate guide to Jewish practice, it had to commit itself on many questions of theology and ritual and social doctrine upon which the Pharisaic teachers in the past had not decided. The destruction of the Temple called for a reorganization of Jewish piety in which the Temple with its sacrificial cult had been an integral factor. Thus, the old ritual for initiating a proselyte to Judaism, still a living issue at the time, called for the offering of a sacrifice, which was now impossible. Jerusalem, as the seat of the Temple and the center of Jewish life, enjoyed certain privileges as compared with the other cities of Palestine, but Jerusalem was now in ruins and the center of Jewish life had shifted to Jabneh. Finally, Pharisaism had to compose its own differences. For it had long been divided into two hostile factions—the conservative Shammaites and the progressive Hillelites. The Shammaites had always been in the minority, but individuals had been permitted full freedom to follow the rulings of either school, with the result that the views of the Pharisees existed in many instances in conflicting traditions. It was clear to the leaders that they could not secure the desired national following, unless they came before the people with a uniform position. To achieve this, they were finally forced to repudiate the Shammaites altogether, declaring the Hillelites alone as authoritative.

This process of adjustment was hampered for a time by the opposition wihch developed against it on the part of one of the Pharisaic leaders, R. Eliezer b. Hyrcanus, also known as R. Eliezer the Great. A member of the upper class, a landed aristocrat, he was rigidly conservative in his conception of Jewish piety, social doctrine, and the champion of a static jurisprudence. R. Eliezer's colleagues fought hard to clarify and defend their views. But R. Eliezer was no less zealous in justifying his opposition. As a great scholar and preserver of traditions, his voice carried great weight. In the face of the national emergency, however, his colleagues were finally forced to repudiate him as they had repudiated the conservative Shammaites. His views were to be studied for their academic value, but as far as practice was concerned, the position of the majority alone was to be authoritative. But R. Eliezer violated this arrangement and publicity sought to defy the majority. To break the impasse his colleagues were in the end moved to a most drastic measure: they excommunicated him. The present work is an effort to reconstruct this clash of views between R. Eliezer and his colleagues, the most decisive contest, no doubt, in the transition of Pharisaic Judaism from the position of a sect, to that of the authoritative world outlook of catholic Israel.

II

Many competent scholars, including Graetz, Weiss, Halevy, Jawitz, Bacher and Moore[1] have written on this period. But though their discussions are immensely valuable for purposes of orienta-

---

1. H. Graetz, *Geschichte der Juden von den aeltesten Zeiten bis auf die Gegenwart*, in 11 volumes, Leipzig 1891-1909, volume IV dealing with our period; I. H. Weiss, *Dor Dor v' Dorshav* (A history of the Orol Law), in 5 volumes, new ed., N. Y. and Berlin 1924, volume II dealing with our period; I. Halevy, *Dorot ha-Rishonim* (A literary history of Israel from the Maccabean through the Geonic periods), Pressburg—Frankfort o. M. 1898-1906, in 3 parts, of which 4 volumes have been published, volume Ie dealing with our period; Z. W. Jawitz, *Sefer Toldot Yisrael* (A history of the Jews) in 9 volumes, Vilna-Cracow 1898-1907, vol. VI dealing wiht our period; W. Bacher, *Die Agada der Tannaiten*, in 2 volumes, volume I dealing specifically with R. Eliezer and his contemporaries, Strassburg 1903; G. F. Moore, *Judaism in the First Centuries of the Christian Era*, in 3 volumes, Cambridge 1927-1930.

tion, they by no means cover the subject. Graetz, Weiss, Halevy and Jawitz mark a significant advance over their predecessors in reckoning with the time factor in the development of the Law. But they do not relate adequately this development of the Law with the facts of social and economic stratification, a most important element, indeed, as the researches of Ginzberg [2] have well demonstrated. Moreover, their works are of a much more extensive scope and their discussions of our more limited problem suffer because of inevitable omissions. The work of Halevy is, in addition, handicapped by a somewhat undisciplined arrangement and a tendency to favor traditional interpretations. Bacher's work, while valuable in individual explanations, omits all halakic material; nor is his collection of the Agada by any means complete. The views of the Tannaim as they are presented in Bacher, therefore, assume a rather distorted form. Moore's aim was to present the institutions of first century Judaism in a systematized form, and he has, indeed, produced a monumental work. But in the very process of systematization, the sense of change, the fact of the individual differences between the Tannaim has in many instances been lost; Judaism as it is presented in Moore tends to appear as an absolute, a crystallized fact, which it certainly was not. There is still need for a presentation that will do justice to the Law as a changing phenomenon, that will deal with the impact of social and economic forces on the Law, and that will indicate the individual differences between the Tannaim in their respective attitudes toward the Law. The present study will try to reckon with all these facts.

Any study of our subject meets with a handicap because of the nature of the only primary sources available: the scattered discussions of Talmudic literature. The tannaitic material (the Mishnah, Tosefta, the tannaitic Midrashim, and the baraitot quoted in the Talmud) is most reliable. Even here, however, there is the problem of doubtful traditions. An opinion attributed to one scholar

---

2. *Mekomah shel ha-Halakah b'Hokmat Yisrael* (The Place of the Halakah in Jewish Scholarship), Jerusalem 1930.

in one source will very often be attributed to another scholar in a different source. In our immediate case there is an additional difficulty in the fact that R. Eliezer b. Hyrcanus, usually written "R. Eliezer" or abbreviated 'R.E.' (ר"א) has often been confused with R. Eliezer b. Jacob or with R. Elazar b. Azariah.

The confusion in names may in many instances be resolved by considering the other scholars taking part in the discussion. Thus, if one of the parties to the discussion is R. Joshua, it may well be assumed that the other is R. Eliezer, because these two scholars were accustomed to engage in such discussions. Similarly, if one of the scholars in the discussion is not a contemporary of R. Eliezer, the other cannot be our R. Eliezer. This is, however, not always reliabel, because the discussions were later rdacted by editors who did not hesitate, in many instances, to place the views of scholars of different generations in immediate juxtoposition. Another criterion in evaluating the accuracy of conflicting traditions, is a knowledge of the general position of the scholars in the halakah. In employing this criterion one must, of course, guard himself against the danger of reasoning in a circle. But where the original positions are established on the basis of uncontested and accurate traditions, they may be used with a large measure ot success. There are, nevertheless, instances where none of these expedients prove helpful; such cases must be left as purely problematic.

Greater difficulties are presented by the later strata of Rabbinic tradition, the Palestirian and Babylonian Talmudim. The material quoted in these sources is often crucial for the construction of a proper biography or the theological and social outlooks of the scholars of our period. But in addition to the fact of conflicting traditions, we have here also the problem of later amplifications. The biographical notes recorded in the Talmud are in many instances clearly exaggerated tales, such as all peoples weave about their great heroes. They may be based on some kernel of fact, but it is not always easy to distinguish between the factual and the legendary. Our problem is even more serious in the case of the later haggadic Midrashim which are even further removed from the actual events of our period. Such material is obviously a legitimate source for our work; great caution must, however, be exercised in using it.

Special problems are presented by the *Pirke d' R. Eliezer*, the *Additions to the Seder Eliahu Zuta*, and the *Midrash Mishle*. The *Pirke d'R Eliezer*, a volume of haggadic comments to Genesis, part of Exodus, and a few sentences to Numbers, describing the workings of God in creation and in the early history of Israel, has traditionally been ascribed to the authorship of our R. Eliezer. This is, however, clearly impossible since the book quotes some forty-five authorities who lived after R. Eliezer, and contains allusions to the Moslem empire. The ascription very likely arose at a later time because the introductory comment to the work is a statement by R. Eliezer. It contains, however, a number of statements which are specifically attributed to R. Eliezer. These may be based on some older sources, and there is no reason to regard them as less genuine than comments by R. Eliezer in other Midrashim of the same period.

The *Additions to the Seder Eliahu Zuta* or *Pseudo-Seder Eliahu Zuta* quotes a number of very elaborate conversations between R. Eliezer and his pupils dealing particularly with the hereafter. In their present form they cannot all be genuine. They clearly betray much later influences. Ginzberg has, however, shown that the *Additions* is an integral part of the *Seder Eliahu*. There is, consequently, no reason for applying to them a criterion other than the one applied to other Midrashim of the same age. While a later hand has apparently tampered with them, they may, nevertheless, be based on genuine comments by R. Eliezer. They should be utilized only with the greatest caution, but there is certainly no justification for discarding them.

The *Midrash Mishle* quotes six discussions between R. Eliezer and R. Joshua in which the former consults the latter for an elucidation of some Biblical verse. The latter, in replying, addresses R. Eliezer as "my son." This is clearly impossible since the two men were approximately of the same age, and R. Joshua was generally the one who deferred to R. Eliezer; not *vice versa*. Clearly apocryphal in form, these discussions may nevertheless presuppose genuine elements. This is certainly possible in the case of the independent expressions by R. Eliezer which are likewise quoted in this Midrash. The significant fact is that by and large these expressions, not only in the *Midrash Mishle* but also in the *Pirke d' R. Eliezer* and the *Additions to the Seder Eliahu Zuta,* are fully consistent with R. Eliezer's general positions in the halakah. Accepting them en masse would, of course, be no more reasonable than rejecting them. These statements should be judged on their individual merits. But they certainly have a place in any study on the life and work of R. Eliezer.[3]

Our study will begin with a biography of R. Eliezer, which will be followed by two discussions, one reviewing the clash between R. Eliezer and his colleagues in the field of Jewish piety, and the other, in the filed of social doctrine. Thereafter will be presented a formal analysis of the systems of jurisjrudence as employed by R. Eliezer and his colleagues. The concluding chapter will evaluate R. Eliezer's place in the history of Jewish tradition.

---

3. *Pirke d' R. Eliezer* and *Midrash Mishle* were probably compiled in the eighth century, and the *Seder Eliahu* in the tenth. But such accepted Midrashim as *Deuteronomy Rabba and Numbers Rabba* were not compiled until the tenth and twelfth centuries respectively. The compilers were, of course, far removed from the tannaitic period but they generally drew on older sources, although they may at times have allowed themselves certain liberties with their texts. Cf. Theodor's survey of Midrashic literature, *J. E. s. v. "Midrash Haggadah;"* Zunz, *Gottesdienstliche Vortraege,* Berlin 1832, pp. 271-278; Weiss, *Dor,* III, pp. 270-294; Friedlander, introduction to his translation of the *Pirke d' R. Eliezer,* London 1916; B. Z. Halper, "Recent Judaica and Hebraica", *JQR,* N. S., VIII 1917-1918, pp. 477-483; Friedmann, introduction to his edition of the *Pseudo Seder Eliahu Zuta,* Vienna 1904; Ginzberg, *Genizah Studies,* I, N. Y. 1928, pp. 188-191; Kadushin, *The Theology of the Seder Eliahu,* N Y. 1932, p. 13ff; Buber, introduction to his edition of *Midrash Mishle,* Vilna 1893; Bacher,*Tannaiten,* I, pp. 193f. Cf. also Gaster, "Araber und Samaritaner," *MG WJ,* LXXVII 1933, p. 305, who places the compilation of the *Pirke d' R. Eliezer* as early as the second century.

Chapter II

R. ELIEZER THE MAN

A halo of legend surrounds the early life of R. Eliezer b. Hyrcanus. Until the age of 22, he is supposed to have lived on his father's estate in total ignorance. One day, while plowing in the field, he met with an accident, which he regarded as ominous. He felt that he should no longer be satisfied with his present condition, and at once there was born in him a great longing for the wider possibilities of a more cultured life. Against the protests of his family he finally made his way to Jerusalem, where he joined the academy of R. Johanan b. Zakkai. His life as a student was beset with many difficulties—he was without means, a stranger in a large city. But Johanan soon learned of his plight and offered both help and friendship. Encouraged by his master, helped by an indomitable will and a remarkable memory, he made rapid strides in his studies. His father Hyrcanus was still opposed to his stay at Jerusalem, and finally, losing patience, decided to disinherit him. To effect his purpose he came before the judicial court of Johanan b. Zakkai; but it so happened that Eliezer was at that very time delivering a learned discourse before a very distinguished audience. The father was, of course, pleasantly surprised, and changed his mind; in fact, he now sought to will his entire property to Eliezer. But the latter refused to take any undue advantage of his brothers and contented himself with a proportionate share. Father and son, completely reconciled, parted again, the former returning to his estate and the latter staying on at the academy to continue with his studies.[1]

---

1. A. R. N. 6, II A. R. N. 13; Gen. R. ed. Theodor 41:1; P. R. E.

11

As it stands, this story cannot be regarded as fact; it has every earmark of legend.[2] But it probably contains some truth which we may accept—that Eliezer came from a family of landowners, that he did not become a professional scholar until of mature age, and that he began his scholarship under the tutelage of the great scholar R. Johanan b. Zakkai. Of Eliezer's distinguished career as a student we also have the testimony of R. Johanan himself. Because of his receptive and retentive mind R. Johanan described him as "a cemented cistern that does not lose a drop." There is a tradition that R. Johanan on one occasion even went to the extent of proclaiming him greater than all the other scholars in Israel combined.[3] Nor was his education one-sided. He enjoyed a reputation among his contemporaries as a great linguist,[4] and judging by some of his exegetical remarks on Scripture, he was certainly familiar with Greek.[5] He was likewise informed on subjects of a scientific

---

1, 2. In Tan. ed. Buber, Lek Leka 10 Eliezer is made to flee to Jerusalem because of some difficulties with the Roman officials who had bestowed upon his father an "honorary" office. Cf. Gaster, *Exempla of the Rabbis,* 170. But this is impossible. Compulsory "honorary" offices were not bestowed on Jews except under the emperors Septimus Severus and Caracalla (3rd century). See Juster, *Les Juifs dans l'empire romain,* Paris 1914, II,p. 243 and note 4, and cf. A. Buechler, *Political and Social Leaders of the Jewish Community of Sepphoris,* Oxford 1909, p. 40 note 3. According to the accounts in P. R. E. and II A. R. N., Eliezer was 28 years of age when he joined R. Johanan in Jerusalem. Cf. also "Maaseh m' de R. Eliezer b. Hyracnus," a collection of seven different versions of the early life of R. Eliezer, by H. M. Horowitz in *Bet Eked ha-Agadot,* Frankfort o. M. 1881, I, pp. 1-16. These include the primary sources already referred to, as well as the modified accounts as they occur in post-Talmudic sources.

2. That R. Eliezer was in complete ignorance before he came to Jerusalem is specifically contradicted in Gen. R. 1:15 where another tradition is reported according to which he exhibited much scholarly ingenuity as a child.

3. Ab. 2:8; A. R. N. 14.

4. San. 17a.

5. Thus he translates נבכי ים (Job 38, 16) to קלומין דימא which S. Krauss, *Griechische und lateinische Lehnwoerter im Talmud,*

nature: his explanation of rain as the transformed mists arising
from the sea, is essentially in accordance with the facts, and he was
aware that Alexandrian medicine had perfected a cure for certain
forms of impotence.[6]

Eliezer was deeply attached to his master R. Johanan. He betrays his master's influence in his religious practices.[7] In spite of
his militant nationalism,[8] he remained loyal to his master during the Roman war, when the latter persisted in his pacifism. And
when Rabban Johanan, on his own initiative, sought negotiations
with the Roman command, Eliezer, in cooperation with his colleague,
Joshua, smuggled him in a coffin, out of the besieged city
into the camp of Vespasian.[9] He, together with his other colleagues,
joined Johannan in Jabneh, where the latter received the permission of Vespasian to reopen his academy, and followed him to Berur
Hayil when the leadership of the Jabneh Academy passed to Rabban
Gamaliel. [10]

The Talmud does not record very much of R. Eliezer's personal
life. From a number of sources it would appear that he was of
levitical descent, although there is no record of his having served

---

Midrash und Targum, Berlin 1899, II, p. 545 relates to the Greek *Kli-
tus.* Cf. Gen. R. ed. Theodor p. 34 and editor's note. Similarly he ren-
ders the word for "fourfold" as   טטראגנו (Mid. Tehil. Ps. 78:15),
which is the Greek *tetraganon.* Cf. Krauss, *op. cit.,* p. 260.

6. See below, p. 40; M. Jeb. 8:4; Jeb. 80a. Cf. Krauss, *Talmudische Archaeologie,* Leipzig 1910, I, p. 247.

7. See below, p. 71.

8. See below, p. 113.

9. Git. 56a; A. R. N. 4; Lam. R. 1:32. According to an ancient
custom, dead bodies were not to be disposed of within the city limits
of Jerusalem, probably a precaution against defiling the holy city with
ritual uncleanliness. See A. Buechler, "La purete levitique Jerusalem" *REJ,* LXIII 1912, pp. 30-40. It is interesting to note that when
Alexandra and her son Aristobulus sought to flee from Jerusalem
to Cleopatra they also used the stratagem of the coffin (Jos. *Ant.*
15,3,2).

10. Ecc. R. 7:15; Cf. A. R. N. 14; See W. Bacher, "Johanan ben
Zakkai," in *J. E.* VII, p. 215, and cf. S. Krauss, "Die Versammlung-

in the sanctuary.[11] According to one source, he was already married when he joined Johanan's academy in Jerusalem. [12] Later he married Imma Shalom, the cultured sister of Gamaliel II.[13] A num-

---

staetten der Talmudgelerten," in *Festschrift Israel Lewy,* 1911, p. 24.

11. Thus, tradition traces his descent to Moses, the Levite. P. R. K., p. 70; Tan. Buber, Hukkath 24; Nu. R. 19:4. Again, his son Hyrcanus received the levitical tithe (j Sota III, 19a). It is true that priests also received this tithe during our period (Jos. *Vita* 12, 15; Hul. 131b; Ket. 26a; Jeb. 86a,b). R. Eliezer, however, cannot have been a priest, since he helped carry R. Johanan B. Zakkai out of the besieged capital in a coffin. A later development of the law pemitted priests to participate in the burial ceremonies of a Nasi (j Ber. III, 6a). It is doubtful, however, whether this dispensation was already established during our period; but even if it was, R. Johanan was then the Ab Bet Din, not the Nasi (Mid. Tann. on Deut. 26:13). It is furthermore unlikely that R. Eliezer was a priest, bcause he married his minor niece (j Jeb. XIII, 13c. Cf. A. R. N. 16), when it was he who prohibited a priest's marriage with a minor girl (Jeb. 61b). Cf. below, p. 104.

That we have no reference to his serving in the Temple is not unusual. There might have been some glory attached to serving in the sanctuary as a priest, but it was principally the revenues that compensated for serving as a levite—the services of the levites in themselves, such as singing in the Temple choruses and keeping the doors, were distinctly of a subordinate nature; in fact, the levites were not even recognized as full-fledged Temple ministers (Jos. *Ant.* 20, 9, 6 and cf. Graetz "Eine Strafmassregel gegen die Leviten", *MGWJ,* XXXV 1886, pp. 100-108). As a rich man R. Eliezer did not need such compensation. Furthermore, R. Eliezer came from a rural family and as such was out of touch with the Temple service, which was largely confined to those priestly and levitical families that lived in Jerusalem. Thus, Phanias b. Samuel, a rural priest who was elevated to the high priesthood during the revolution, had apparently never taken part in the Temple service and was totally ignorant of the duties of his office (Jos., *Wars* 4, 3, 8). It is significant that R. Eliezer generally spoke of the levites in very complimentary terms and accorded them a place of great importance in Jewish society.

12. A. R. N. 6. But this is specifically contradicated in the account in *Pirke d' R. Eliezer.*

13. Shab. 116a; B. M. 59b; Er. 63a. It is not likely that he

ber of children came to him by his marriage with Imma Shalom.
They were all famed for their physical beauty,[14] but none of them
seem to have shown any great aptitude for scholarship. Only one
of them, Hyrcanus, is occasionally mentioned by name in the
Talmud,[15] and even he, according to one account,[16] carried on his
studies only at the insistence of his father who threatened to disinherit him. Later in life, after much urging by his mother, R.
Eliezer married his minor niece also, but he did not live with her
until she reached puberty.[17] We have the testimony of Imma Shalom
herself describing the extreme chastity of his marital life.[18]

R. Eliezer was a man of great wealth, a slave owner and a
landed proprietor. His holdings included plantations of flax, vine,
date, palm, and olive trees. He made his home in Lydda, a loca-

---

married Imma Shalom before joining R. Johanan's academy in Jerusalem. R. Simeon b. Gamaliel I would not have given his daughter in
marriage to an ignorant person. Moreover, R. Eliezer's going to his
father-in-law's home, as related in A. R. N., suggests that the two
families were neighbors; this cannot be since R. Simeon did not live
in Galilee. For Imma Shalom's learning, cf. Shab. 116a which relates how she and her brother Gamaliel exposed the corrupt practice
of a sectarian judge who had made pretensions to honesty and impartiality. Cf. Halevi, *Dorot*, Ie, p. 131, Buechler, *The Economic Conditions of Judea After the Destruction of the Second Temple*, p. 37.
Imma Shalom also helped her husband in his rabbinical work (Nidda
48b).

14. Ned. 20a.

15. Men. 35a; San. 68a; j Sota III, 19a.

16. Shab. 127b; P. S. E. Z., p. 6f. These texts speak of Hyrcanus
as the son of a rich landowner and a scholar, whose name is, however, not mentioned. In *Sheiltot* on Exodus, section 40, where the
same incident is quoted, the name of the father is expressly mentioned as R. Eliezer. Cf. Buechler, *op. cit.*, p. 37 and note 1, p. 45.

17. j Jeb. XIII, 13c; A. R. N. 16. Imma Shalom must have
been alive when he married his niece, since she survived his death
(San. 68a). Polygamy was considered permissible among the Pharisees. See below, p.

18. Ned. 20b. Cf. A. Buechler, *Types of Palestinian Piety*, London
1922, p. 43. Cf. also Nidda 13a and Buechler, *op. cit.*, p. 47f, note 2.

tion that seems to have been particularly popular with the emigré aristocracy, both lay and sacerdotal, who had fled from the scene of war.[19]

During the Anti-Christian persecutions in Palestine, R. Eliezer was suspected of the heresy and brought before the Roman court for trial. He was released, so the story relates, when, upon being rebuked by the judge that as a great man he should not have engaged in "idle things," he replied, "the Judge is right." R. Eliezer meant that God was just in having inflicted the trial on him, but the judge understood it as a denial of all connection with Christianity. That he should have been suspected of heresy, grieved him sorely, but he finally came to regard it as a merited punishment when it was recalled to him that he had at one time listened with pleasure to a halakah transmitted to him in the name of Jesus by a secretary at Sepphoris. A man, R. Eliezer generalized from this experience, should keep away not only from that which is unbecoming, but even from that which only appears so.[20]

---

19. San. 68a, 101a, R.H. 31b; Best 5a b; Tos. M. Sh. 5:16 p. (96); Ber. 16b; j Ber. II, 5b; Sem. 1:10; Git. 38b; Shab. 127b; P. S. E. Z. p. 6f; *Sheiltot*, section 40. Cf. Buechler, *Die Priester und der Cultus*, Vienna 1895, p. 26ff. From the description in the Talmud. it would seem that the house in which he lived was built in Greek style and consisted of at least an upper chamber, a dining room, and a third room. Cf. Buechler, *Economic Conditions*, p. 27.

20. A. Z. 16b; Tos. Hul 2:24 (p. 503); Ecc. R. 1:24. Eusebius, *Ecclesiastical History*, III, 32, refers to a persecution of Christians that took place in Palestine during the reign of Trajan, in 109 C. E. S. Zeitlin, "Jesus in the early Tannaitic Literature," in *Chajes Memorial Volume*, Vienna 1933, p. 297, following R. T. Herford, *Christianity in Talmud and Midrash*, London 1903, p. 141f, argues that the arrest and trial of R. Eliezer took place during this persecution. The recollection of R. Eliezer was stimulated by his conversation with R. Akiba, quoted in the Talmud as follows: R. Akiba spoke to R. Eliezer, "Will you permit me to make a statement on the basis of what you taught me (ממה שלמדתני)? He (R. Eliezer) said to him (R. Akiba): "Speak". R. Akiba said to R. Eliezer: "Perhaps some heretical sentiment was expressed in your presence and you enjoyed it?" Replied R. Eliezer, "Akiba, you have recalled it to me."

There are a number of passages in the Talmud which certain scholars have interpreted as proving that R. Eliezer was actually sympathetic to Christianity, and that the suspicions which led to his arrest were, therefore, well founded. Thus, some[21] see a reference to Jesus in the "Ben Stada" because of whose practice in scratching certain magic spells on his skin, R. Eliezer tried to extend the prohibition of writing on the Sabbath to include the scratching of skin marks as well.[22] Even if this identification were correct, it would be inconclusive as to R. Eliezer's sympathies for Christianity. What we know of the career of Jesus does not, however, harmonize with Ben Stada whom the Rabbis describe as a "fool," and who is supposed to have introduced certain magic practices from Egypt.[23]

This does not mean as Toettermann, *R. Eliezer b. Hyrcanus sive de vi qua doctrina Christiana primis seculis illustrissimos quosdam Judaeorum attraxit,* Leipzig 1877, p. 23f, explains, that R. Eliezer's dealings with the Christians had become common knowledge. Had that been the case, he would not have needed R. Akiba to remind him of it. R. Akiba made his suggestion on the basis of the well known principle of talio, i.e., that God's penalty is in accordance with man's sin, without having any specific incident in mind. As to the identity of the sectary, the Talmud gives his name as *Jacob ish-Kefar-Sekanya.* We also meet the same Jacob, a *min,* in A. Z. 27b, Tos. Hul. 2:22, 23 (P. 503), j A. Z. II, 40d, 41a, where he tried to cure a nephew of R. Ishmael, who had been bitten by a serpent. R. Ishmael did not permit it. Jacob, active at the time of R. Ishmael, cannot have been a direct disciple of Jesus. When he remarks כך למדני ישו "Thus Jesus taught me", he simply means that he is quoting a current Christian tradition, as is indeed the explicit reading in the Tosefta. Cf. S. Zeitlin, *ibid,* p. 297f.

21. Herford, *op. cit.,* ppp 35-41; Kohut, *Aruk,* II, 118; Levy, *Woerterbuch, s. v.* בן סטרא.

22. Shab. 104b; San. 67a. Cf. Tos. Shab. 11:15 (p. 126).

23. The complete statement runs as follows: R. Eliezer said to the Wise: "Did not Ben Stada bring spells from Egypt by a cut in his flesh?" They answered: "He was a fool, and you cannot adduce proof from fools". The Amoraim seem to have identified Ben Stada with Jesus. Thus, the Amoraic discussions which follow the above passage in the uncensored editions of the Talmud (see Rabin-

Far more plausible appears the hypothesis, suggested by Chajes,[24] identifying this Ben Stada with the Jewish Egyptian "prophet" mentioned in Josephus and in the New Testament,[25] who was routed by the procurator Felix at the Mount of Olives, where he had assembled a crowd of followers for a display of his "miraculous powers."

Similarly, some[26] see a reference to Jesus in the "P'loni" ("a certain one"), an unnamed person, about whom R. Eliezer was asked whether he would have a share in the world to come, and which R. Eliezer evaded answering,[27] presumably because he was afraid to state his true views, which were in the affirmative. But this identification is not supported by any facts. We would be more justified in identifying P'loni with Solomon. There is actually a tradition that some rabbis had moved for including Solomon among the royal sinners (Jeroboam, Ahab and Manasseh) who were not to share in the life of the world to come.[28] It was apparently this

---

owicz, *Dikduke Soferim, ad locum*), speak of Ben Stada also as Ben Pandira, by whom they may have meant Jesus. Cf. Tos. Hul. 2:22 (p. 503), where there is a specific reference to Jeshu Pandira or Jesus. But the Amoraic identification of a term is, of course, no criterion as to what meaning the Tannaim attached to it. Cf. M. Joel, *Blicke in die Religionsgeschichte*, II, Breslau 1883, p. 55f, Derenbourg, *Essai sur l' histoire et la geographie de la Palestine*, Paris 1867, p. 468ff, Zeitlin, *op. cit.* p. 301. Cf., however, Origen, *Contra Celsum*, 1:28-32 which shows that already Celsus (2nd century) knew of the tradition that Jesus was the illegitimate son of a certain Panthera and that he had learnt magic spells while in Egypt. Cf. also Zuckermendel, *Gesammelte Aufsaetze*, Frankfort o. M. 1912, II, pp. 193 ff.

24.   "Ben Stada", in *ha Goren*, IV 1903, p. 35ff.

25.   *Ant.* 2, 8, 6; *Wars* 2, 13, 5; Acts XXI 38.

26.   Herford, *l. c.*; A. Edersheim, *Life and Times of Jesus the Messiah*, N. Y. 1910, II, p. 193; J. Klausner, *Jesus of Nazareth* (translated form the Hebrew by H. Danby), N. Y. 1927, p. 36f.

27.   Yoma 66b. Cf. Tos. Jeb. 3:3,4 (p. 243).

28.   j San. X, 29b; Tan. Buber, Mesora 1; Nu. R. 14:1. Cf. P. R. 23b. Cf. San. 104b where the name of Solomon has already been deleted, the text speaking anonymously about a move to include

question which was put to R. Eliezer, but he refused even to discuss it.   The high regard of tradition for the dynasty of David which defeated this move was, very likely, also responsible for the later substitution of the anonymous P'loni for the name Solomon.   Any supposed sympathies on the part of R. Eliezer toward Christianity are further unlikely, in the light of his own explicit condemnation of the *minim*, a term meaning sectarians, and certainly including the Judeo-Christians.[29]

Nor is there any merit in the hypothesis according to which

"one more king." A Geonic tradition, based upon a text which re-peated the question about P'loni, identified the first P'loni with Absal-om (Cf. A. R. N. 36 where Absalom is excluded from a share in the world to come) and the second, with Solomon (Ginzberg, *Geonica*, II, pp. 7, 14). But the best manuscripts of the Talmud and Tosefta have only one question about P'loni.   Cf. Rabinovicz and Zucker-mandel, *ad loca*.   Ms. B. in Rabinovicz, *ad locum*, interpolates a com-mentary on the P'loni question into the text, explicitly identifying him with Solomon.   Cf. below, p. 109.   Cf. also the very interesting suggestion by L. Finkelstein, "Is Philo mentioned in Rabbinic Litera-ture?" *JBL*, LIII 1934, pp. 144 ff, that P'loni may refer to the Jewish Alexandrian philosopher, Philo.   One would, however, have to ex-plain how פלוני was misread for פ י ל ו נ . It is moreover difficult to see why Philo's participation in the life of the world to come should have been in doubt and, particularly, why R. Eliezer should have regarded it as definitely out of the question (according to Fin-kelstein's interpretation of R. Eliezer's answer).   In spite of all the vagaries of his metaphysics, Philo was always a thoroughly observant Jew.

29.   He referred to them the Scriptural phrase (Deut. 32:21) "a vile people".   Mid Tann., *ad locum;* Jeb 63b.   In our editions of the Talmud R. Eliezer refers the epithet to the Sadducees.   This is no doubt a change introduced into the text by the censor.   The 1522 Venice edition of the Talmud retains the reading *minim*.   Older in-terpreters were inclined to refer *minim* to the Judeo-Christians exclu-sively.   Cf. for example Graetz, *Geschichte*, IV, pp. 90-93 and especi-ally note 11 p. 433.   More recent investigations have led to an exten-sion of the term, applying it to sectarians in general, Judeo-Christians being of course included. See L. Ginzberg, *Eine unbekannte juedische Sekte*, N. Y. 1922, p. 2 note 1; G. F. Moore, *Judaism*, III, p. 68. Cf.

R. Eliezer was suspected and arrested, because a number of his statements betray a striking similarity to parallel expressions in the New Testament.[30]   Thus, his dictum,[31] "He who has a morsel of food in his basket and worries, 'What shall I eat to-morrow,' reveals a lack of faith," is supposed to correspond to *Matthew* VI, 30-34 "...how much more you, O ye little of faith; therefore be not anxious, 'What shall we eat and what shall we drink...' be not anxious therefore for the morrow."   The short prayer of R. Eliezer, "Do thy will in heaven above and give comfort to them that fear thee here below and do what is good in thine eyes,"[32] is cited as a parallel to the prayer which Jesus taught to his disciples: "Our father in heaven... Thy will be done, as in heaven so also on earth."[33] While there may be a certain similarity in sentiment between these expressions, there is nothing peculiarly Christian about them. They represent part of that general piety which Jesus imbibed from his Jewish environment. All that the story of R. Eliezer's suspicion and arrest probably illustrates, is—what Joel observed long ago— that, in the eyes of pagan officials, Jews and Christians were not as yet well defined groups during that period, permitting at times of strange confusions between them.[34]

It is with the return to the Jabneh academy after the death of R. Johanan b. Zakkai that R. Eliezer's public career began.   The national crisis had made much new legislation necessary.   Much of the older law existed in varying traditions and was scattered in different sources; a good deal of it was not even clear in meaning.   It was obvious to the Jewish scholars under the leadership of R.

---

also, *Schuerer, Geschichte des juedischen Volkes*, Leipzig 1907, III, p. 438f.

  30.   Klausner, *op. cit.*, p. 43f; Chajes, *op. cit.*, p. 34, note 2.
  31.   Mek. R. Simeon p. 75; Sota 48b; Yalkut on Zechariah ch. 4. Cf. Mek. Beshalah 2 (Friedmann p. 47b) where this statement is quoted in the name of R. Eliezer of Modin.
  32.   Tos. Ber. 3:11 (p. 7); Ber. 29b.
  33.   Matt. VI 9-11, Luke XI 2.
  34.   *Blicke*, I, Breslau 1880, p. 32ff, note 1.

Gamaliel, that if Jewry was to survive the loss of a political center
and national autonomy, another agent must be found for the pro-
motion of unity and homogeneity—a common religious and social
practice, a common law. They therefore undertook to re-edit the
Mishnah, to transform the scattered legal opinions transmitted by
tradition into an authoritative code of law. R. Eliezer joined in
every effort that this task involved—the assembling of old material,[35]
the tracing of authorities for many of the legal opinions that were
known anonymously,[36] the removal of ambiguities in the formulated
language of the old law,[37] and the further application of that law
to new facts and new situations.[38]

In addition to taking part in the deliberations at the academy
of Jabneh, R. Eliezer also conducted his own school and judicial
court, called Beth Mothba Rabba, in what had formerly been a
public arena in Lydda.[39] R. Akiba, who was later accepted to full
membership in the council at Jabneh, began his scholastic career
under R. Eliezer and R. Joshua.[40] Among R. Eliezer's many dis-

---

35. M. Shek. 4:7; M. Orla 1:7; M. Nidda 1:3, 4:7; Tos. Nidda
1:5 (p. 641); Nidda 7b. Cf. Halevi, Ie, p. 268.

36. M. Jeb. 3:1; Tos. Jeb. 5:1 (p. 245); Jeb. 28a; M. Ed. 5:5;
Tos. Ed. 2:9 (p. 458); M. Ed. 5:4; Tos. Y. T. 1:3 (p. 201); Besa 4a;
j Besa I, 60a; Tos. Shev. 1:5 (p. 61).

37. M. Jeb. 8:4; M. Bek. 4:7; M. Ar. 3:8, 6:3; M. B. K. 6:5.
Cf. Mek. Mishpatim 14 (Horovitz p. 297); Tos. Ar. 4:24 (p. 548),
4:6 (p. 547). Cf. Halevi, ibid, pp. 250-254, 267.

38. M. Pea 5:4; M. Ohol. 9:15; M. Para 10:3; M. Pes. 3:1. Cf.
Halevi, ibid, pp. 259-262.

39. San. 32b; Sifre, Deut. section 144; Mek. Beshalah 1 (ed.
Friedmann p. 53b); R. Simeon p. 82; Bek. 5b; Cant. R. to 1:3. In Cant.
R. Eliezer's seat in the schoolroom is a stone. Cf. S. Klein, "Laמותבא
רב א de Lydda," REJ, IX 1910, p. 107ff, and S. Krauss, "Die Ver-
sammlungstaetten der Talmudgelehrten", pp. 26ff. Krauss thinks that
because the school was housed in an arena it was called "Bet Motba
Rabba"—the house with many seats. It is interesting that in Justin
Martyr Dial. 9, the pupils of Tryphon, who may indeed be based on R.
Eliezer's colleague in Lydda, R. Tarfon (See S. Krauss "Tryphon"
in J. E. VII p. 395), sit about their master on stone seats.

40. A. R. N. 6; j Pes. VI, 33b, Nazir 56a; D. E. Z. in Masektot

ciples may be mentioned: Rabbis Ilai,[41] Nathan[42] Joseph b.
Perida[43], Jose b. Durmaskes,[44] Abba Hanin,[45] Johanan b. Nuri,[46]
Judah b. Batira,[47] Haninah,[48] and Judah b. Gadish.[49] The decisions
rendered in his court were held up for their equity, their impartiality,
and their correct interpretation of the Law.[50] The administrator
of the domains of King Agrippa II, when in search for religious
enlightment, turned his questions to Eliezer.[51]

Zeirot ed. Higger, 4:10; Sem. 4:19. P. S. E. Z., p. 6f. describes R.
Akiba as a farm laborer in the employ of R. Eliezer. This is lack-
ing in Shab. 127b and *Sheiltot* on Exodus, section 40, where the
same episode is related.

41. Men. 18a; Tos. Pes. 3:9 (p. 21); j Ter. X, 47b; M. Er. 2:6:
Pes. 38b *et seq.*

42. Tos. Pes. 2:8 (p. 159); Pes. 48a. It is rather strange that
R. Nathan should have been a pupil of R. Eliezer while his colleagues
R. Meier and R. Judah were not. The chain of tradition as quoted
in our source may be incomplete.

43. Er. 11b-12a. Cf. j Er. 18b; Tos. Er. 1:2 (p. 138).

44. Hag. 3b; M. Yad. 4:3; Tos. Yad. 2:16 (p. 683); Mid. Tehil.
on Ps. 25:13. Durmaskes means a woman of Damascus. R. Jose
was apparently called after his mother.

45. Mid. Tann. on Deut. 16:3; 19:20; 21:16; 25:15; Nazir 45a;
San. 17a.

46. Sifra, Shemini, p. 54a, Tos. Kel. 6:4 (p. 575).

47. M. Neg. 9:3, 11:7.

48. Mek. R. Simeon, p. 82; Bek. 5b. Cf. Mek. Beshalah 1 (Horovitz p. 177).

49. Tos. M. Sh. 1:14 (p. 87); Er. 27a.

50. Sifre, Deut. section 144; San. 32b.

51. Sukka 27a. The Hebrew reads אפיטרופוס. This word
אפיטרופוס, the Greek *epitropos*, generally means a guardian
or one who administers the property of a widow or an
orphan during his minority. When used in connection with a king,
it has the meaning of a procurator or one who administers the
affairs of state in the king's absence. Cf. S. Krauss, *Monumenta
Talmudica*, V, Vienna and Leipzig 1914, p. 159, note 376. It is therefore probable that our incident goes back to the years 70-79 when
Agrippa II was in Rome. Our text does not suggest the identity of
this official of Agrippa, but in Shab. 121a there is a reference to a

R. Eliezer also played an important role as a communal worker. We find him in years of drought proclaiming public fast days to supplicate God for rain.[52] It was he, together with R. Joshua and R. Akiba, who induced Aquila, the Greek proselyte from Pontus, to undertake a new and more literal translation of the Bible which would bring the Greek text into closer harmony with Jewish tradition. Such a translation had become necessary because of the danger of Christological interpretations that the Septuagint, with its free and inaccurate renderings, had made possible.[53] We find R. Eliezer twice at Antioch, also in conjunction with R. Joshua and R. Akiba, collecting funds for needy scholars.[54] We also find him travelling to Abelia, Caesarea, Sepphoris, and Tiberias, and while his mission may not have been in each instance of a public nature, he generally utilized his stays everywhere for religious guidance and instruction.[55]

R. Eliezer also took part in a Jewish embassy to Rome under the leadership of the patriarch R. Gamaliel.[56] Our sources do not indicate specifically the circumstances under which this embassy

---

Joseph b. Simoi serving as the אפיטרופוס of the king, and Graetz, "Agrippa II und der Zustand Judaeas nach dem Untergang Jerusalems", *MGWJ*, XIII 1881, p. 484ff, argues that it is this same Joseph who is meant in our text too. In Agadat B'reshit 17:2 and Tan. Lek Leka (end), R. Eliezer is consulted by King Agrippa himself, but in P. R. 117a this same question is asked by the proselyte Aquila. See below, p. 64.

52. Taan. 25b; j Taan. III, 66c-d.
53. Meg. 3a. Cf. M. Joel, *ibid*, pp. 43ff, 67, and L. Ginzberg on Aquila in *J. E.* II, p. 36f.
54. j Hor. III, 48a; Lev. R. 5:4; Deut. R. 4:8.
55. Tos. Er. 1:2 (p. 138); Er. 11b, 12a; j Er. I, 18b; Tos. Sukka 1:9 (p. 192), Sukka 27b; A. Z. 16b; Tos. Hul. 2:24 (p. 503); Ecc. R. 1:24; j San. VII, 25d.
56. Deut. R. 2:15; j San. VII, 25d. Cf. Gen. R. 13:6 and Ecc. R. 1:15 where only R. Eliezer and R. Joshua are spoken of. This need not surprise us since the reference is to the observation of a scientific phenomenon for which R. Eliezer and R. Joshua had a common explanation. R. Gamaliel was left in the background.

made the trip to Rome. But the Midrash relates[57] that after they had reached Rome, the senate passed a decree that "within thirty days there shall be no more Jews in the world," and that rescue was effected through "a god-fearing" senator who committed suicide so that the senate should be dissolved, the decree in the meantime falling into abeyance. There is also a report[58] quoting R. Eliezer and R. Joshua, both participants in this embassy, as engaged while in Rome, in a scientific discussion with Hadrian, "may his bones rot." In the light of these facts we would probably be justified in placing the embassy in 116-117,[59] immediately following the uprisings against Trajan. These uprisings in which the Jewish communities of the diaspora had taken part could very well have formed the background for a severe decree against the Jewry of the empire as a whole. The trip of the rabbis was for the purpose of

---

57. Deut. R. *ibid*. Our text has נטל which S. Krauss, *Monumenta,* V, p. 138, note 315, correctly explains as a corruption for בטל. Cf. also Taan. 29a where a Roman official, on the promise of a share in the world to come, commits suicide to rescue R. Gamaliel from a death sentence that had been decreed against him, the Talmud remarking, "When one of those who took part in the issuing of the decree dies, the decree is abrogated".

58. Gen. R. *l. c.*; Ecc. R. *l. c.* Cf. S. P. Rabinowitz, note 2, on Graetz, *History,* II (Hebrew), p. 234, who points out that Hadrian was accustomed to indulge in discussions with the leaders of the different races and religions of the empire in an effort to learn their customs and ideas.

59. Graetz, "Die Reise der vier Tannaiten nach Rom," *MGWJ,* I 1851-52, pp. 192-202, *Geschichte,* IV, p. 110f and note 12, p. 103ff, dates this embassy in the reign of Domitian. He arrives at this conclusion by identifying the friendly senator mentioned in our sources with the consul Flavius Clemens who was executed for his conversion to Judaism in 95. The severe decree against the Jews mentioned in the text he identifies with Domitian's vigorous collections of the ficus, his suppression of Jewish propaganda and his arrest of certain Jews who traced their descent from the house of David. It is however difficult to see how these measures of Domitian could have been enlarged by the Midrash into a decree purposing to exterminate all Jewry. Nor is there any support for the identification

guarding Jewish interests against such measures of retaliation that they were afraid would follow. The story about the senator's suicide is clearly unhistorical since that, as far as we know, would have had no effect on the sessions of the senate or on its legislation. It may, however, allude to the help that some friendly senator extended to these ambassadors, and to the death of Trajan whose punitive plans against the Jews were thereupon discarded. It was with Hadrian's ascendancy to the throne that their mission was finally successful, and, as we indeed know from other sources, Jewish rights were, for the time being at least, again made secure. The so called *Yom Tyrianus* (Day commemorating the fall of Trajan), a semi-festival whereon mourning and fasting were to be prohibited,[60] was probably

---

of the God-fearing senator in our text with Flavius Clemens. Indeed, it may even be that the conversion of Clemens was not to Judaism but to Christianity (Schuerer, *Geschichte,* III, pp. 64 note 97, 168 note 57). There is, furthermore, the conversation with Hadrian which Graetz seems to have overlooked entirely. Graetz also denies that R. Eliezer took part in this embassy, resorting to a correction of the text from R. Eliezer to R. Elazar b. Azariah. There is no support for this whatever. S. Krauss, *Monumenta, l.c.,* follows Graetz in dating the embassy in the reign of Domitian but he interprets "there shall be no more Jews in the world" as a contemplated expulsion of the Jews from Rome, our sources having confused the Latin *urbs* (city) with *orbis* (world). This expulsion, he explains, citing Vogelstein-Rieger, *Geschichte der Juden in Rom,* I, Berlin 1896, p. 26, actually occurred in 95 C. E. as part of the general expulsion of "philosophers". But a reading of Vogelstein-Rieger does not support the assertion that the decree expelling the "philosophers" from Rome included Jews as well. Nor is it likely that our phrase "in the world" is the rsult of a confusion between *urbs* and *orbis* because the amplification of the story must have been the work of Jews who employed Hebrew, not Latin.

60. Megillat Taanit 12; j Meg. I, 70c. In the *Scholiast,* the *Yom Tyrianus* is accounted for by the fact that Papus and Lulianus were rescued on that day from an impending execution through a rescript from Rome which decreed death for the Roman governor instead. Papus and Lulianus were apparently active in the Palestinian phase of the Trajanic wars and the Roman governor (Quietus)

instituted in honor of this occasion.   It was, however, later abolished

---

was planning to execute them.   With the success of the mission, his
plans too were foiled.   We indeed know from other sources that
Quietus was executed shortly after the rise of Hadrian as emperor.
Taan. 18b, Sem. 8:15, Ecc. R. 3:23 wher the same narrative is reported, involve Trajan himself in this incident with the two Jewish
leaders, and not the governor.   But this is clearly a confusion.   Trajan was never in Palestine.   Furthermore, as emperor he could not
have been subject to a "rescript from Rome".   (Cf. Schuerer, *Geschichte*, I, p. 668).   We must likewise reject as inaccurate the report
in the above texts that Papus and Lulianus were actually executed
before   the   rescript   from   Rome   became   effective;   both   these
men were active in Jewish affairs under Hadrian (Gen. R. 64:8).
Graetz, *Geschichte*, IV, p. 126, 411ff, thinks that the *Yom Tyrianus*
was in honor of the rescue of Papus and Lulianus and that instead
of *Yom Tyrianus* our sources should really have *Yom Quietus*.   Zeitlin, *Megillat Taanit as a source for Jewish Chronology and History
in the Hellenistic and Roman Periods*, Philadelphia 1922, p. 110, has,
however, argued correctly against this, on the ground that such a
confusion, possible in the later *Scholiast* and Amoraic sources, could
not have occurred in the almost contemporary Megillat Taanit.   P.
Cassel, "Anmerkungen zu Megillath Taanit," in his *Messianische
Stellen des alten Testaments*, p. 84ff, corrects the "T" in Tyrianus to an
"S" and argues that the holiday was in commemoration of the victory
of Judas Maccabeas over the Syrian commander Seron.   Zeitlin (*l.c.*)
has argued against this, too, since the occasion is not mentioned in
II Maccabees, a book that is essentially concerned with the holidays
originating in the Hasmonean struggle against the Seleucids

Zeitlin himself (*op. cit.*, p. 111), instead *Yom Tyrianus*, reads
Yom Tyrion (the version in some texts), which he relates to the Syr-
iac and the Greek *tiro*, meaning a military recruit.   The holiday, according to him, was instituted in honor of the Jewish young men who
joined the revolutionary forces at the outbreak of the war against
Rome.   This is, however, unlikely.   It is difficult to see why a per-
manent holiday should have been decreed in honor of recruits, in
the light of the disastrous ending of the war.   Moreover, the holiday
was obviously decreed by the Rabbis, and they were unfriendly to the
war.   To maintain his view, Zeitlin is, of course, also forced to reject
the narratives in the Talmud about the incident with Papus and
Lulianus as entirely unhistorical.   Joel, *Blicke*, p. 15ff, thinks that

when Hadrian reversed himelf and adopted a hostile policy against the Jews.[61]

For his achievements in the different fields in which he was active R. Eliezer won the respect and reverence of his contemporaries. He came to be called R. Eliezer the Great.[62] At one of the sessions of the council at Jabneh the consensus of opinion among the scholars deemed him one of the two men in his generation who were worthy of "divine inspiration."[63] R. Tarfon, on a visit during R. Eliezer's sickness, greeted him as "more precious to Israel than even God's gift of rain," and others on the same occasion paid him similar tributes.[64] R. Joshua in one instance referred to him as the

the occasion for the holiday was Trajan's permission to rebuild the Temple. But most scholars are of the opinion that the tentative permission to rebuild the Temple was given not by Trajan but by Hadrian. *Yom Tyrianus,* furthermore, is used as a parallel to the next mentioned Yom Nicanor and must, therefore, mean not an anniversary in his honor, but the anniversary of his downfall. Cf. H. Lichtenstein, "Die Fastenrolle," in *HUCA,* VIII-IX 1932, 272f, who rejects all the above hypotheses without however offering any identfication of his own.

61. j Taan. II, 66a; j Meg. I, 70c:
"The *Yom Tyrion* was abrogated on the day when when Papus and Lulianus were killed." Papus and Lulianus were apparently active in the uprisings against Hadrian and they were finally executed. These executions are, however, only indicative of the general perscutions that now set in.

62. Mid. Tann. on Deut. 34:4; Ber. 6a, 32a; Tos. Orla 1:8 (p. 45); Taan. 31a; M. Sota 9:15; Kid. 39a; A. R. N. 15; B. K. 83a; B. M. 59b; B. B. 121b; Men. 38b; Yirat Het, Masektot Zeirot, 80:18; II Yirat Het, *ibid,* 87:4, *et seq.* Kraus, *Archaeologie,* II, p. 16, points out that while such an epithet may signify largeness of body or seniority in point of age, its general meaning was prominence. Cf. also A. R. N. 17 where the text speaks of "R. Eliezer the Great who was greater than R. Akiba."

63. j Sota IX, 24c; j Hor. III, 48c; j A. Z. III, 42c. Cf. San. 11a.

64. San. 101a-b. Cf. Sifre, Deut. section 32; Mek. Jethro 10 (Horovitz, p. 240), where this greeting is quoted by R. Joshua, and

"ark of the covenant" and kissed the place on which he was accustomed to sit in the academy as "The Mour.tain of Sinai."[65] Public opinion, on one occasion, demanded the commutation of a death sentence against a criminal because he had at one time studied under R. Eliezer. At R. Eliezer's death, the people lamented that a scroll of the law had been destroyed.[66]

Nevertheless, R. Eliezer s relationships with his fellow scholars were far from happy. One disturbing factor was his character, his unpolished manners, the crudeness of his speech, and his bullying at the slightest provocation. Thus, in consoling his teacher R. Johanan ben Zakkai, who had lost a son, he suggested crudely that R. Johanan follow Adam's example when Abel died—bring another son into the world. To his favorite disciple, R. Akiba, when he refuted him in an argument, he cried out in anger, "From the laws of shehita (slaughter) have you refuted me; by shehita may you perish." When Simon the Chaste, a learned pirest, reported one of his Temple practices to him, R. Eliezer summarily asked him: "Who is more worthy, you or the High Priest?" And when Simon did not reply, R. Eliezer continued: "Do you not admit that even the dog of the High Priest is more worthy than you? Even if the High Priest himself had practiced as you did, his head would have been split for him."[67] At the same time R. Eliezer was never diffident about speaking in his own praise. According to his own admission, he was the most diligent of students. He compared his two hands to the two scrolls of the Law. "If all the reeds were pens, and all the seas were ink, and the heavens and the earth were parchment, and all mankind were scribes," so R. Eliezer is supposed to have declared, "it would still be impossible to record all the Torah

---

R. Joshua's greeting is quoted in the name of R. Tarfon. It is more likely that R. Tarfon, a wealthy landowner, to whom rain was a matter of supreme importance, should have made that the point of comparison for his beloved colleague. This is the reading preferred by Horovitz.

65. Cant. R. 1:20.
66. Er. 54a; Tos. Sota 15:3 (p. 321); Sota 49b; j Sota IX, 24c.
67. A. R. N. 14; Pes. 69a; Tos. Kel 1:6 (p. 569).

I have learnt."[68] Tradition has probably exaggerated, but these statements, nevertheless, reveal a side of his character, the product no doubt of the rural environment from which he had emerged, but which must have interfered with the formation of any happy relationships with his colleagues.

Far more serious was R. Eliezer's general position in the halakah. We have already learnt that in the name of Jewish unity the scholars at Jabneh finally repudiated the conservative Shammaites with all that they had stood for in the history of the halakah. But as the deliberations at Jabneh proceeded, it became apparent that in R. Eliezer there was a Shammaite all over again. He set himself up as a great bulwark of tradition, and as we shall discover in our detailed discussion of his conception of Jewish piety, social doctrine, and his system of jurisprudence, he resisted every effort at change, at new adjustment and development. That R. Eliezer should have taken this position is not surprising. He was, it is true, a disciple of an ardent Hillelite, R. Johanan b. Zakkai. A world outlook, however, is not determined by a party label but by a social orientation. As a wealthy landowner, an aristocrat, a member of the upper class, he was only insisting on what upper classes who have stakes in the continuity of the status quo have always insisted—religious and social stability as opposed to change. It is equally clear, however, that with such divergent philosophies at play, Jabneh could not long continue as a united body.

At first a modus vivendi was tried by recognizing R. Eliezer's views for their academic value, repudiating them, however, as far as practice was concerned, for being Shammaitic. To make the repudiation more effective they even etxended it to such individual decisions where R. Eliezer was admittedly justified.[69] But this was not entirely satisfactory. For there was the danger that certain

---

68. Sukka 28a; San. 68a; Cant. R. 1:20. This was a current proverbial comment. R. Joshua, in Cant. R. l.c. applies it also to himself.

69. Shab. 130b; Nidda 7b; j Nidda I, 49a. R. Eliezer was a Sham-

communities would disregard the majority decision of the rabbis and withdraw from the orbit of a common Jewish practice, so indispensable now to Jewish survival, and follow the views of R. Eliezer.   We have a record of such a community following the halakah of R. Eliezer; the rabbis resented it, even expressing surprise that such a community should escape divine punishment.[70] R. Eliezer's wranglings, his policy of continued and determined opposition and dissent was, of course, also a great hindrance to the constructive work which the Jabneh scholars were trying to do.

The hostility which had been gathering for some time finally culminated in an open break during a discussion concerning the levitical uncleanliness of the so called 'Akhnai' stove.[71] This was apparently a pottery stove which had become contaminated with levitical uncleanliness, and the owner cut it into tiles which were separated from each other by sand but externally plastered over with cement. This was a loose arrangement, but could still be used as a stove, and at the same time, as a "broken" vessel, it would no longer be susceptible to uncleanliness.[72] R. Eliezer's colleagues were unwilling to see the priests evade the laws of levitical uncleanliness and objected to the arrangement.   What was important to

---

maite in the sense that he adhered to those principles which were peculiar to the Shammaite school. Where he seemed to deviate from these principles, the usual Talmudic reconciliations were resorted to. Cf. j Nazir VI, 55d; j Sukka II, 53a-b; j Besa III, 62b; j Ter. IV, 43b. In individual instances R. Eliezer nevertheless freely modifies the view of the Shammaites. See M. Er. 1:2; M. Nidda 5:9; Jeb. 89b; Tos. M. K. 2:9 (p. 230). Cf., however, M. K. 20a; Jeb. 80a; Tos. Ed. 2:7 (p. 458). Cf. Weiss, Dor, II, p. 83 and note 2; Graetz, Geschichte, IV, p. 42, and V, pp. 394f; Jawitz, Toldot Yisrael, VI, p. 286f. After R. Eliezer's death, the scholars reconsidered their decision and ruled in his favor in those individual instances where his views seemed justified.

70.   Shab. 130a.

71.   M. Ed. 7:7; Tos. Ed. 2:1 (p. 457); M. Kel. 5:10; B. M. 59a-b. S. Krauss is of the opinion that Akhnai may be the name of the stove's owner. See Archaeologie, I, p. 438, note 168.

72.   Cf. Krauss, op. cit., p. 88.

them was not so much the objective fact that the stove was "broken," as the intention of the owner who continued to use it. The owner's intention made it again into a "whole" vessel, and its impurity, therefore, persisted. R. Eliezer, more friendly to the priests, and generally more concerned with the objective facts than with the intention of the doer, regarded the stove as actually broken and, therefore, ritually pure. The controversy that raged over this question was prolonged and bitter. Finally the matter was put to a vote and R. Eliezer was dramatiaclly defeated by a great majority. But R. Eliezer refused to yield. He defied the majority and publicly continued to argue and to teach his own views. Behind this impasse stood not only a difference in attitude toward the Akhnai stove but a clash of two totally different philosophies of Jewish life.

To break the impasse the rabbis finally responded with the ban. In demonstration they held a public burning of all types of priestly food which he, in defiance of their opinions, had persisted in considering ritually pure. Akiba, his own disciple, carried the news of the decision to him. Seated in mourning dress, at some distance from him, Akiba spoke: "My master, it appears to me that thy colleagues keep aloof from thee." R. Eliezer understood the message but remained unyielding to the end. With a keen sense of wrong in his heart he retired to his own school at Lydda, an outcast from the council of scholars where he had played a leading role for many years.[73]

The fact that so learned and pious a man as R. Eliezer should have been excommunicated created a stir in the Jewish world. The general failure of crops which came the following year was explained by many as God's answer to his indignant outcry against the injustice that was done him. R. Gamaliel himself, when overwhelmed by a storm at sea, feared that he was being punished for what he, as the head of the Jabneh council, had done to R. Eliezer; and he prayed to God, "O Master of the Universe. . . it is not for

---

73. B. M. 59b; Ber. 19a; j M. K. III, 81d.

my honor or for the honor of my father's house that I have done it, but for Your honor—that strife shall not continue in Israel." His wife, Imma Shalom, anxious for her brother Gamaliel's safety, requested Eliezer not to offer prayers for deliverance from his enemies. He complied with her request, which she repeated at the proper time each day. When one morning, before she had an opportunity to repeat her request, she found him in the midst of such a prayer, she sorrowfully exclaimed: "Cease, thou hast killed my brother." And indeed, her apprehension soon proved to have been well-founded— Gamaliel's death actually occurred a short time thereafter. In spite of the resentment that R. Eliezer bore him during his life time, he neverthless, took part in Gamaliel's funeral and accorded him the usual honors as a brother-in-law and the patriarch of Israel.[74]

R. Eliezer felt his isolation most keenly. The terms of his excommunication apparently left him free to continue teaching in his school at Lydda,[75] but he realized that the centre of Jewish learning and authority was at Jabneh. From his pupils, who occasionally travelled thither, he sought to learn what went on there, but such conversation would only pain him, reminding him that he was an outcast. Once, when he was told that the council of Jabneh had deliberated on a question concerning which he felt himself qualified to speak authoritatively, he actually shed tears, and although the decision of the scholars was in accordance with his own opinion, he dispatched to Jabneh a message of acquiescence.[76] Moved, no doubt, by his own experience, he warned his disciples, "Be as careful about the respect due to your colleagues as about the respect due to yourselves—and do not permit yourselves to become easily provoked to anger." "Warm yourselves before the hearths of scholars, but see that you are not burnt, for when they

---

74. B. M. *l. c.;* j Ber. III, 5d.   Cf. M. K. 27a and see Graetz, *Geschichte*, IV, p. 130, note 4.

75. For an excommunicant's right to teach, cf. M. K. 15a.

76. Hag. 3a; M. Yad. 4:3; Tos. Yad. 2:16 (p. 683).

bite, it is the bite of a fox, and when they sting, it is the sting of a scorpion.[77]

It is difficult to approximate the date of R. Eliezer's death. We have seen that during 117-118 he was in Rome. A number of years must have elapsed between then and the time of his death to allow for the events leading up to his excommunication and to the death of R. Gamaliel, whom he survived. It would seem from the account in the Talmud that he died in Caesarea and was thence taken for burial to Lydda.[78]

---

77. Ab. 2:10.

78. Graetz, *Geschichte,* IV, p. 47, places the date of R. Eliezer's death between 116-118. He bases his view on the fact that R. Eliezer spoke to the scholars who came to visit him while on his sick bed about "troubled conditions" (San. 101a), which Graetz identifies with the Trajanic wars against the Jews. But this cannot have been the sickness from which R. Eliezer finally died, because the scholars would not have drawn close to him or conversed with him intimately, as they are reported to have done, since he was then an excommunicant. In the report about the illness from which R. Eliezer actually died (San. 68a), the visiting scholars kept aloof, restrained by the ban. Cf. Halevi, Ie, p. 297; S. R. Hirsch, *Gesammelte Schriften,* V, p. 244.

Weiss, *Dor,* II, p. 131f, dates R. Eliezer's death about 130. His reason is a reference by Eliezer to a time when it was dangerous to expose the knife used in circumcision (Shab. 130). Weiss identifies this with the Hadrianic persecutions when the general Roman edict against castration was applied to prohibit circumcision. But if R. Eliezer died about 130, R. Joshua, who survived him, will have lived to over 100 years of age, since he performed services in the Temple before seventy—a levite began serving in the Temple at the age of thirty. The danger alluded to need not refer to a ban of circumcision, but to a time of revolutionary unrest when it was dangerous to expose a weapon, which the ordinary סכין was. This might have been during the uprisings in 68-70 or 116-117. Supporting this identification is the tradition of R. Judah who quotes R. Eliezer: "When it was dangerous, we used to cover the knife" (Shab. 130. Cf. Rabinovicz, *ad locum*). This suggests that R. Eliezer was referring to what had happened long ago. If the incident involved were the Hadrianic persecutions, R. Judah would have given a first-hand

A pathetic description is given of his dying moments.[79]   R. Joshua, R. Akiba, and a number of other scholars, hearing of his illnes, came to pay him a visit. They could not draw close—he was still under the ban—and they, therefore, stood at some distance. But he recognized them. "Why have you come?", he demanded summarily. "To study Torah," they replied. "And why have you not come until now?", he continued. Embarrassed, they apologized that they had been busy. Still smarting under the sense of wrong, and perhaps thinking of the Hadrianic persecutions that had set in,[80] R. Eliezer burst forth: "I doubt if you will die a natural death"—true to his temperament to his last day. "And what of me?" queried R. Akiba, who having been Eliezer's particularly devoted pupil, felt a greater measure of responsibility for his master's isolation. "Your fate will be even more severe," he replied. R. Eliezer recalled

---

report, without attributing it to R. Eliezer's authority. It is, of course, also possible that circumcision was prohibited even before Hadrian, perhaps during the disturbances under Trajan. Cf. M. Jeb. 16:7 which refers to a situation during the life time of R. Gamaliel, when R. Akiba was forced to go to Parthia in order to intercalate the calendar, presumably because it was unlawful to do so in Roman territory.

   In Git. 57a R . Eliezer is quoted as describing a great slaughter of Jews that took place at *Bik'at Yadaim*. Graetz, *Geschichte*, IV, note 16, p. 425ff, identifies this *Bik'at Yadaim* with the last strong-hold which fell in the Bar Kokeba war. This is impossible, since the author of the description is R. Eliezer, who died before the Bar Kokeba war. Rappaport, *Erek Millin, s. v.* "Alexander Tiberius," identifies it with the massacre of Alexandrian Jewry under Alexander Tiberius in 60. Possibly it refers to the massacre that took place at the fall of Jerrusalem in 70. R. Eliezer's description of the fall of Bethar in the late source of the Seder Eliahu (ch. 29, p. 151) is clearly unhistorical. In the passage preceding it R. Eliezer gives the same description ofr a massacre in Alexandria. Obviously both cannot correct. It is possible that in a presently deleted passage R. Eliezer described the fall of Jerusalem in 70, which was subsequently amplified with the latter two descriptions.

   79.   San. 68a.   Cf. A. R. N. 25; j Shab. II, 5b.
   80.   Cf. Toetterman, p. 13f; Weiss, *Dor,* II, p. 129f.

the days when he was still the great teacher in Israel, and looked back upon the time when Akiba was still his devoted disciple. To erase the pain induced by these recollections the visiting scholars drew him into a legal discussion. In the midst of it he expired. Forgotten now were all the dissensions; only Eliezer's great sincerity, his profound learning and his piety remained. Overwhelmed with grief, R. Joshua arose and formally dissolved the sentence of excommunication that had been between them. R. Akiba applied the verse spoken by Elisha at the passing of Elijah: "My father, my father, the chariots of Israel and the horsemen thereof" (II Kings 2:12). A great but turbulent personality had passed from Israel.

Like the other teachers of the Talmud, R. Eliezer did not leave any formal writings to present a coherent description of his views. But, posterity, impressed by his outstanding personality, has attributed to him a number of works of a psedo-epigraphic nature. We have already learnt that the *Pirke d' R. Eliezer*, attributed to our R. Eliezer, is really a geonic work not preceding the eighth century. The *She'elot R. Eliezer*, ten questions concerning resurrection and the life of the hereafter, likewise generally ascribed to R. Eliezer, is really an abridgment of the concluding section of the seventh chapter of Saadia's philosophic work *Emunot V'deot* (10th century).[81] R. Eliezer is also the putative author of the *Orhot Hayim*, an ethical treatise in the form of a will to his son Hyrcanus, which is for that reason also known as *The Will of R. Eliezer the Great*. Modern scholars have generally attributed this book to the authorship of R. Eliezer b. Isaac, a German scholar of the eleventh century who was also known as R. Eliezer the Great and was, therefore, confused with our R. Eliezer. The dedication to his son Hyracanus has been regarded as the work of a later hand.[82] The *Sefer ha-Gan*, ascribed to R. Eliezer b. Hyrcanus in

81. Jellinek, *B. H., VI*, p. 35 (introduction); Malter, *Life and Works of Saadia Gaon*, p. 365f.

82. Menahem di Lonsano, *Shete Yadot*, Venice 1618, p. 122a; Zunz, *Zur Geschichte und Literatur*, Berlin 1845, I, p. 124; Weiss, *Dor*, IV, p. 280; Steinschneider, *Cat. Bodl.*, cols. 957-958; Jellinek,

the Hanover edition 1620, is a moralistic work written originally in German by Isaac b. Eliezer of Worms, a fifteenth century scholar and pupil of R. Moses b. Eliezer ha-Darshan.[83]

While this material as ascribed to R. Eliezer is not genuine, there are a large number of genuine statements by him scattered throughout the entire field of Rabbinic literature. It is out of these statements, by the process of orderly disposition, that we may reconstruct his views, his system of Jewish piety, social doctrine, and jurisprudence—a system of which he may have been totally unconscious but which these statements, analyzed critically, certainly betray. To this we shall turn in the following pages.

B. H., III, p. 28 (introduction); J. Freiman, "Eliezer ha-Gadol b. Isaac", in *Eshkol*, II, p. 568f.

83. Steinschneider, *ibid*, col. 628; Zunz, *ibid*, p. 130.

Chapter III

R. ELIEZER THE RELIGIOUS CONSERVATIVE

Pharisaic piety was a development in the direction of individualism and universalism in both its elements—theology and ritual. To the extent that this was already achieved by the time that R. Eliezer appeared on the scene of Jewish life, he, no less than his colleagues, accepted it. Wherever flexibility still prevailed however, we generally find a difference of opinion. R. Eliezer's colleagues try to continue the old tendency. They strive after a more thorough-going individualism and a broader universalism. R. Eliezer, on the other hand, objects. He demands a halt to these developments and defends the more conservative point of view.

1. *Conception of God.*—The complete universalization of the God idea had already been achieved long before the first century. The comments concerning God, consequently, furnished very little occasion for disputes between R. Eliezer and his colleagues. Like his colleagues R. Eliezer was a complete monotheist. Because the Scriptural reference to idols as "other gods" (Deut. 5:7) seemed inconsistent with the doctrines of pure monotheism, R. Eliezer reinterpreted the term "other." Idols, he explained, may properly be called "other gods," because they are constantly superseded by others —when the idolator needs gold, he supersedes his golden idol with an idol of silver; and when he needs silver, he supersedes that idol with an idol of copper, etc.[1]

Because of the exalted conception which he had of God, R.

---

1. Mid. Tann. on Deut. 5:7; Tan. Jethro 16; Mek. Jethro, Bahodesh 6.

Eliezer, like his colleagues, did not make use of His proper name, except in prayer.[2]   Generally he employed synonyms: 'the holy One blessed be He,' 'the King of kings, the holy One blessed be He,' 'He who spoke and the world came into being,' 'the holy Spirit,' 'the Place,' 'Heaven,' 'our Father in heaven,' and 'Strength.'[3] In the

---

2.   j Ber. IV, 4d quotes a prayer of R. Eliezer's composition and it includes the term   ה' אלהי .   Cf. L. Finkelstein, "The Develop_ment of the Amidah," *JQR*, N. S., XVI, 1925, p. 4f, who states that "the contemporaries of R. Gamaliel II never used the term   ה' אלהי in their prayers", and makes the presence or absence of this one of the criteria in the dating of prayers.

3.   Ber. 3a; San. 97b, 98a; P. R. K. 172b; Ecc. R. 11:5; Tan. Beshalah 21; Mid. Tehil., Psalm 78:18; Yalkut, Proverbs, section 943; P. R. 28b; Cant. R. 1:55; San. 44a; Mid. Tehil., Psalm 1; Mek. Jethro, Bahodesh 8; Lev. R. 4:2; Mek. R. Simeon. p. 82f; P. S. E. Z., p. 10; Sem. d'R. Hiya 1:4 (Sem. Ed. Higger, p. 214:41-45)); M. Sota 9:15; Mek. R. Simeon, p. 71f; Lekah on Ex. 15:22 and Mek. *ad locum.* A. Marmorstein, *The Old Rabbinic Doctrine of God,* London 1927, pp. 97, 108-148, assumes that the name "The Holy One, blessed be He" was first introduced in the third century and that where this name occurs in earlier sources it is either an addition or an alteration. The name is however used not only by R. Eliezer but by all the first century scholars—R. Johanan b. Zakkai, R. Gamaliel II, R. Joshua, R. Elazar b. Azariah and R. Akiba (Mek. on Ex. 20:22; Tan. Jethro, end; P. R. 40a; Ex. R. 30:6; Mek. on Ex. 16:28, 17:26; Ber. 5a; Gen. R. 33, end, *et seq.*). It is not likely that alterations or additions should have occurred in each of these instances Similarly Marmorstein, *op. cit.,* p. 99f, thinks that "the holy spirit" as a name for God was not used until Amoraic times and that where it is used in Tannaitic sources it means prophecy or the prophets. But the dialogues quoted by R. Eliezer and R. Joshua in Lev. R. 4:2 clearly use this name for God. *Ha-Makom,* "the place," as a synonym for God, is very old and it has generally been traced to Hellenistic-Alexandrian influence. See already A. F. Dæhne, *Geschichtliche Dar-stellung der Alexandrinische Religionsphilosophie,* I, Halle 1834, pp. 72, 282. Geiger, *Juedische Zeitschrift,* XI, p. 228, *Nachgelassene Schriften,* Breslau 1885, IV, p. 324f, has however, argued against this theory on the ground that with the Alexandrians the use of Place as a synonym for God is isolated; while, on the other hand, in Jewish literature it is much more popular.   Far more plausible appears the

Temple service, R. Eliezer suggests, they used an abbreviation of God's proper name, Ja.[4]

The principal attribute of divinity to R. Eliezer was strength. Thus, he suggested that if the pagans should urge the Israelites to worship idols their retort should be: if these idols can cause the heaven and the earth to pass away, we shall worship them, but if not, then "may they perish from the earth."[5] God's strength manifests itself in His complete mastery over the events of history, but even more so in the universe which is His creation. In discussing the creation R. Eliezer, like his colleagues, betrays the influence of the general cosmological notions that were current at the time. He maintains that there were two primal substances out of which the heaven and the earth were respectively formed.[6] In its shape,

---

suggestion of J. A. Montgomery, who calls attention to the native Hebrew use of *ha-Makom* for "the place of the deity," or a shrine. Its application as a synonym for the proper name of God would then be merely a derivative from the identification of God with the place of His worship. See his article, " 'The Place' as an Appellation of Deity," *JBL*, XXIV 1905, pp. 22-27, and cf. F. R. and C. R. Conder, *A Handbook to the Bible*, p. 187.

4. M. Sukka 4:5. The name *Ja* was already used in the Bible. It is the regular name for the deity in the Elephantine papyri, where it also occurs in compounds. Diaspora Jewry, in general, made extensive use of this name, and it is often found in magic formulae. See Bousset, *Die Religion des Judentums in neutestamenlichen Zeitalter*, Tuebingen 1926, p. 63, note 2; H. Gressman, *Die Aufgaben der Wissenschaft des nachbiblischen Judentums*, Giessen 1925, p. 13ff. According to a Talmudic tradition the discontinuance of the pronunciation of God's proper name goes back to the time of the death of Simon the Just. See Tos. Sota 13:8 (p. 239) and Yoma 9b. It was likewise discontinued in the Septuagint. Cf. Marmorstein, *op. cit.*, p. 19f and Boussett, *op. cit.*, p. 307ff.

5. R. Joshua suggests another retort: 'if they can create heaven and earth we will worship them.' Tan., Mishpatim 12.

6. Ecc. R. 3:26; Gen. R. 12:11; Yoma 54b. R. Joshua in all these instances accepts one primal substance. The rabbis, of course, assumed that these primal substances were not eternal but created. In certain Greek conceptions the primal substances were eternal. Cf.

the world resembles an exedra, the northern side of which is un-
covered; and it was formed from the center outward.[7] In common
with his colleague R. Joshua, R. Eliezer entertained notions of a
bottomless abyss located somewhere in the sea which swallows all
other water that comes in contact with it, something like the Greek
conception of Charybdes.[8] He knew the correct explanation for the
genesis of rain: that it is the transformed mists gathering in the
air from the evaporated oceanic waters.[9]

Gen. R. 1:12 where a "philosopher" is quoted arguing with R. Gamaliel. Your God, said the "philosopher", is a great artist but he found
good materias which helped him: waste (*tohu*), desolation (*bohu*),
darkness, wind, water, watery depths (*t'homot*). R. Gamaliel then
cited a number of text-proofs to demonstrate that these materials
had themselves been created. For the cosmologies of the Greek philosophers, see E. Zeller, *Die Philosophie der Griechen*, Leipzig 1892,
I[1], pp. 73-101, 187-196; I[2], 643-650, 783-787, 1001-1007, 1033f; II[2],
Leipzig 1879, pp. 435-447. Cf. also Aptowitzer, "Zur Kosmologie in
der Agada", *MGWJ*, LXXII 1928, pp. 364-366. According to a tradition in the Midrash ha-Gadol on Genesis, p. 14, the two primal substances of R. Eliezer were the snow under the throne of God's glory
and the light emanating from His garments; the one primal substance
of R. Joshua the same tradition identifies as snow. Yoma 54b supports snow as the one primal substance of R. Joshua, but there seems
to be no parallel for snow and light as the two primal substances of
R. Eliezer. The compiler of the Midrash may, however, have used a
source which is no longer extant.

    7. B. B. 25a-b; Yoma 54b; Yalkut on Job 38:5. The Pytha-
goreans pictured creation as having begun through a fire operating
at the center and spreading outward. Cf. Zeller, II, p. 412.

    8. Gen. R. 13:6; Ecc. R. 1:15.

    9. Taan. ed. Malter, Philadelphia 1928, p. 64 and note 159; Gen.
R. 13:9; Tan. Mikes 1. Cf. Gen. R. 13:6. R. Joshua imagined the
clouds as sieve-like vessels which receive the water from above the
firmament and let it come down in the form of rain. R. Eliezer was
incorrect however in attributing the removal of the salty taste of the
sea water to the activity of the clouds. The salt, being heavier, does
not enter the mists from which the clouds are formed. See S. Krauss,
"Conception of Wind, Rain, and Dew in the Talmud" (Hebrew), in *ha-
Sofeh l'Hokmat Yisrael*, X 1916, p. 308.

In common with his colleagues, R. Eliezer also taught the doctrine of God's providence. History was to him no more than the process whereby God's plans and decisions are unfolded.[10] The main concern of God's providential ordering of history is the well being of His people, Israel. The relationship of Israel to God, R. Eliezer on one occasion compared to the relationship of a daughter to her kingly father. If it had not been for Israel the whole creation would not have taken place, and Israel will, in spite of all vicissitudes, endure under God's special protection forever.[11]

In the true spirit of Rabbinic edification, R. Eliezer loved to dwell on the acts whereby God delivered Israel in the past. The Egyptian plagues were not the simple episodes related in the Bible; each plague was really of a fourfold nature, and the total that was visited on Egypt was not ten, but forty. Nor was this all. When the Egyptians, in pursuit of the Israelites, came to the Red Sea, they were again punished, and this time the plagues numbered fully two hundred.[12] God parted the waters of the Red Sea for the Israelites, and the news of the event resounded from one end of the world to the other. It was then that God made Himself manifest to His people in all His glory. "When a king comes into a province, men wonder, 'who is the King?', for he is no more than flesh and blood, even as they are. But when God revealed Himself to the Israelites as they had crossed the Red Sea, they were not obliged to ask that He be pointed out to them; for when they saw Him, majestic and glorious, they recognized Him. It was then that they, pointing at Him, burst forth in song, 'This is my God and I will glorify Him, the God of my Fathers and I will exalt Him'" (Ex. 15:2).[13]

God fed the Israelites with manna for forty years in the desert until the death of Moses on the seventh of Shebat; and even for

10. P. R. 117a; Tan. Buber, B'reshit 28.
11. Cant. R. 1:49; Tan. Buber, Tesaveh 9. Cf. Vehiz. p. 199f.
12. Mek. Beshalah 6; R. Simeon, p. 55; Mid. Tehil. Ps. 78:15.
13. Mek. on Ex. 15:2. Cf. R. Simeon, ad locum.

seventy more days thereafter.[14] Nor were those trying experiences of the long journey, the episode with the Egyptians at the Red Sea, and the tedious march through the desert, without their providential significance: they were really the devices by which God tested and trained Israel in the discipline of a united national life. When they came to the mountain of Sinai, God formed the Israelites into a perfect people: the blind saw, the dumb spoke, the deaf heard, the lame stood up, and the foolish understood. When they entered Canaan, God continued His fostering care over them. Thus, He defeated for them the hosts of Sisera, and annihilated the mighty army of Sennacherib when they tried to break into Jerusalem.[15] In the future, too, God will arise "like a mighty man stirred with wine" to battle for His people and redeem them. Then it will be the turn of Edom-Rome to give way; she, also, will finally be crushed by the vengeance which God Himself will administer against her.[16]

God's providence, however, is not limited to the group; it ex-

---

14.   Mek. Jethro, Amalek 1; R. Simeon p. 85; Lekah on Ex. 17:1; Mek. Beshalah, Vayasah 5. R. Eliezer is the only authority who places the death of Moses on the seventh of Shebat. Josephus (*Ant* 4, 8, 49) places it on the first of Adar. All other authorities place it on the seventh of Adar. Cf. Ginzberg, *Legends of the Jews,* Philadelphia 1909—28, VI, p. 167, note 966.

15.   Mek. Beshalah 1: R. Simeon p. 38; P. R. 117a, 160b; Mek. Jethro, Bahodesh 9 (ed. Horovitz, p. 235). Cf. R. Simeon, p. 113.

16.   Mid. Tehil. Ps. 78:18, Tan. Buber, B'reshit 28, Mid. Tann. on Deut. 32:39, P. S. E. Z. p. 26. Cf. L. Ginzberg, *Legends,* V, pp. 272f, note 19, who points out that the use of the term Edom as well as of such related terms as Esau and Seir for Rome, was old and was probably coined at the time of Herod, whose designation the Idumean was applied to his masters, the Romans. Early Christian authorities likewise applied these Biblical applications to Rome. Cf. Jerome, Is. 21:2, who takes Dumah and Seir to refer to Rome exactly as does R. Meir in j Taan. I, C4a. Later on, when Rome adopted Christianity the same appelations were transferred to the Christians and Christianity. Cf. Zunz, *Die synagogale Poesie des Mitelalters,* Berlin 1855, pp. 437-448 and *Literaturgeschichte der synagogalen Poesie,* Berlin 1865-67, p. 620.

tends to individuals as well. God was with the patriarchs, and He
always interceded to give them His protection. R. Eliezer enlarged
particularly on the punishment God visited on Pharaoh and the
Philistine king Abimelech, when they detained and sought to molest
Abraham's wife, Sarah. God likewise interceded for Moses. Thus,
when his enemies tried to betray him to Pharaoh, God smote them
with lameness, deafness, and blindness.[17] To the deserving God
is similarly prepared to offer His care and protection in all generations to come, and reliance upon God is indeed one of the virtues
that pious men must cultivate. "Any one who has a morsel of bread
in his basket and worries as to what he will eat the following day,
manifests a lack of faith in God's providence," was a famous dictum
of R. Eliezer.[18]

R. Eliezer and his colleagues clashed in their conception of the
other attribute generally posited of God, His justice. Absolute and
self-consistent justice had always been posited of God by the ancient
Hebrews, but with the development of prophecy God's mercy was
likewise assumed.[19] The Pharisees inherited both doctrines, but in
the very nature of things, they could not define the exact limits
where the one was to end and the other begin. Here R. Eliezer
and his colleagues differed. With their deeper concern for the
individual, they, in a certain sense, extended the doctrine of providence and placed their emphasis on the side of God's mercy.
R. Eliezer's emphasis was on the side of justice.

The chief factor in the working of God's providence, as taught
by R. Eliezer, is man's merits. When the Israelites live by the
will of God, prosperity and peace reign in the land, but when they
do not, strife and hunger set in instead. Indeed, just as every sin
is followed by some punishment, so conversely, every misfortune

---

17. Gen. R. 52:14; Mek. on Ex. 18:4; R. Simeon, *ad locum*.

18. Sota 48b; Mek. R. Simeon p. 75; Yalkut on Zech. 4. Cf.
Mek. Beshalah 2 (ed. Friedmann p. 47b) where this statement is
quoted in the name of R. Elazar of Modein.

19. Cf. W. R. Smith, *The Prophets of Israel*, London 1919, pp.
71ff, 161ff; H. P. Smith, *The Religion of Israel*, N. Y. 1928, pp. 101ff,
145ff.

befalling a person or a people may be regarded as the consequence
of some sin. It was, upon ultimate analysis, the sinfulness of the
people that was responsible for the destruction of the Temple and
all the tragedy consequent upon it. Indeed, God could not have
avoided that tragedy even if He had wanted to. For God's con-
duct is in a sense limited by the principle of justice which is inherent in His nature, as well as in that of the world which He has
made. Thus, God, reports R. Eliezer, 'roars like a lion' at each
watch in the night, in grief for His abode which is in ruins, but
He can do nothing, for the Israelites are in sin and a 'just' sentence
must be executed. Against His own will God must contain Himself,
pretending indifference, 'as if He sleepeth.' "I must act according
to justice," R. Eliezer quotes in the name of God, "for even if by
one step I deviate from justice, the world would at once collapse."[20]
The rewards and punishments of God are, however, not confined to
this world. As far as the individual is concerned, they prevail
after death as well. It is then that the souls of the righteous find
repose under the throne of God's glory, while the souls of the wicked
wander on in filth without finding rest.[21] Different fates are similarly awaiting the righteous and the wicked in the new age in the
hereafter: for the former there will be endless blessedness and peace;
for the latter, the endless terrors of Gehenna.[22]

As a consequence of God's justice, R. Eliezer emphasized the
doctrine of talio, the doctrine that God's punishments are in some
way analogous to man's sins. R. Akiba repeated it as one of R.
Eliezer's favorite teachings; and it was on the basis of this doctrine
that R. Eliezer later attributed his arrest on the suspicion of Chris-

---

20. Mek. Kaspa, Mishpatin 20 (ed. Horowitz-Rabin p. 329);
Mid. Tehil. Ps. 72:3; j Yoma I, 38c. Cf. Mid. Tehil. Ps. 137, end; Ber.
3a; Mid. Tehil. Ps. 78:18; Tan. Buber, B'reshit 28; Tan. Mishpatim 5;
Gen. R. 26:14; Mid. Tann. on Deut. 32:41. Cf. Deut. R. 5:4; Tan.
Buber, Mishpatim 4.

21. Shab. 152b. Cf. Rabinovicz, ad locum. Similarly in IV
Ezra 7:80. Cf. also Rosenthal, Vier apokryphische Buecher, Leipzig
1885, p. 64.

22. See below, p. 53ff.

tian heresy to the fact that he had at one time listened with satis-
faction to a halakah transmitted to him in the name of Jesus.[23] Nor
do God's punishments come suddenly, without due warning. God
never inflicts punishment on Israel unless He has previously warned
them. These warnings also come to men individually through different signs and portents. "A man does not see a wild beast,"
runs a homily by R. Eliezer, "unless he has merited death by a
wild beast, and he does not see a serpent unless he has merited
death through a serpent." Sickness should always be a warning
to man; he should look upon it as a summons to an indictment, and
he should at once take effective steps to clear himself.[24]

The principal medium for clearing one's self, whether as an individual or as a group, is, of course, repentance, to which God is always responsive. For God is really loathe to punish; He would much
prefer that men reform, and then punishment would be unnecessary.
"Repent the day before you die," R. Eliezer advised his followers.
"Does a man know when he is to die?" his disciples wondered.
"Indeed," replied he, "a man should, therefore, repent every day,
since he may die the day following. 'Let thy garments always be

---

23. A. Z. 16b; Tos. Hul. 2:24,25 (p. 503); Ecc. R. 1:24. See above,
p. 16. It is possible that R. Akiba was only deferring to R. Eliezer
when in speaking to him about this doctrine, he described it as "what
you have taught me."

24. Introduction, Lam. R. 27; Sifra, Behukottai, p. 11b; Sem.
d'R. Hiya 1:45 (in Sem. ed. Higger, p. 214:41-52). Notions of talio
were entertained in Biblical times. Cf. Deut. 28:47; Lev. 26:34f ;I Sam.
15:23. These notions occur in much more elaborate form in Apocryphal and Talmudic writings. See the discussion of Heinemann, *Philons
griechische und juedische Bildung*, Breslau 1929, pp. 364-383. It may
have been for reasons of talio that R. Eliezer confined the selling of a
thief as a slave to such instances where the price offered for him
was equivalent to the amount of the theft. See Abadim 2:9 (in Seven
Minor Treatises); Kid. 18a. Cf. Mek. Mishpatim 12 where R. Eliezer is
quoted as sanctioning his sale where the price offered exceeds the
amount of the theft.

white, and thy head lack no oil (Ecc. 9:8)' "[25] Exactly how one
was to repent R. Eliezer does not tell us. But apparently one
ought to go through some visible acts that would indicate his regret
for past transgressions, in addition to the inner resolve for moral
improvement in the future. Thus, Reuben, the first man to have
repented, fasted and sat in sackcloth. Because he was first in this
practice, God rewarded him with the prophet Hosea, who was an
offspring of the Reubenite tribe.[26]

Repentance should be the concern of every one since sin is so
universal. One who comes from righteous ancestry will be able to
exercise a greater check on himself; he will be less prone to sin.
But sin in one form or another cannot be escaped; it is the normal
lot of all mortal men. Even the patriarchs were not entirely blameless. The verse in Ecc. 7:20: 'For there is no righteous man on
earth who does not sin,' was impressed by R. Eliezer on his disciples, and R. Akiba so repeated it in his name.[27] There is, however, no justification for the theory[28] that R. Eliezer believed in
the doctrine of original sin as a consequence of Adam's fall.

R. Eliezer's remedy for sin was, as suggested before, repentance.
But since sin was so universal and so much a part of human nature,
how could one hope to be in right relations with God on the basis
of merit, even with the remedy of repentance? Moved by a deeper

---

25. Shab. 153a, Yalkut, Ecc. section 979. Cf. also Ecc. R. 9:6;
Ab. 2:10; A. R. N. 15 (end); II A. R. N. 29; Sem. d'R. Hiya 2:1 and
editor's note on p. 61. For the efficacy of repentance cf. also P. S. E.
Z. ch. 22, 23.

26. Gen. R. 84:18. Cf. P. R. 199a.

27. Midrash Mishle 11:21; Yalkut, Proverbs, scetion 947; Ar. 17a;
San. 101a; Cf. P. S. E. Z. ch. 20, which describes the specific "sins"
of the patriarchs. Abraham and Isaac were the fathers of unworthy
children in Ishmael and Esau respectively. Jacob transgressed Lev.
18: 18 by marrying two sisters, Rachel and Leah. There were many
other rabbis who permitted themselves to find faults with the patriarchs. Cf. J. Wohlgemut, "Zur Charaketristik des Suendenbewustseins im talmudischen Judentum", *Jeshurun,* XI 1924, pp. 97-112.

28. Rosenthal, *op. cit.,* p. 60f.

concern for the individual, R. Eliezer's colleagues invoked the principle of God's mercy, and assured men that even regardless of deserts, when a soul cries out in anguish to God, it is certain to be heard and responded to. R. Joshua went out of his way to assure his generation that, repentance or no repentance, when the proper time comes, God, in His own wisdom and mercy, will redeem Israel. R. Eliezer, however, continued to defend the doctrine of justice, ruling that without full repentance salvation was not possible. Indeed, he did not even hesitate to suggest, that should the Israelites never repent, they would never be redeemed. Confronted with the vigorous protests of the more tender R. Joshua, R. Eliezer finally modified his position. He conceded that when the proper time comes God will force upon Israel cruel treatment from unfriendly governments, and then they will have to repent, even if they should not be minded to do so. He still maintained, however, that redemption without repentance was not possible.[29]

2. *Intermediaries and Magic.*—Modifying the doctrine of monotheism was the notion of intermediaries between God and man which was finally admitted within the purview of Pharisaic Judaism. To some extent this was a concession on the part of Pharisaism to the old folk religion of Israel. It was reinforced by the very triumph of monotheism and the constant exaltation of the God idea, which, in spite of the doctrine of Providence, tended to remove the divine from the realm of men. In addition to this, there was the pressure

---

29. San. 97b, 98a; j Taan. I. 63d. Cf. Tan. Buber, Behukottai 5. That the redemption must be preceded by reprentance was also taught by the author of IV Ezra, 4:35ff. Cf. Rosenthal, *op. cit.,* p. 61f and Moore, *Judaism,* II, p. 351. Cf. also San. 44a where R. Eliezer suggests that Phineas, in trying to stay the plague that was ravaging Israel, did not pray, as the text suggests, but protested instead that the plague was "unjust," that the magnitude of God's punishment was not justified by the extent of Israel's sin. Cf. also P.S.E.Z. ch. 22, where R. Eliezer limits the efficacy of prayer and charity as compared with repentance, and P.R.E. ch. 3 where he describes repentane as the stabilizing element of the world without which creation could not endure.

brought to bear by contemporary syncretism, in which the notion of mediating forces played a significant role. God's own attributes, for example, were hypostasized and given independent status, somewhat after the fashion of Platonic ideas.[30] Angelology, in its larger developments, which already the rabbis themselves traced back to the influence of the post-exilic period,[31] grew into even wider ramifications. There were the notions of the Chaldean astral religion, which, after achieving complete sway over the whole Hellenistic world, invaded Palestine as well.[32] Together with these, there also flourished what was equally popular in the Hellenistic world, the occult practice of magic by which men sought a greater control over their en-

---

30. Moore, "Intermediaries in Jewish Theology," *HTR*, XV 1922, pp. 41-62, is probably correct, that the uses of "the word of God," "the glory of God" or "the presence of God," as substitutes for the tetragrammaton in the Targum, are but a phase of the general diffidence of the period to employ God's proper name, as well as an effort to remove anthropomorphisms. But when it comes to God's attributes of justice and mercy, the מדת הדין and the מדת הרחמים, we are dealing with distinct entities whose functions do not differ significantly from those of mediators. The rabbis generally understood *Jahveh* as referring to the attribute of mercy and *Elohim*, to the attribute of justice. Philo reverses this, regarding *Elohim* as referring to mercy and *Jahveh* to justice (see Siegfried, *Philo*, p. 213f). Cf. Bousset, *op. cit.*, p. 342, note 1, and p. 350f; Joel, *Blicke*, p. 114ff.

31. "The Israelites brought with them the names of angels from Babylonia." j R. H. I, 56d; Gen. R. 48:9. The angels mentioned in the early portions of the Bible are anonymous, and represent no more than self-manifestations of God. It is symbolic of a large development when after the exile angels with specific names and definite functions appear. The post-exilic period meant, of course, not only contact with the Persian religion where angelology was extensively developed, but also a great impetus to the growth of monotheism with its increased need of mediators. Cf. Bousset, *op. cit.*, p. 320ff.

32. See Bousset, p. 476ff; H. Gressman, *Die Aufgaben der Wissenschaft*, p. 19ff; *The Tower of Babel*, N. Y. 1928, pp. 69-73; Moore, *Judaism*, I, p. 457f, and *idem*, "Fate and Free Will in the Jewish Philosophies," *HTR*, XXII 1929, p. 379ff.

vironment and an escape from the tyrannies of astral fate or from evil spirits.[33] These developments are strikingly illustrated in the popular literature of our period as well as in the utterances of the later Amoraim. That they are not so conspicuous in the Tannaitic literature is probably due, for one thing, to the nature of that literature. This consists essentially of authoritative legal maxims with which beliefs about angelology and magic could not very well be classified. The Tannaim undoubtedly steered clear of the extremes reached by the general public. Expressions of R. Eliezer and his colleagues leave no doubt, however, that in their basic elements these beliefs had long been shared by them as well.

R. Eliezer speaks of hosts of angels standing like the hosts of an army, each under its own banner.[34] These angels act as God's executives, carrying out His will on earth. It was Gabriel, appearing like a small disk of fire, who annihilated the army of Sennacherib. He reappeared in the camp of the Chaldeans; it was God's decree, however, that Jerusalem be destroyed and he therefore left Nebuchadnezzar's army undisturbed.[35] It was an angel who dragged the bodies of Nadab and Abihu after their death out of the sanctuary. And it was similarly an angel who spoke through the mouth of Balaam when, against his original intent, he invoked his blessings upon Israel.[36]

---

33. Cf. Tarn, *Hellenistic Civilization*, London 1927, p. 291f.

34. Mid. Tehil. Ps. 22:12.

35. P. R. 160b. Cf. San. 95b where R. Eliezer says that Sennacherib's army was destroyed by the "hand of God." See Ginzberg, *Legends*, VI, p. 363, notes 58 and 59, who cites other accounts as to how the Assyrians were destroyed. The view that Gabriel destroyed the Assyrians suggests that R. Eliezer considered him the guardian angel of Israel. Cf., however, Ginzberg, *ibid*, V, 75, note 19, who thinks that this view of R. Eliezer agrees with Origen who regarded Gabriel as the angel of war.

36. Lekah, Shemini, p. 54; Sifra, Shemini, p. 45b. Cf. Mid. ha-Gadol on Lev., p. 191 (ed. Rabinowitz); Nu. R. 20:16. In the P. S. E. Z. R. Eliezer also alludes to angels who are in charge of the storehouse where the souls are kept (p. 32). He also mentions by name the

R. Eliezer believed in the malevolent effects of the "evil eye," which may cause even the death of its victim.[37] Tradition has transmitted a number of stories which picture R. Eliezer as an active magician. On one occasion, R. Eliezer, R. Joshua, and R. Akiba are supposed to have come under the spell of a sectarian magician who was with them in a bath house in Tiberias. At the direction of R. Eliezer, R. Joshua is reported to have reciprocated with a spell upon the magician. The latter then agreed on a mutual release. While on

---

angels Metatron (p. 31) and Gabriel (pp. 32, 35). Gabriel we have already met elsewhere in the theology of R. Eliezer. In Sifre, Deut. section 338, Mid. Tann. on Deut. 32:49 (Cf. Sifre, Nu. section 136) R. Eliezer states that God's finger was a Metatron to Moses when He pointed out to him the promised land. Here, however, the word Metatron does not stand for the proper name of the angel. It is still used in its original meaning of scout or guide, like the Latin *metator* from which it seems to be derived. Cf. Moore, "Intermediaries," pp. 62-79, who argues that Metatron, in its original meaning of scout or guide, was first used as an appellative of God Himself because He guided the Israelites on their way from Egypt. It was only later on that metatron came to stand for a distinct angel. Cf. also P. S. E. Z. p. 40, where R. Eliezer refers to the hypostases of the מדת הדין and the מדת הרחמים, and *ibid*, p. 10, where he describes the different phases of the sun's eclipse as betokening evil for the pagans, and of the moon, for the Jews. This is an interesting deviation from the general Hellenistic belief where the eclipse not merely betokened but actually determined evil. The Israelites are also assured in our passage that should they live in accordance with God's law, they will be totally free from the planetary influences. Cf. Tos. Sukka 2:6 (p. 194) and Sukka 29a where the same passage about the eclipses is quoted ananymously. Cf. also Mek. Bo 2 and Yalkut on Genesis, section 188.

37. San. 93a. The Amoraim Rab and R. Jose b. Hanina propose the same explanation. See San. *l. c.* and Yalkut on Zechariah, section 570. The belief in the malevolent effects of the "evil eye," still surviving among many people today, was very popular among all primitive races. It is alluded to in the Bible (Deut. 28:54, 56; Is. 13:18 and Psalm 92:11). Cf. F. T. Elworthy, "Evil Eye," in Hasting's *Encyclopaedia of Religion and Ethics*, V 1912, p. 608ff, and cf. L. Blau, *Das altjuedische Zauberwesen*, Strassburg 1898, p. 152ff.

their journey to Rome, R. Eliezer, R. Joshua, and R. Gamaliel are
said to have been implored by their host to help his son who was
childless. R. Joshua, again at the direction of R. Eliezer, performed
a magic act and identified the witch who had worked the spell upon
the childless man. "Release the knot," demanded R. Joshua of
the witch, threatening to expose her. "I cannot," the witch protested, "I cast the knot into the sea." Once more R. Joshua resorted to magic and the sea returned the knot, which was now released. In time a child was born to that man, and it grew up to be
no other than R. Judah b. Batira. At the request of R. Akiba,
R. Eliezer is at one time supposed to have exercised a charm, thereby filling an entire field with gourds; by means of another charm
he is then supposed to have transferred them to a single place.[38]
These stories are, of course, clear legend. But they probably pre-
suppose some genuine interest on the part of R. Eliezer in the practical workings of magic.

   3. *Eschatology.*—We also meet with Pharisaic universalism in
the elaborate doctrines of eschatology. Developing from what was
no more than a hope for national vindication in the prophets, these
doctrines, by the first century of our era, also included the beliefs
in the general resurrection of the dead, the day of Judgment, notions
of a cosmic transformation, and the final consignment of the righteous to a life of endless peace in the garden of Eden and of the
wicked to a life of everlasting torments in Gehenna. As far as the
general outline of these beliefs was concerned, they were shared by
R. Eliezer as much as by his colleagues. Thus, R. Eliezer speaks

----

   38. j San. VII, 25d; San. 68a. The knot figures prominently
in the magic lore of all primitive peoples. The tying of the knot
implies something "bound"; it, therefore, becomes a spell impeding
the actions of those against whom it is directed. The loosing of the
knot implies the removal of the impediment caused by its original
tying. See W. J. Dilling in Hasting's *Encyclopaedia of Religion and
Ethics*, VII 1912, p. 747f. For the use of the knot as a magic symbol
in Biblical literature, see S. Gandz, "The Knot in Hebrew Literature,"
in *ISIS*, XIV 1930, p. 192.

of the final redemption of Israel, when Rome, the last of the four
ungodly kingdoms, will be destroyed.[39]   This redemption will be
preceded by a period of world distress, darkness, and moral decline,
the throes of the race, laboring to bring forth the Messiah ('the
travails of the Messiah').   There will be a war—the war of Gog
and Magog, when a mighty coalition of peoples will endeavor for
the last time to harass Israel.   But they will all be overcome, and
Israel under the leadership of the Messiah, will emerge triumphant.
This will be followed by the Day of Judgment, when the living and
the dead, now risen from their graves, will be summoned before God
to trial so that the proper rewards and punishments might be al-
loted to them.   The cosmos itself will be rebuilt on new foundations.   The ultimate stage in the new world order—the 'Olam Haba'
or 'l'atid labo' of traditional literature—will finally be ushered in,
with its store of bliss for the righteous and suffering for the wicked.[40]

---

39.   Mid. Tann. on Deut. 32 :39.   Cf. P. S. E. Z., p. 26.   Cf. Moore,
Judaism, II, p. 331, note 2, and Bousset, *op. cit.*, p. 218.   Cf. also P.R.E.
ch. 28, where R. Eliezer similarly alludes to "four kingdoms."   The
identifications are, however, the work of a later hand since the fourth
kingdom is identified with the Moslem empire!   R. Eliezer is the
authority for this statement in the manuscript underlying Friedlander's translation.   The printed texts attribute it to R. Akiba.

40.   Mek. Vayasa, B'shalah 4 (Horovitz, p. 169).   Similarly in
IV Ezra 5:1ff, 6:13ff, 7:10-35.   Cf. Rosenthal, *op. cit.*, p. 65, and
note 2; Moore, *Judaism*, II, p. 360ff; Tan. Buber, Tesaveh 9.   Cf. Tan.
Tesaveh 13, and Vehiz, p. 199f; P. R. E. ch. 51.   The rabbis differed
in estimating the duration of the transition period.   In Mek. Amalek
B'shalah 2 (Horovitz, p. 187) R. Eliezer fixed it at "three genera-
tions"; in Tan. Ekeb 7, at 100 years; in San. 99a, at 40 years; in
P. R. p. 4a-b, at 400 years; in Mid. Tehil. Ps. 90:17, at 1000 years.
Rosenthal, who maintains that IV Ezra was written by a pupil of
R. Eliezer, accepts the reading in the Pesikta as genuine since IV
Ezra (4:28) also fixes this time at 400 years (*op. cit.*, p. 64 and note
2).   His theory about the author of IV Ezra, is, however, by no means
well established, and we cannot therefore follow him in his determination of sources either.   Cf. P. R. *l. c.*, editor's note 54.   Cf. also P.R.
E. ch. 33, where R. Eliezer states that the dead will be resurrected
in their shrouds.

R. Eliezer and his colleagues, however, clashed sharply in determining who will be eligible to share in the Judgment Day and the blessedness of the world to come—questions which tradition had not as yet decided. Prophecy had succeeded in modifying the more ancient Hebraic conception, and established the principle that "the soul that sinneth, it shall die." Adult offspring of sinners will, therefore, according to this, be tried on their own merits. What, however, of the minor children of sinners, who are not as yet responsible for their own doings, and cannot be tried on the basis of individual merit? Would, for instance, those upon whom God had already pronounced a special sentence—the inhabitants of Sodom, the generation that died in the desert because of their rebellion against God and Moses, Korah and his followers, the northern tribes of Israel—would they, too, be summoned for trial on the Day of Judgement? What will be the fate of righteous gentiles—those who were not technically affiliated with Israel, but who, nevertheless, led blameless lives? R. Joshua, moving toward a greater indvidualism, ruled that the minor children of sinners will have a share in the world to come, regardless of the fate befalling their parents. R. Joshua similarly declared, that in the hereafter all special sentences would be disregarded, and that all the dead without any distinction would be resurrected and have the opportunity for trial on the Day of Judgment on the basis of their individual merits. He likewise transcended all particularism and pronounced righteous gentiles eligible for a share in the golden age of the hereafter on a footing of equality with righteous Israelites. R. Eliezer in each instance took the narrower view. Allying himself with the more ancient tendency, he visited the guilt of sinful parents upon their minor children, and denied them a share in the world to come. Similarly, he ruled that the special sentences would remain, and that those suffering under them would not be included in the general resurrection and judgement. Likewise, he consigned all gentiles to Gehenna, regardless of the lives they lived, and even without giving them the chance for a trial on Judgment Day.[41]

The *Pseudo-Seder Eliahu Zuta* describes, in a number of passages attributed to R. Eliezer, some of the detailed events marking the transition from the present life to the world of the hereafter, and they betray boldly the narrow, particularistic position of R. Eliezer. As the first step in the final judgment of the world, the heavens and the earth will be confronted with charges. "You were my first creation" (Gen. 1:1), God will say to them: "You saw my shekinah depart, my abode destroyed, and my children banished into exile— why did you not intercede in their behalf with a plea for mercy?" God will repeat this to all the planets, the angels, the patriarchs, and even to His own throne. Finally He will in anger destroy the world but He will soon rebuild it on new foundations. The resurrection will follow, and the judgment of the dead, with the earth itself testifying against the sinners. Then God will cast all the heathens into Gehenna. But Gehenna will protest, asking that the sinners in Israel be cast into it as well. God will reply:

---

41. I A. R. N. 36, San. 105a and Tos. San. 13:2 (p. 434). Cf. Mid. Mishle 17:1 and Bacher, *Tannaiten*, I, p. 143f, note 4. M. San. 10:3 transmits another tradition as to the dispute concerning the participation of the inhabitants of Sodom, *etc.* in the final judgement, the dispute being between R. Akiba and R. Eliezer, with R. Eliezer maintaining the more lenient view. Cf. also Tos. San. 13:10 (p. 435). In the light of R. Eliezer's general position, the reading in A. R. N. seems more plausible. Cf. Bacher, *ibid*, p. 142 and note 4. According to IV Ezra 13:38-48, the gentiles will have no share in the world to come but the ten tribes of Northern Israel will. The Apoc. of Baruch 72:2 accords a share in the world to come to righteous gentiles. In Tos. San. 13:1 (p. 434) the dispute concerning the minor children of sinners is between R. Gamaliel and R. Joshua, with Gamaliel maintaining the position that is in our sources attributed to R. Eliezer. In San. 110b the dispute is between R. Gamaliel and R. Akiba, R. Akiba maintaining the view that is attributed in the other sources to R. Joshua.

"I have filled you with the heathen and you have no more room."
After further pleading from Gehenna, God will increase its space
and sinners in Israel will then be cast there too.

The righteous will then be invited to an elaborate banquet in
the garden of Eden, with which their new life will begin. God and
David will preside at the feast, both sitting side by side on chairs
set for them by the angel Gabriel. After the banqueting is over,
the patriarch Abraham will be invited to lead in saying grace, but
he will decline as being unworthy, since he was the father of a son
who provoked God (Ishmael). Isaac, Jacob, Moses, and Joshua will
each be invited in turn, but they will all decline: Isaac, because he
was the father of a son who destroyed God's abode; Jacob because he violated the law in being married to two sisters, Rachel and
Leah, at the same time, against Lev. 18:18; Moses, because he had
not been privileged to enter the holy land; and Joshua, because
he left no posterity. The invitation will then be extended to David
who will accept. The banquet will finally conclude with a learned
discourse in halakah and aggadah in which David will lead and all
the assembled guests join with appropriate responses. At the suggestion of Gabriel, which will be seconded by the Messiah, God
will open the portals of Gehenna, so that the heathens may look
on with envy at the blessedness of Israel. Israel will, at last, have
been vindicated.[42]

4. *Particularism vs. Universalism.*—The universalism of the
Pharisees also manifested itself in their gradual detachment of religion from the territorial unit and the national self. Throughout the
latter part of the Second Commonwealth, when there seems to have

---

42. P. S. E. Z. ch. 20, 21. It would seem from this account
that R. Eliezer identified the future Messiah with David. There are
probably a number of later amplifications in this description. Its con-
signing all the non-Jews to Gehenna, its fault-finding with the patriarchs, its apotheosis of David, its emphasis of the duty of procreation, and its notions of a cosmic renewal, are however fully consistent
with R. Eliezer's general position, and there is no reason to dismiss
them as spurious. In its basic elements, at least, the passage is very
likely genuine.

been a continued flow of emigration from Palestine to the diaspora, the rabbis had tried to emphasize the greater holiness of Palestine, and the merits of living in the holy land.[43] They were particularly solicitous about Jerusalem, which served as a focal point for the far-flung Jewries scattered throughout the Hellenistic and Parthian worlds, and in their legislation endowed the holy city with all sorts of privileges.[44] Nevertheless, diaspora Jewry grew until it more than outnumbered the Jewish community in Palestine. Closely related to this was the extensive propaganda which was carried on among the pagans of the Empire, with the result that a vast number of proselytes and semi-proselytes were brought within the orbit of Judaism. Both these factors cooperated to transform Judaism from a cult limited to a territory and a nation, into a cosmopolitan religion of world significance. It was inevitable that the catastrophe of the year 70 C.E., involving the destruction of Jerusalem as a center and the further integration of Jewry with the rest of the empire, with a consequent increase in the importance of the diaspora factor, should have stimulated continued developments in the direction of universalism—a further detachment from territory and nation. It is equally clear, however, that a bloody war in which Jews had lost so much was bound to produce in the minds of others a reaction against the outside world and an effort to retire back into the national self.

It is precisely on this point that R. Eliezer and his colleagues were divided. R. Eliezer's colleagues moved toward further universalism. Already R. Johanan b. Zakkai had transferred some of the religious privileges formerly enjoyed by Jerusalem to the new

---

43. Thus, the ruling of the diaspora lands as levitically impure, which goes back to Maccabean times (Shab. 15b, j Pes. I, 27d), has been explained as an effort to discourage Jewish emigration following in the wake of the persecutions of Antiochus. See Weiss, *Dor*, I, p. 105 and Ginzberg, *Mekomah shel ha-Halakah*, p. 5.

44. See S. Krauss, "La defense d'elever du menu betail en Palestine," *REJ*, LII 1907, pp. 14-55, *Kadmoniot ha-Talmud*, Odessa 1914, I, pp. 93-113 and cf. A. Buechler, "La purete levitique de Jerusalem,*REJ*, LXII 1911, pp. 201-215, LXIII 1912, pp. 30-50.

center in Jabneh. But the Jabneh scholars now declared themselves prepared to shift these privileges again, should Jabneh also have to be abandoned for some new center.[45] The rabbis, similarly, abolished the old custom of carrying the fourth year products of neighborhood vineyards for consumption to Jerusalem.[46] They were likewise anxious to continue the old proselytising propaganda. True enough, many of the proselytes and semi-proselytes had proven themselves during the recent events disloyal to Judaism; it was also from their ranks prinicipally that the Christian missionaires were drawing their recruits.[47] Yet the mere fact that the competition of an active Christian propaganda existed, must have moved the rabbis to redouble their own efforts. R. Joshua was particularly active in championing this position. The great obstacle in the way of Jewish propaganda was the harsh requirements of circumcision, and R. Joshua therefore advocated that it be done away with.[48] The Jews had been defeated in the field of battle. But there were other fields where they might yet conquer—in the realm of the spirit. At any rate the propaganda was to go on.[49]

R. Eliezer opposed all this. To him Judaism was to remain

---

45. M. R. H. 4:1, 3.

46. In accordance with Lev. 19:24 these products were regarded as sacred. Cf. M. M. Sh. 5:2, R. H. 31b. Cf. Halevi, *Dorot*, Ie, 69f.

47. See Moore, *Judaism*, I, p. 342 and III, note 106. Cf. Jos., *Against Apion*, 2:11

48. See below note 65.

49. There is no justification for the assumption of Bousset, *op. cit.*, p. 84f, and others, that after 70 C. E. a great reaction against the propaganda set in. The conversions of Aquila and Flavius Clemens took place after 70. The expressions of the leading scholars are friendly to the proselyte, and, for that matter, to the non-Jew. There is no doubt that the extreme to which R. Eliezer's unfriendly attitude proceeded, was to some extent, at least, inspired by the recent events. But R. Eliezer was here as elsewhere betraying his general conservatism, his kinship to Shammaism, which had never been friendly to the propaganda. Cf. Graetz, "Agrippa II und der Zustand Judaeas" pp. 488-491, and Moore, *Judaism*, I, p. 342ff.

rooted in Palestine and in the holy city. He required postponing
the use of the new crops in the diaspora until after the offering
of the first fruits of the harvest (Omer) in the Temple in Jerusalem.[50] At the same time, he was severe in discriminating against
imported diaspora products as levitically unclean.[51] He did not
challenge the reform of R. Johanan b. Zakkai—that was now part
of tradition which he accepted—, but he declared himself ready to
oppose any further shifting of the religious privileges from Jabneh,
even though the center of Jewish life should have to be transferred
elsewhere.[52] He likewise demanded that the fourth year products of
neighborhood vineyards continue to be consumed in Jerusalem,
though the city was now in ruins.[53] Jewish piety was still to re-
volve about the holy land and the holy city. "All that good,"
which Jethro saw befalling Israel and which moved him to become
a proselyte (Ex. 18:9) was, according to R. Eliezer, God's promise

---

50. This was, of course, the regular law with regard to Palestine
crops (Lev. 23:10-14), but R. Eliezer extended it to the diaspora.
His colleagues agreed with him, however, in extending to diaspora
agriculture the required rejection of the first three year crops of
the fruits of trees (Lev. 19:23), and the prohibition of growing
diverse products in the same field (Lev. 19:19). See M. Kid. 1:9;
Sifre, Deut. section 59; Mid. Tann. on Deut. 12:1; j Orla III, 63b;
Kid. 37a. R. Elazar b. Jose reported a tradition in the name of R.
Jose b. Durmaskes, who in turn learnt his tradition from R. Jose
the Galilean, who learnt it from R. Johanan b. Nuri, that R. Eliezer
did not require rejecting the first three year crops of the fruits
of trees in the diaspora. On the basis of this, the Amoraim correct
our texts, making R. Eliezer exempt diaspora products from the prohibition of growing diverse seeds in the same field as well (Tos.
Orla 1:8 [p. 45]; Kid. 39a). It is more likely, however, that the
inaccuracy came into R. Elazar b. Jose's statement, which was so far
removed from its original source, than into the report of the
Mishnah, Sifre and the Midrash Tannaim. The Mishnah in Kid. 37a,
ed. Venice 1520, reads "R. Elazar" instead of "R. Eliezer." The Amoraic correction of the text clearly argues, however, for the reading
"R. Eliezer."

51. M. Ohol. 17:5.

52. M. R. H. 4:1.

of the holy land.[54] He who does not include in his benedictions
of grace after a meal, thankfulness to God for that 'pleasant, good
and spacious land' of Palestine has, he ruled, been derelict in his
religious duty.[55] R. Eliezer did not permit the selection of Ezekiel
ch. 16 as the prophetic reading in the synagogue, because it de-
nounces the vices of contemporary Jerusalem; and when on one
occasion he found a man reading that chapter, he rebuked him
sharply for it.[56]

Similarly, R. Eliezer objected to proselytising. There was very
little, he felt, to be expected from a gentile. Essentially he would
remain an idolator.[57] His sex life was on a consistently low moral
level—he was subject to the suspicion of cohabiting with animals.[58]
He was always prepared to deceive a Jew. Even in the occasional
good deed that the non-Jew performs, he is not moved by noble
impulses, but by a desire to boast about it later on.[59] And the
proselyte is not much better. He attributed the mass desertions of
proselytes from Judaism to their innately perverse nature. It was,

---

53. R. H. 31b and cf. Halevi, *Dorot*, 1e, p. 69.

54. Mek. Jethro, Amalek 1; R. Simeon, p. 88.

55. Ber. 48b. This liturgical formula is not an original composition of R. Eliezer; it was well known at the time. Its Greek
equivalent seems to be alluded to in the *Letter of Aristeas*, section
107, the Bok of Jubilees 13:6, and Jos. *Ant.* 4, 8, 22, (sections 242-
243). Cf. J. Weil, *Gen Agathen Kai Pollen, REJ*, LXXXII 1926, pp.
129-131, and L. Finkelstein, "The Birkat ha-Mazon," in *JQR*, N. S.,
XIX 1929, p. 230, note 39.

56. M. Meg. 4:10; Tos. Meg. 4:34 (p. 228); Meg. 25b; j Meg.
IV, 75c; Soferim 9:11. The colleagues of R. Eliezer did not object
to the reading of that chapter.

57. M. Hul. 2:7; Git. 45b; Men. 42a; Hul. 13a, 116b; A. Z. 32b;
j A. Z. II, 41b.

58. M. Para 2:1 and cf. commentary of Bartinoro, *ad locum;*
A. Z. 24a, Tos. Para 2:1 (p. 631). Cf. P. R. 56a, Sifre Zuta, p. 124.

59. P. R. *l. c.,* B. B. 10b. Cf. P. R. K. 12b and Tan., Ki Thisa 5.
Basing his interpretation on the same verse as R. Eliezer, R. Johanan
b. Zakkai explained: just as a sin offering atones for the sin of a
Jew, so good deeds, such as charity, atone for the sins of the non-Jew
(B. B. 10a). Cf. Bacher, *Tannaiten,* I, p. 37f.

indeed, for this reason, R. Eliezer suggested, that Scripture found it necessary to admonish the Israelites so often against offending them. It was a relapsed proselyte, according to him, that Ex. 23:4 and Deut. 20:1 meant by the word 'enemy'.[60] R. Eliezer was even unkind to those proselytes who remained Jews and suffered the persecutions of the Roman State; he regarded these persecutions as falling on them deservedly because they had probably embraced Judaism not out of love of God but out of fear of His punishments. Unlike R. Joshua, he commended the famous eighteen "measures" which the Shammaites had forced through a session of the academy in order to discourage social and religious intercourse between the Jews and the pagan world. According to R. Joshua these measures "had overstepped all limits."[61]

R. Eliezer could not, of course, ban proselytism altogether— that was too much a part of tradition. But he emphasized the caution that must be used to determine the proselyte's sincerity. Even Jethro, R. Eliezer explained, was not accepted as a proselyte until

---

60. Mek. Mishpatim 18, on Ex. 22:20. Cf. R. Simeon, p. 156; B. M. 59b; Lekah on Ex. 22:20; Vehiz, p. 138; Mid. Tann. on Deut. 19:20.

61. Jeb. 48b; Tos. Shab. 1:7 (p. 111), Shab. 153b; j Shab. I, 3c. The reference to a persecution of proselytes may go back to the reign of Domitian when many proselytes had their property confiscated or were actually executed as atheists. Cf. Graetz, "Die Reise der vier Tannaiten nach Rom," p. 194ff. Cf. M. Lerner, "Die achtzehn Bestimmungen, MWJ, IX 1882, pp. 113-144, X 1883, pp. 121-156, who refutes the theory, suggested by Graetz, Geschichte, III4, pp. 802-811, note 26, and accepted with minor reservations by S. Zeitlin, "Les dix—huit mesures", REJ, LXXVIII 1914, pp. 22-36, relating the "eighteen measures" with the revolutionary movement against Rome in 70 C. E. Certainly, R. Eliezer, who smuggled R. Jonahan out of the besieged city into the camp of Vespasian and surrendered with him to the Romans, would not have commended revolutionary enactments. Our sources furnish no adequate evidence for the specific dating of these measures. Lerner places them in the early years of Agrippa II's reign, but his arguments are by no means conclusive.

God had given Moses due assurance of his sincerity.[62] Tradition has recorded a number of incidents illustrating the extremes to which R. Eliezer went in exercising this 'caution' with those who sought conversion to Judaism. Once a gentile woman came asking that he convert her. He requested that she review for him the record of her past life. When he discovered that she had cohabited with her own son, and had given birth to a child by him, he dismissed her summarily with sharp rebukes, to the amazement of his own pupils. She then turned to R. Joshua. The latter was more sympathetic, and made her a convert to Judaism.[63] On another occasion, the proselyte Aquila came to R. Eliezer with the question: "Is the whole reward of a proselyte to consist in receiving food and raiment?" (see Deut. 10:18). R. Eliezer angrily answered him, that what had been sufficient for the patriarch Jacob (Gen. 28:20) ought to be sufficient for Aquila. When Aquila put the same question to R. Joshua, the latter reassured him by expounding "food and raiment," as meaning metaphorically "Torah and tallit." The Midrash adds that if Joshua had not been so gentle, Aquila would have forsaken Judaism.[64]

R. Eliezer demanded that the rite of circumcision be retained in the ritual of a proselyte's initiation into Judaism.[65] This prob-

---

For R. Eliezer's attitude toward gentiles and proselytes, cf. also I. Levi, "The Attitude of the Talmud and Midrash Toward Proselytism" (Hebrew), ha-Goren, IX 1923, p. 9ff.

62. Mek. R. Simeon on Ex. 18:6. Cf. Mek., ad locum. Cf. I. Levi, l. c., p. 10, note 1.

63. Ecc. R. 1:25. Incest, including even mother-son relations, were not unknown in the Hellenistic world, particularly among the upper classes. See the material cited by L. Blau, "Die aelteste Eheform," in Chajes Memorial Volume, pp. 13-16.

64. Gen. R. 70:5; Nu. R. 8:10. Cf. Ex. R. 19:4.

65. Our sources are not very clear on this. Jeb. 46a reads: גר שמל ולא טבל, ר"א אומר הרי זה גר, טבל ולא מל ר"י אומר הרי זה גר, וחכמים אומרים טבל ולא מל מל ולא טבל אינו גר עד שימול ויטבול. "A proselyte who was circumcised but not baptized, R. Eliezer says we may consider him a legal proselyte; one who was baptized but not circumcised, R. Joshua says we may consider him a legal proselyte.

ably accounts for R. Eliezer's generally great emphasis on the ceremony of circumcision. The covenant between Israel and God referred

---

The *Hakamim* say, whether he was circumcised but not baptized or
baptized but not circumcised, he is no legal proselyte until he has
gone through both circumcision and baptism." The Amoraim interpret this to mean that both R. Eliezer and R. Joshua agree in accepting baptism without circumcision as adequate. R. Eliezer, however,
accepts circumcision without baptism as equally valid but R. Joshua
does not. Were this the correct interpretation, our text could certainly have been much more explicit. There is, furthermore, an
altogether different reading in j Kid. III, 64d: גר שמל ולא טבל
טבל ולא מל הכל הולך אחר המילה דברי ר"מ ר"י אומר אף המילה מעכבת
"Whether a proselyte was circumcised but not baptized or baptized
but not circumcised, circumcision alone determines his legal status
as a proselyte"—this is the view of R. Eliezer. R. Joshua says,
"Baptism too is a prerequisite." Ginzberg has therefore suggested
that both Talmudim pre-suppose a common archetypal text which
probably read: גר שמל ולא טבל ר"א אומר הרי זה גר ר"י אומר
טבילה הרי היא כמילה   "A proselyte who was circumcised but
not baptized, R. Eliezer says we may consider him a legal proselyte.
R. Joshua says, baptism has the same status as circumcision."
The Palestinian Talmud interprets R. Joshua's remark as an insistence on both rites for legal proselytism. This interpretation is also
quoted in the Babylonian Talmud, but it is ascribed to the *Hakamim,*
(R. Joshua's view when in dispute with that of R. Eliezer is often
ascribed to the *Hakamim.*) But the Babylonian Talmud also quotes
another interpretation, according to which R. Joshua accepted R.
Eliezer' view that one rite was enough, but insisted that baptism
be accorded the same status as circumcision, i. e., that baptism without circumcision ought to be as adequate as circumcision without
baptism. I accept the latter interpretation. If the former were
correct, R. Joshua could have expressed his view more explicitly
by dissenting, i. e., by merely saying   אינו גר,   "he (the proselyte
who was circumcised but not baptized and whom R. Eliezer declared
a legal proselyte) is not a legal proselyte." Cf. I. Levi, *ibid,* p. 16.
This would be fully in consonance with R. Joshua's general esteem
for the proselyte. Cf. Jos. *Ant.* 20, 2, 4 describing the conversion of
the ruler of Adiabene, Izates. The merchant-missionary Ananias
thought circumcision unnecessary but Eleazar, a Galilean Jew, urged
the king to go through with it. Jeb. 47a-b describes the ritual of

to in Ex. 19:5, R. Eliezer explained as applying not to the Sabbath, as was suggested by R. Akiba, but to circumcision.[66] According to R. Eliezer's interpretation, Elijah in his prayer for rain on Mount Carmel, urged that the Israelites had merited God's favor in observing the two commandments of the Sabbath and circumcision.[67] Just as it is the duty of every father to circumcise his son, so is it the duty of every master to circumcise his slave, whether born in his household or acquired by purchase. Uncircumcised slaves one may not keep at all. But more: any one whose son or slave remains uncircumcised in violation of the law, may not eat of the paschal lamb. For the uncircumcised Jew himself, there was of course the Biblical punishment of excision.[68]

In the light of the importance that R. Eliezer attributed to circumcision, the question naturally arose why it was not com-

initiating a proselyte and it includes circumcision. Gerim 1:1 (in Seven Minor Treatises) quotes another version of the ritual, omitting circumcision. Very likely these two accounts go back to the varying opinions of R. Eliezer and R. Joshua.

66. Mek. R. Simeon , p. 95. In Mek. Bahodesh 2, the attributions are reversed, and Moore, *Judaism*, I, p. 16, follows the reading in the Mek. But we have a number of other references, where, in a different connection, R. Eliezer takes the "covenant" as refering to circumcision. See P. R. 116b-117a; Agadat Breshit, p. 36, and Tan. Lek Leka, 20. Cf. Graetz, "Agrippa II und der Zustand Judaeas," pp. 488-491. For R. Eliezer's emphasis of circumcision cf. also P. S. E. Z., p. 40,46; P. R. E., ch. 29 (Friedlander's text), 39; Mid. ha-Gadol on Gen. p. 251.

67. Er. 40b; P. R. K., p. 172b; Ecc. R. 11:5; Yalkut, Pinhas, sec. 782. Cf. Moore, *Judaism*, II, p. 16f and notes. Jerome, in his commentary on Ecclesiastes 11:2, quotes this as the generally accepted Jewish interpretation (*Hebraei ita hunc locum intellegunt*). See Ginzberg, "Die Hagada bei den Kirchenvaetern," in *Chajes Memorial Volume*, p. 43. It is interesting to note that R. Joshua, who minimized circumcision, took the "seven" and the "eight" as refering

68. Mek. Bo 15. This view was also shared by R. Akiba. Cf. Feast of Booths.
Jeb. 48b.

manded in the decalogue. In one source[69] this question is put to
R. Eliezer by Aquila, the proselyte; in another,[70] by King Agrippa.
R. Eliezer's reply is in both instances the same: the law of circumcision preceded the decalogue, being presumed in Ex. 19:5,
'and ye shall observe my covenant,' which was spoken before the
theophany at Sinai and which refers to the rite of circumcision.

5. *Asceticism.*—R. Eliezer opposed the practices of asceticism.
In a measure this opposition was shared by his colleagues as well,
since it was fully in consonance with the general trend of Pharisaism
which, in spite of its individualism, never sanctioned the with-
drawal from the world to search for a purely personal salvation.
With R. Eliezer, however, the opposition was much more pronounced. He opposed vowing, an ascetic practice recognized in the
Bible, by which individuals assumed certain restrictions on themselves. It was, no doubt, in order to accord it greater authority
that he sought Biblical support for the later custom of vow annulment.[71] He was extremely lenient in his definition of the grounds

---

69. P. R. 116b-117a.
70. Agadat B'reshit p. 36 and Tan. Lek Leka. Graetz, *l. c.* has
pointed out that this question may actually have been asked by both.
Both, the king and Aquila, were naturally interested in missionizing,
and may have favored the doing away with the requirement of
circumcision. As the leading opponent of this, R. Eliezer was asked
to justify his position.
71. M. Hag. 1:8; Hag. 10a; j Hag. I, 76c; Nazir 62a. R. Joshua
too found Biblical support for it. The general view in the Mishnah
is, however, "The annulment of vows hovers in the air; it has no
Biblical support." In Biblical times vows could not be invalidated
under any circumstances; thus, Jephtah, because of his vow, offered
up his own daughter as a sacrifice (Judges 11). The Rabbinic development of the law provided that vows made by mistake were not to
be valid. Acting on this provision, people who regretted their vows
declared before some competent religious authority that they had
originally vowed by mistake; if an adequate explanation justified this
claim, the vow would be annulled. Josephus, looking at the past in
the light of the later development of the law, finds that Jephtah's
act was "neither comfortable to the law, nor acceptable to God"

for which annulment might be pronounced. He sanctioned annulment where the votary proved that his act had created unanticipated embarrassment to his parents.[72] He similarly sanctioned it where the votary proved an unforseen change in the status of the object or the person with whom he vowed not to associate: that the house he vowed not to enter had since become a synagogue, or the person whose services he vowed not to enjoy had become a scribe. This leniency on his part actually provoked one of his disputants to exclaim, "You have rendered vows obsolete altogether."[73]

The despair generated by the social and political unrest of our period seems to have driven many people to abandon their property or to consecrate it to the Temple. R. Eliezer inveighed against this. One may, of course, consecrate a portion of his property. To consecrate it entirely would, however, be improper. Indeed, he ruled such consecrations invalid.[74]

In common with his colleagues R. Eliezer also emphasized the duty of marriage as a means of procreation. To abstain from recreating is a crime equivalent to the shedding of human blood.[75] He limited the time that a man, while travelling, may stay away from his wife. He also prohibited a person who was not living

---

(*Ant.* 5, 7, 10). Philo, on the other hand, regarded vowing as praiseworthy. See I. Heinemann, p. 88.

72. M. Ned. 9:1. The assumption of a vow seems to have been attributed to an irritable and impulsive temper. It is one of the derogatory things said of the Galileans that they were prone to take on vows at the slightest provocation.

73. M. Ned. 9:1, 2; Nazir 32b.

74. M. Ar. 8:4; Tos. Ar. 4:24 (p. 548); Ar. 28a. According to R. Judah b. Batira, consecrated property belonged to the Temple treasury. The general view of the rabbis is, however, that it belonged to the priests. (M. Ar. 8:6). It is therefore possible to speak of consecrations to the Temple after 70.

75. Jeb. 63b. The text has "any Jew who does not beget children..." This is a correction of the censor, who regarded the original statement as derogatory to the celibate clergy. See Rabinowicz, *Dikduke Soferim,* VI, p. 353, and Bacher, *Tannaiten,* I. p. 113, note 4. Wedlock was shuned by the Therapeutae and the larger sections of

with his wife to exercise the functions of a school teacher.[76]

    6. *Prayer.*—Even more characteristic of Pharisaic Judaism was its development, beside the Temple with its sacrificial cult, of those ritual observances which centered in the individual and revolved about personal life. The most important of these was the synagogue with its institutions of prayer, both private and public. These prayers were still in a certain measure free and informal, but they enabled the laity to approach God much more intimately than they could through the medium of the Temple service. Prayer became, however, much more important after the Temple was destroyed and the service of sacrifice discontinued. It was inevitable that corresponding to this new importance, prayer should also go through certain new developments in legal status. Whatever in the realm of prayer was traditional, R. Eliezer accepted. But whatever represented change or development, he generall opposed.

    R. Eliezer emphasized the importance of prayer. A man should pray to God, he taught, because God, when properly approached, is responsive to prayer. Through prayer, as well as through repentance and righteous deeds, God may be induced to commute an evil decree.[77] One must, however, make sure to pray properly. The mood of prayer should be one of concentration and awe. "When you pray, know before whom you stand" was one of the three maxims spoken by R. Eliezer from his sick-bed to his visiting disciples, when they asked that he teach them the way leading to eternal life.[78]

---

the Essenes. There were many others who shunned it in the general Hellenistic world. See Strathman, *Geschichte der fruechristlichen Askese,* Leipzig 1914, I, p. 307f, and Heinemann, p. 266ff. That the principal aim of marriage was procreation was also taught by Philo as well as by many general writers in the Hellenistic world. See the discussion in Heinemann, pp. 261-273. R. Eliezer, however, did not favor divorcing a barren woman, as did Philo. See M. Sota 4:3, and below, p. 89. Cf. also Testament Issacher, section 2.

   76. M. Ket. 5:6. Cf. Ket. 62b; M. Kid. 4:13.

   77. Tan., Buber, Noah 13; Ecc. R. 5:4; P. R. 200b.

   78. Ber. 28b; Kal. R. 6. Cf. D. E. R. 3.

The true efficacy of prayer is determined not by its volume but by the sincerity of feeling with which it is uttered. When told of one of his disciples who had gone to undue length in prolonging his public prayers, R. Eliezer justified him by explaining: He has not prolonged more than Moses who on one occasion prayed to God for forty days and forty nights (Deut. 9:18). He similarly justified another of his disciples who had abbreviated his prayers, by citing the fact that Moses, on another occasion, confined his prayers to five words. "There is a time for prolonging as well as a time for abbreviating," was his customary comment concerning prayer. Indeed, God actually rebuked Moses for indulging in lengthy prayers, while the Israelites were being overtaken by the Egyptians at the Red Sea. "My children are in great distress," R. Eliezer quoted God as having spoken to Moses; "they are hemmed in by the sea on the one side and by the pursuing enemy on the other. Yet you stand and indulge in lengthy prayers. There is a time to prolong and a time to shorten." [79]

R. Eliezer agreed with his colleagues in requiring the recitation of the shema as part of one's private prayers. One who neglects the *Shema*, he ruled, stamps himself as an Am ha-Ares, religiously the lowest type of individual.[80] The records in the Talmud de-

---

79. Ber. 34a; Mek. B'shalah 3, R. Simeon, pp. 47, 72f; Sifre, Nu. section 105; Ex. R. 21:7.

80. Ber. 47b. The term *Am ha-Ares* means literally the "people of the land" or the rural population. Because the rural population was generally backward in their adherence to Pharisaic piety, the term *Am ha-Ares* gradually came to mean a religiously lax person in general, as the term is here used by R. Eliezer. Zeitlin's theory ("The Am ha-Ares," *JQR*, N. S., XXIII 1932, p. 58), that R. Eliezer meant by the term *Am ha-Ares* in our pasage a Judeo-Christian, does not appear justified. The non-reading of the Shema was certainly no sine qua non of Christianity. While many Christians may have omitted the Shema, there were undoubtedly many others, in the Judeo-Christian colony at least, who recited it; there must have been also many non-observant Jews who neglected the Shema, but who had no connections with Christianity. In M. Sota 9:15, San. 20b. and Pes. 49b, R. Eliezer uses the same term as referring explicitly

scribe R. Eliezer as attending the public service in the synagogue
and in several instances, during years of drought, leading in the
public prayers for rain. He seems to refer to the prayers known
as "Malkuyot," "Zikronot," and "Shofrot," which were part of the
traditional synagogue ritual of the new year.[81] From his discussions we may judge that, to the extent it had already developed, he
also recognized a fixed ritual of the Amidah.[82]

But he generally opposed every effort that represented change.
Moved probably by the higher esteem in which the Sabbath and
the festivals were held after 70, many of the rabbis tried incorporat-
ing into he formula of the Amida prayers, the *Habdalah* and the
Kedushat ha-Yom[83] of the new moon and of the intermediate days of
a festival when coinciding with the Sabbath. R. Akiba insisted that
the *Habdalah* should be made into an independent benediction, to
be recited fourth in the order of the ritual. According to another
view, quoted anonymously in the Mishnah, it was to be integrated
with *"Honen hadaat,"* the already accepted, regular, fourth benediction. The *"Kedushat ha-Yom,"* the Rabbis demanded, should be
incorporated into the *Abodah, t*he seventeenth benediction. R.
Eliezer certainly appreciated the Sabbath and the festivals, but he
objected to innovations. He therefore demanded that these prayers
be left for insertion at the *"Hodaah,"* virtually the last benediction,

---

to the religiously ignorant and lax person. (The Munich Mss. reads
in the Sanhed. passage, instead of our R. Eliezer, R. Eliezer b.
Sadok, and the Tos. San. 4:5, citing the same passage, has the reading
R. Eliezer b. Jose. In the Pesahim passage our reading is R. Elazar
but the Munich Mss. reads Eliezer. Zeitlin himself [*ibid,* p. 57],
prefers the latter reading of the Munich Mss.). Cf. below, p. 100.

81. Tos. Meg. 4:34 (p. 228); Meg. 25b; j Meg. IV, 75c; Taan.
25b; j Taan. III, 66c-d; R. H. 32a.

82. M. Ber. 5:2; Tos. Ber. 3:1 (p. 7); j Ber. IV, 7d; Besa 7a;
Er. 40b; A. Z. 7b; Lekah, Deut. p. 10. Cf. below, p. 69, note 85.

83. The *Habdalah,* recited at the outgoing of the Sabbath, praises
God for dividing between "the holy ond the profane... the Sabbath
and the six working days..."; the *Kedushat ha-Yom* is a prayer
solemnizing some special religious occasion.

being followed only by the priestly blessing, and where many in-
terpolations were always made to suit individual temperament and
local need.[84] R. Eliezer similarly opposed the move of R. Gamaliel
to include the Amidah in the ritual of the individual's private devotion.[85] He also differed with R. Joshua as to the relative order in
which private and public prayers are to be recited. According to

---

84. M. Ber. 5:2; Tos. Ber. 3:1 (p. 7); Besa 17a; Er. 40b. Cf.
Elbogen, *Der juedische Gottesdienst*, Frankfort o. M. 1924, p. 57f.
Similar to this was the dispute concerning the *Kedushot ha-Yom*
in the grace after meals. R. Eliezer's colleagues tried to find for it
a fixed place in the ritual. R. Eliezer permitted its recitation with
any one of three prayers: with the prayer of consolation, the prayer
of thanks for Palestine, or "the benediction ordained by the scholars
at Jabneh" (*Hatob v'Hametib*). The fact that R. Eliezer refers to
this prayer not by name, but as "the prayer instituted by the scholars
at Jabneh," may mean that he was opposed to its original introduction. The circumstances that moved the scholars to ordain the
benediction *Hatob v'Hametib* we do not know. Finkelstein, "The
Birkat ha-Mazon," p. 222, suggests that it may have been Hadrian's
permission to rebuild the Temple. The benediction is obviously an
expression of gratitude for some happy event, but it would be difficult
to connect it with Hadrian's permission to rebuild the Temple, since
that permission was soon revoked. Buechler, "The Origin of the
Benediction *Hatob v'Hametib*" (Hebrew), in *Chajes Memorial Volume*,
p. 144, thinks that it came after the Jews were excused from setting
up the statue of Caligula in the Temple. But R. Eliezer's connecting
it with Jabneh shows that it came after 70 C. E. Possibly it was
ordained after the Jewish embassy succeeded in warding off the contemplated anti-Jewish legislation after the Trajanic wars. We recall
that it was also, in all likelihood, in honor of this occasion that the
holiday *Yom Tyrianus* (Trajan Day) was instituted when mourning
and fasting were to be prohibited. See above, p. 25.

85. M. Ber. 4:3, 4. R. Eliezer did not dispute the requirement
of the Amidah in public prayer, which was already fixed long before
his time. R. Gamaliel merely re-edited the Amidah text which was
extant in varying versions and also introduced it into private prayer.
Cf. Halevi, *Dorot*, Ie, pp. 144-170, against Weiss, *Dor*, II, p. 73f.

him private prayers should precede; according to R. Joshua, they should follow.[86]

The Talmud has preserved a number of prayers of R. Eliezer's own composition. "Do Thy will in heaven above and give composure of spirit to those who revere Thee here below, and what is good in Thy sight, do." This is the prayer R. Eliezer recommended for a time of danger when meditation for a greater length of time was not possible.[87] After his regular prayer of the Amidah, R. Eliezer was accustomed to conclude with the following: "May it be the will before Thee, O Lord my God and God of my fathers, that no man shall entertain hatred toward us, and that we shall not entertain hatred for other men; that no one shall envy us, and that we shall not envy others; that our toil shall be in Thy Torah throughout the days of our life, and that our words shall be acceptable as a plea for grace before Thee."[88]

Connected with the institution of prayer was the custom of wearing the *tephillin* or phylacteries on arm and forehead.[89] We do not know when the custom arose. Philo apparently did not know of it.[90] But a contemporary of Philo already refers to the *tephillin* of his grandfather.[91] They are likewise alluded to in the *Letter of Aristeas*,[92] and *Josephus*.[93] The custom probably arose at an early time among the common people who regarded the phylactery as an amulet.[94] The rabbis, however, in accordance with their usual prac-

---

86. A. Z. 7b; Lekah on Deut., p. 10. Cf. Moore, *Judaism*, II, p. 219; Bacher, *Tannaiten*, I, p. 109f.

87. Ber. 29b. Cf. Tos. Ber. 3:10, 11 (p. 7) and see editor's note.

88. j Ber. IV, 7d.

89. But the name *tephillin* is not related to *tefillah*, the Hebrew word for prayer. Cf. K. Kohler, *The Origin of the Synagogue and the Church*, N. Y. 1929, p. 62.

90. See Heinemann, p. 166ff.

91. Shammai in Mek. on Ex. 13:10; Hillel in j Er. X, 26a.

92. Section 159.

93. *Ant.* 4, 8, 13.

94. M. Shab. 6:2, Shek. 3:2, where the *tephillin* are mentioned

tice of counteracting popular superstitions, changed its character and converted it into a symbol of submission to God and Torah. The custom, of course, enjoyed the support of the literal interpretation of Deuteronomy 6:8, "And thou shalt bind them for a sign upon the hand and they shall be for frontlets between thy eyes."[95]

Like his colleagues, R. Eliezer was emphatic in stressing the importance of this custom. It is to the phylactery worn on the head, according to R. Eliezer, that Deut. 28:10 alludes: "And all the peoples of the earth shall see that the name of the Lord is pronounced upon thee, and they shall fear thee (because the name of God is inscribed on that phylactery).[96] When the Israelites complained to God that it was impossible for them to meditate on the Torah "day and night" (Joshua 1:8), R. Eliezer reports, God suggested to them that they put on phylacteries on arm and head, and He would regard it as of equivalent merit.[97] R. Eliezer himself, following the practice of his teacher R. Johanan b. Zakkai, wore his phylacteries constantly, refusing to move even four ells without them. Indeed, he even had them on while on his death bed.[98]

7. *The Sabbath and Holidays.*—In the same spirit as the other scholars, R. Eliezer eulogized the Sabbath as a cardinal observance of Judaism. By a proper observance of the Sabbath one will be saved from the terrors preceding the inauguration of the messianic age of the Hereafter.[99] The prophet Elijah in his famous prayer for rain, we find a homily of R. Eliezer explaining, invoked

---

side by side with the *kemiot* (amulets). Cf. K. Kohler, *ibid*, p. 61f.

95. Cf., however, Jacob Mann, "Changes in the Divine Services of the Synagogue due to Religious Persecutions," *HUCA*, IV 1927, p. 294ff. Cf. also Buechler, *Am ha-Ares*, p. 23 and notes.

96. Ber. 6a, 57a, Sota 17a; Meg. 16b; Men. 35b; Hul. 89a; Lekah on Ex. 13:9.

97. Mid. Tehil. Ps. 1:17; Yalkut on Psalm 1:1; Tephillin, 20 (in Seven Minor Treatises). Cf. Lekah on Ex. 13:9.

98. j. Ber. IX, 16a; P. R. 112a; Tephillin, 19; San. 68a. Cf. A.R.N. 25; j Shab. II, 5b.

99. Mek. on Ex. 16:29 (ed. Friedmann, p. 51a).

Israel's observance of the Sabbath, in addition to circumcision, pleading with God that for their observance of these two commandments alone, rain ought to descend for them. R. Eliezer followed his colleagues in reaffirming the general laws as to how Sabbath observance should properly be carried out. Thus, he accepted the thirty-nine categories of works that were forbidden on the Sabbath.[100] He extending the Sabbath regulations to begin some time on Friday befcre sundown.[101] He prohibited carrying from one domicile into another, as well as into the alley. Likewise he restricted the walking outside of the city limits for more than 2000 ells, and he recognized the *erub*, the legal fiction by which a person deposited before the Sabbath certain edibles at some point outside of the city, which became his theoretical abode, so that his movement on the Sabbath would then be computed from that place as the starting point.[102] He

----

100. R. Eliezer and his colleagues merely differed on the definition of these categories. M. Shab. 10:6, 12:4; Shab. 95a; Tos. Shab. 9:12 (p. 122), 11:15 (p. 126), *et seq.* For the formulations of the ctegories themselves, see Mek. Vaykhel 1; Shab. 49b; B. K. 2a; M. Shab. 7:2. Cf. below, p. 130.

101. M. Shab. 1:10. The antiquity of this institution is seen by the fact that Augustus exempted Jews from court proceedings on Friday beginning with 3 P. M. (*Ant.* 16, 6, 2). The institution was also followed by the Damascan sect, as Ginzberg, *Sekte,* p. 80f, has shown. According to Tos. Sukka 4:11, 12; Shab. 35b, the signal for stopping work on Friday was sounded before sundown. Cf., however, Jos., *Wars* 4, 9, 2, who reports that this signal was given at sunset; Ginzberg, *op. cit.,* p. 152f, regards this report as inaccurate.

102. M. Er. 1:2, 2:5, 6; 3:6; 9:2. Tos. Er. 1:2 (p. 138); 3:7 (p. 140); 5:1 (p. 143); Ket. 31b and cf. Shab. 6a, where the same statement is quoted in the name of R. Eliezer b. Jacob; Er. 11b-12a; j Er. I, 18b. These prohibitions were followed by the Damascan sect. See Ginzberg, *op. cit.,* pp. 155, 159. The Book of Jubilees (11:30) prohibits even carrying from house to house, which is explicitly permitted in Tos. Shab. 1:3 and Shab. 6a. The Dositheans, a Samaritan sect, prohibited all locomotion on the Sabbath. See Montgomery, *The Samaritans,* Philadelphia 1907, p. 255f, and Ginzberg, *op. cit.,* pp. 199f. Geiger, in consonance with his theory that the Sadducees were the conservatives and the Pharisees the progressives, argues that the

forbade the use of any object on the Sabbath unless it was prepared the day before.[103] He also accepted the law that when human life was at stake, all Sabbath restrictions were to be suspended.[104] R. Eliezer and his colleagues were often divided in their detailed interpretations of these general laws, but the basis for the division was usually a varying methodology of legal reasoning, and we shall treat of this in our discussion of formal law.

In the discussions concerning the celebrations of the festivals R. Eliezer, in disagreement with his contemporaries, tended to emphasize the restrictive and ritualistic features as opposed to the social. He objected to making the festivals an occasion for exchanging visits. He rebuked his own pupil Ilai, who on one occasion came to pay him a visit on a holiday, with the comment: "Are you not among those who repose on a festival day, Ilai? It is not proper to leave one's home on a holiday, as it written: 'And thou shalt rejoice (on a festival day), thou and thy household' " (Deut.

Sadducees did not recognize the *erub* and prohibited all carrying on the Sabbath (*Urschrift und Uebersetzungen der Bibel in ihrer Abhaengigkeit von der innern Entwicklung des Judentums*, Breslau 1857, pp. 147-148; *Nachgelass. Schriften*, III, p. 290, *Juedische Zeitschrift*, II, 24, *Kebusat Maamarim*, p. 147). *Halevi, Dorot, Ic*, pp. 436f, has however called attention to M. Er. 6:2 which refers to a Sadducee carrying even without the fiction of the erub. Cf. also Ginzberg, *op. cit.*, pp. 194f.

103. M. Besa, 4:6, 7. R. Eliezer and his colleagues merely differ on their definitions of this "preparation." Jos., *Wars*, 2, 8, 9, reports that Jews prepare food on Friday as they cannot cook on the Sabbath. The explanation is only partially accurate, since preparation was required even where cooking was not involved. Such preparation was likewise required by the Damascan sect. See Ginzberg, *op. cit.*, pp. 84, 155.

104. R. Eliezer merely tries to establish a derivation for this law, in which he differs from a number of his colleagues. Tos. Shab. 15:16 (p. 134). Cf. Mek. Ki Tissa 1 (ed. Friedmann, p. 103b); Yoma 85a. See Bacher, *Tannaiten*, I, 260 and note. The law itself was already invoked by the Maccabees, when they took up arms on the Sabbath to defend themselves against the Syrians. See I Macab. 2,

14:26).[105] The only legitimate occupation on a festival day, for a scholar at least, is to devote one's self to study. On one festive occasion R. Eliezer actually tried lecturing all the day but the strain proved too great and successive members in his audience tired and walked out, to the accompaniment of his sharp criticism.[106]

R. Eliezer discussed some of the festivals individually. He recommended a quick disposal of the Passover meal so that the children shall not fall asleep before the Seder is over.[107] He emphasized greatly the commandment of dwelling in booths on the feast of Tabernacles. Every one, he ruled, must build his own booth and construct it firmly and comfortably enough to last him for the full seven day period of the holiday.[108] In the event of rain or excess of heat one was permitted to leave the booth. Neverthless, when R. Eliezer on one occasion left his booth for such a reason, he immediately reentered it, hoping for a change. He repeated this all night.[109] He likewise stressed the importance of Hanukkah. The Talmud records an instance, where the Lyddan authorities on one occasion proclaimed a fast for rain during Hanukkah. R. Eliezer and R. Joshua, who apparently had not been consulted, publicly defied them; R. Joshua even rebuking the people that they ought to do penance for having fasted on such an occasion.[110]

32ff. Cf. Geiger, *Urschrift,* p. 217ff, and Moore, *Judaism,* II, p. 30. This law was likewise followed by Philo, Josephus, and the Damascan sect. See the discussion of Ginzberg, *op. cit.,* pp. 97, 161 and note 2.

105. Tos. Sukka 2:1 (p. 193); Sukka 27b; j Sukka II, 53a.

106. Besa 15b; Pes. 68b. The moderate R. Joshua counselled a division of the time between study and the social pleasures. Heinemann, *op. cit.,* p. 137 and note 2, calls attention to the fact that both views are represented in Philo. In j Shab. XV, 15a, R. Eliezer's view is quoted anonymously.

107. Mek. Bo 18; Tos. Pes. 10:9 (p. 172); Pes. 109a.

108. Sukka 27a-b, 31a. Cf. below, p. 133f.

109. j Sukka II, 53b.

110. Tos. Taan. 2:5 (p. 217); j Taan. II, 66a; j Meg. I, 70d; j Ned. VIII, 40d; Buechler, *Palestinian Piety,* p. 210, note 2, thinks that the Lyddan authorities followed the view of R. Gamaliel, who permitted completing on Hanukkah a series of fast days for rain,

8. *The Temple and the Priesthood.*—The ritual of personal observances as developed by Pharisaism represented, in a sense, a movement away from the Temple service and the cult of sacrifices. Consistent with their general individualism the Pharisees had also introduced into the Temple service itself such elements as would make for a greater measure of lay participation. They, nevertheless, continued to look upon the Temple with its sacrificial cult as a focal point in Jewish religious life. For one thing, the Bible accorded the Temple a place of central importance in the divine service. The Temple, moreover, symbolized in a very effective manner, the basic religious solidarity of Israel throughout the world. Inevitably, therefore, the destruction of the Temple was looked upon as a great catastrophe by all the Pharisaic leaders of our period, including R. Eliezer.

But while the other scholars considered the destruction a great calamity and looked forward to a restoration, they, nevertheless, reckoned in a practical way with the new conditions and sought to recognize the non-sacredotal observances as a self-sufficient formula of Jewish worship. R. Eliezer opposed this, maintaining that without the Temple an adequate Jewish religious life was impossible. In contrast to the champion of more progressive Pharisaism, R. Johanan b. Zakkai, who declared explicitly that the practice of

---

provided that they had been proclaimed and begun before the holiday. R. Joshua, and apparently also R. Eliezer, opposed the fasting even in such a case (M. Taan. 2:10; Tos. Taan. 2:5; Er. 41a). Our text, however, speaks clearly of the fast being proclaimed on the holiday itself. It is, furthermore, unlikely that R. Eliezer and R. Joshua would have been so harsh with their rebukes, had the Lyddan authorities acted in accordance with the views of the patriarch. The Lyddan authorities had, in all likelihood, violated the law completely. This need not surprise us when we recall that Lydda was the colony of the emigre aristocracy. As great landowners, a drought held out to them a serious menace; and as Sadducean sympathizers they, very likely, did not consider the festival significant enough to be in the way of the usual method of dealing with such a situation—fasting and praying to God for rain.

charity was as acceptable to God as the offering of sacrifices,[111] R. Eliezer commented gloomily that "as long as the cult of sacrifices flourished there was peace in the world, but since its extinction there has not been a day without its curses and woes".[112] Indeed, God Himself, declared R. Eliezer, roars like a lion at each watch of the night, in grief for His abode that is in ruins.[113] He painted in dark colors the general deterioration that followed the destruction of the Temple. "Since the day the Temple was destroyed the learned began to be like school masters, the schoolmasters like sextons, the sextons like the ignorant masses and the masses go their way to ruin and no one cares. And who is there for us to lean upon? Our father who is in heaven".[114] R. Eliezer opposed any reorganization of Jewish worship that would detach it from the Temple. Thus, he insisted that since the proselyte could no longer offer the prescribed sacrifice of initiation, he should, for the time being, set aside a sum of money equivalent to the cost of such a sacrifice and guard it as sacred property (hekdesh) until the time when the Temple would be restored and the appropriate sacrifice could be brought.[115]

---

111. A. R. N. 4.

112. Tan., Toldot 1.

113. Ber. 3a.

114. M. Sota 9:15. The Cambridge Mss. of the Mishnah (printed by Lowe) and the Munich Mss. of the Talmud attribute this comment to R. Joshua. To R. Eliezer they attribute the gloomy comment which is in our text attributed to R. Pinhas b. Yair. The passage is in Aramaic with the exception of the words "and who is there for us to lean upon? Our father in Heaven," which are in Hebrew. The Aramaic portion may be a quotation from an apocalyptic source, the Hebrew words alone being the addition of R. Eliezer.

115. Sifre Zuta, p. 94. Cf. Gerim 2:4, where the same controversy is reported in the name of R. Eliezer b. Jacob and R. Simeon. Higger records, however, a variant in Ms. Adler 2237, which reads R. Eliezer, instead of R. Eliezer b. Jacob. According to j Shek. VIII, 51b; R. H. 31b; Ker. 9a, the original reform was introduced by R. Johanan b. Zakkai. During the lifetime of R. Johanan, R. Eliezer did not dare disagree, but after the death of R. Johanan, R. Eliezer

Hopeful of speedy restoration,[116] R. Eliezer like his colleagues, devoted himself to a careful study of all matters pertaining to the Temple and its administration.[117] His rulings betray, however, a decided tendency to favor the interests of the Temple as opposed to those of the laity. Thus, in spite of his general leniency with regard to the annulment of vows, he refused to void any vow by which a person consecrated property to the Temple. To further protect the Temple against any losses through legal manipulations he also ruled that should the votary divorce his wife he must vow never to remarry her. This was to preclude any abuse of an old law which permitted the divorcee to collect the amount of her dower rights even from her husband's consecrated property.[118]

R. Eliezer emphasized the paramount position of sacrifices in Jewish ritual. According to an old law, the duty of giving proper burial of a dead body found lying on the road, was to take precedence over the injunctions not to defile himself through contact with the corpse, which applied both to the priest, and to the nazarite. If, however, both a priest and a nazarite came upon such a dead body, the general opinion of the rabbis was that the nazarite shall occupy himself with the burial, the priest being the more 'sacred' person. R. Eliezer, on the other hand, insisted that even

---

challenged the innovation, while R. Joshua defended it.

116. It is interesting to note that in spite of all his solicitousness about the Temple he seems nevertheless to have objected to the ordinance decreed by his colleagues, forbidding to plaster Jewish houses with lime, as a symbol of mourning for the Temple's destruction. See B. B. 60b; Yoma 66b; Tos. Jeb. 3:4 (p. 243), and cf. below, p. 108, note 54.

117. M. Yoma 7:3; Yoma 70a; Tos. Yoma 4:19 (p. 189); M. Sukka 4:5; Tos. Kel. 1:6 (p. 569); M. Yoma 5:5; j Yoma V, 42d; Yoma 58b-59a; Sifra, Ahrē Mot, p. 81b, and cf. Buechler, *Economic Conditions,* p. 9; Tos. Yoma 4:1 (p. 186); Yoma 68a; Tos. Men. 1:5 (p. 512); B. B. 121b; Taan. 31a; Sifra, Vayikra, p. 7a; P. S. E. Z., p. 10; Lament. R. (Introduction) 1:33 *et seq.*

118. The views of R. Eliezer and his colleagues follow respectively the position of the Shammaites and the Hillelites. See M. Ar. 6:1; Tos. Ar. 4:5 (p. 547); Ar. 23a, and cf. B. B. 120b and Nazir 30b;

if it were a question between the nazarite and the high priest himself, the high priest and not the nazarite shall attend to the burial.
He held that contact with a corpse was a more serious violation
wiht the nazarite than with the high priest, since the former must
in such a case offer a sacrifice, while the latter is excused from it.[119]
This emphasis on the significance of sacrifices likewise explains
R. Eliezer's position with regard to the status of the feast of Pentecost in a period of mourning. According to an ancient halakah, any
one of the major festivals suspends the law regarding the seven
day period of mourning. This applied not only to Passover and the
Feast of Booths, which are of seven day duration, but also to
Pentecost. In Temple days this was, of course, a logical rule, for
with regard to the holiday sacrifices, Pentecost was also of seven
day duration—one was permitted to offer them for the six days
following the one day of Pentecost. The other scholars nevertheless
continued this rule even after the destruction; they were apparently
moved by the inherent importance of the occasion as one of the
three major festivals. R. Eliezer reckoned only with the factor of
sacrifices. Since sacrifices were no longer offered, he maintained
that Pentecost, like the Sabbath, suspends the period of mourning
for only one day.[120]

R. Eliezer encouraged the offering of sacrifices by enlarging
the sphere of their efficacy. He, for example, required a sin offering from a person who was uncertain whether he had desecrated the
Sabbath or the Day of Atonement. R. Joshua, on the other hand,
insisted that a sacrifice is efficacious only when brought with the
full knowledge of the specific sin which it is to expiate.[121] Similarly

---

j Nazir V, 54a. Cf. also M. Bek. 5:3. Where, on the other hand,
it was not a matter of safeguarding a cherished institution, R. Eliezer
opposed the enactment of precautionary or deterrent legislation. See
below, p. 129.

119. M. Nazir 7:1. Cf. Sem. 4:7 and editor's note.

120. M. M. K. 3:6. Cf. Maimonides, *Mishneh Torah*, Laws of
Mourning 10:3.

121. Sifra, Vayikra, pp. 20a, 26b; Ker. 17b, 19a; Hor. 5a; M. Ker.

with regard to a "suspensive trespass offering," required for the doubtful commission of a sin, the consensus of opinion among the scholars was that at least the doubt be specific, i. e., whether the fat one had eaten, was of the permitted or prohibited kind. R.Eliezer, however, taught that a person may volunteer such a sacrifice at any time, since one may always have committed a sin without suspecting it.[122]

R. Eliezer required great devotion on the part ot the priest officiating at the sacrificial service. Thus, an old custom invalidated a sacrifice if the priest intended that its flesh be eaten outside of the confines of the Temple area or beyond the time limit set for its consumption. The other scholars, however, limited this rule to the edible portions of a sacrifice, excluding from it those portions which are normally burnt on the altar. R. Elieezer extended it to the latter also.[123]

In cases where, through some accident, the ritual fitness of sacrificial flesh or blood became doubtful, R. Eliezer zealously searched for ways and means whereby the offerings on the altar might, nevertheless, take place. His colleagues, on the other hand, refused to sanction any doubtful offerings and ordained that such flesh or blood must be discarded. Where portions of a burnt offering and a sin offering became mixed and their identity lost, he ruled that the total mixture must be burnt on the altar. Although the flesh of the sin offering is normally eaten by the priests, he maintained that no sin would be committed in burning it; it would be equivalent to burning wood, having no sacrificial significance. The other scholars demanded that all the flesh be discarded. Similarly, where several sacrificial bloods, each requiring a different number of sprinklings on the altar, became mixed, R. Eliezer called for a maximum number of sprinklings with the whole mixture. He argued

---

4:2; Tos. Ker. 2:12 (p. 564). Cf. ibid, 2:15 (p. 564), 3:6, 7 (p. 565).

122. M. Ker. 6:3; Tos. Ker. 4:4 (p. 566). Cf. M. Ker. 6:1; Sifra, Vayikra, 27a; Men. 102b.

123. M. Seb. 3:3; Tos. Seb. 2:14 (p. 483), 4:9 (p. 486); M. Men. 3:1 and cf. Men. 17b, 18a; Tos. Men. 2:16 (p. 515).

that any other procedure would violate Deuteronomy 13:1, which forbids any diminutions in the observances of the law. R. Joshua, on the other hand, pointed out that the same verse also forbids any unauthorized additions to the law, and, therefore, ruled that only the minimum number of sprinklings be made.[124]

R. Eliezer and his colleagues also clashed in their attitudes towards the priesthood. The perquisites accruing to the priests had always been a great burden upon the rural population of Palestine; and according to strict law the priests were to continue receiving these perquisites even after the Temple was dstroyed and their functions ceased. What undoubtedly made this situation even more irritating was the fact that the priesthood of this period had, in many instances, degenerated to a low moral level, shocking more sensitive people with their worldliness and their resistance to Pharisaic piety.[125] The privileged position of the priestly order as such was explicitly recognized in the Bible, and the Rabbis respected it. A number of decisions by R. Eliezer's colleagues, nevertheless, betray a certain opposition to the priests. They sought to limit the priestly perquisites to what was specifically covered in the Bible. They exempted all articles of export and all bread baked in units of less than a certain size from the priestly share in the dough. Similarly, they exempted the dill plant and the caper tree from tihting. Furthermore, they enacted numerous precautionary measures to make certain that the perquisites which did reach the priests would be eaten in accordance with the prescribed laws of levitical purity.[126]

---

124. M. Seb. 8:4, 10; Tos. Seb. 8:23 (p. 492); Mid. Tann. on Deut. 13:1; Er. 100a. Cf. M. Seb. 8:5, 8, 9; Tos. Seb. 8:15, 20, 21 (p. 492); Seb. 76b, 77a, 80b-81a; Jeb. 100a; Sota 23a; Men. 106b; Yoma 47b. Cf. also j Pes. III, 30a, where M. Pes. 3:3 is explained on the basis of the same principle. Cf., however, below, p. 102, note 36. Cf. also M. Men. 3:4; Tos. Men. 4:2, 5, 6, (p. 516); Tos. Seb. 4:1 (p. 484); Seb. 104a; Mid. Tann. on Deut. 12:17; Pes. 34b, 77b, 87a.

125. Jeb. 61a; Jos. *Ant.* 20,8,8 and 20,9,2; Pes. 57a; Tos. Men. 13: 21 (p. 533); j Yoma I, 38c; M. Pes. 5:8. Cf. Buechler, *Priester und Cultus,* p. 67ff.

126. These regulations did not affect the laity, since they neither

R. Eliezer, on the other hand, was much more favorably disposed toward the priests. He required the priestly share in the dough from articles of export and from loaves of bread regardless of size, when collected in one vessel; and he similarly required the tithe from the dill plant and the caper tree.[127] He also objected to the many ramifications of the laws of levitical uncleanliness.[128] It was fully in consonance with this that he demanded immediate restitution to the priests for any tithes consumed by a layman. If the species consumed was no longer available, one was to repay with a more costly product. R. Akiba held that the restitution should be with the same kind. Where this was no longer available, he permitted waiting until the gathering of the new crops the follow-

---

ate priestly foods nor came into the Temple area. Cf. Buechler, *Am ha-Ares*, pp. 3, 48, 124f; S. Zeitlin, "Les dix-huit Mesures," pp. 31-35. The rabbis also enacted a number of other measures against the priests. R. Johanan b. Zakkai required that the priests contribute the annual shekel to the Temple, even as the laity (M. Shek. 1:4). The rabbis likewise tried to break down the social stratification of Jewish society in which the priests occupied the highest rank. See below, p. 109.

127. M. Hal. 2:14; Sifre Nu. section 110; Tos. Ter. 2:13 (p. 28); M. Maas. 4:5, 6. Cf. also M. Ter. 11:2; Ber. 38a; Tos. Ter. 9:8 (p. 41); j Ter. X, 47b. In the case of the caper tree R. Akiba required a tithe from the fruits but not from the leaves and flowers.

128. Tos. Ed. 1:12 (p. 456). Cf. M. Ed. 2:7; M. Ed. 7:7; M. Kel. 26:4; Tos. Kel. 4:7 (p. 594) Tos. Ed. 2:1 (p. 457); San. 68a; M. Kel. 2:8; Tos. Kel. 2:8 (p. 571); M. Kel. 15:2; M. Kel. 8:1; Tos. Kel. 6:2 (p. 575); Sifra, Shemini, p. 54a; M. Tahar 9:5; M. Para 5:4; Tos. Para 5:6 (p. 634); M. Ok. 2:3; M. Zab. 2:2; M. Para 9:3; 10:1, 3; 11:7; Tos. Para 9:5; 10:2 (p. 638); M. Hag. 3:8; Nazir 66a; Hag. 23a. M. Ohol. 6:1 *et seq.* Many of these issues are discussed in detail in our chapter on formal law. It does not, of course, mean that R. Eliezer was invariably lenient in matters of levitical impurity. Operating with a specific method of legal reasoning, he was often moved to a more severe position. See below, p. 121. It is significant that R. Eliezer's excommunication was demonstrated by a public burning of sacred foods, which he, against the opinions of his colleagues, had persisted in regarding as levitically pure.

ing year.[129]   Indeed, R. Eliezer included the priests and the levites among "the six precious things that God gave to Israel," and which like Israel, were destined to endure forever.[130]

R. Eliezer demanded that great care be taken in handling priestly foods.   If doubt ever arose concerning the levitical cleanliness of a barrel of priestly wine, R. Eliezer insisted that though that wine can no longer be used, it must nevertheless be treated with all the deference due to regular priestly food, i.e., it must be kept covered, and in a place where it will not be in contact with objects of impurity.   R. Joshua, refusing to burden the owner with such an inconvenience, suggested that the wine be exposed so that it may become definitely impure, whereupon its destruction will be lawful.   Similarly, if a barrel of priestly wine is broken, and there is danger that the wine will trickle into another barrel of ordinary levitically unclean wine standing below, and thereby will render it ritualistically prohibited even to a layman, R. Joshua permitted to catch the priestly wine in an unclean vessel if no clean vessel was available. R. Eliezer, however, objected to such liberties with priestly food, and refused to make any concessions whatever. If, to cite another instance, a traveller carrying with him several loaves of priestly bread, is met by an 'idolator' who demands that he surrender one of the loaves for desecration, threatening that, in the event of a refusal, he will employ force to desecrate all the loaves, R. Joshua recommends compliance.   R. Eliezer, however, dissents, objecting that a Jew shall contribute directly to the desecration of priestly food.[131]   Even where the levitical cleanliness of a priestly food is only doubtful and it is destined to be burnt anyway, R. Eliezer demanded great solicitude for it. Thus, at the approach of Passover, he prohibited the burning of priestly leavened bread that is

---

129.   M. Ter. 6:6; Tos. Ter. 7:9 (p. 37).

130.   Mek. Jethro, Amalek 1; R. Simeon p. 88. Cf. Tan. Tesaveh 13 and Vehiz. p. 199f.

131.   M. Ter. 8:8, 9, 10, 11. Similarly R. Eliezer was much less inclined to permit sacred food to be "lost" in a mixture. M. Ter. 4:7, 8, 9; 5:2, 4, 5, 6; Tos. Ter. 5:10 (p. 33), 5:12 (p.34); j Ter.

definitely unclean together with priestly leavened bread whose levitical cleanliness is doubtful; R. Joshua sanctioned a common burning.[131]

9. *Torah.*—The concept which linked, not only theology and
ritual, but all social customs and usages as well, into the whole complex of Jewish thought and practice, was Torah. This concept of
Torah represented the ideas, laws, and customs themselves, as well
as the literature, written and oral, in which they were embodied.
In so far as Torah represented tradition, R. Eliezer was passionately
devoted to it. Without Torah, he declared, the heavens and the
earth could not endure. Indeed, it was for the sake of the Torah
that the whole creation came into being.[133] The observance of the
Torah, R. Eliezer regarded as fundamental to national well being.
What was the significance, R. Eliezer asked, of the fact that the
Israelites met with victory against the Amalekites while Moses held
his hands upraised but suffered defeat when his hands were lowered
(Ex. 17:11)? When the hands of Moses were upraised, God was
mindful of Israel's devotion to the Torah which the hands of Moses
were to bring down to them, and He blessed them with success;

IV, 43a. R. Eliezer was likewise cautious in the care of a sacrifice
to which he also attached great sanctity. Cf. M. Tem. 3:1, 3. Cf. also
R. Eliezer's very stringent regulations for a sacrifice to change from
its first state when it is still entirely sacred and any lay use of it
would involve sin, to the second state when, after disposing of the
altar's share, the priest or layman may eat it. M. Meil. 1:2.
Seb. 4:5 (p. 485); Tos. Men. 4:10 (p. 516), 4:14 (p. 517). Seb. 89b-
90a; Tos. Men. 4:15 (p. 517); Men. 47a. Cf. also M. Men. 7:3; Tos.
Men. 8:19 (p. 524); Men. 79a. Cf. M. Meil, 1:3; Tos. Meil. 1:6
(p. 557).

132. M. Pes. 1:7, Tos Pes. 1:5 (p.155). Cf. M. Shek. 8:7,
Sifra, Sav, p. 33a. R. Eliezer was close to the general position of
the Shammaites while R. Joshua was closer to the position of the
Hillelites. Cf. Tos. Shek 3:6 (p. 178) and see variant cited by
Zuckermandel.

133. Ned. 32a. Cf. Pes. 68b, where this statement is quoted
in the name of R. Elazar; Yalkut on Ecc. 12:13.

when the hands of Moses were lowered, God considered that Israel would also neglect the Torah, and they met with reverses.[134]

R. Eliezer's zeal for the study of Torah often led him to extremes. Attending the celebration in honor of the circumcision ceremony of Abuyah's son, Elisha, R. Eliezer found the guests engaged in light conversations and friendly chatter. He objected to such a "waste of time", and induced his colleague R. Joshua, who was also present, to withdraw with him for study.[135] R. Eliezer himself is reputed to have always been the first to arrive in the academy and the last to leave.[136] He would apparently have been willing that people should abandon their daily occupations to devote themselves entirely to study. Moses, runs a homily of R. Eliezer, caused a jar of manna to be set aside and preserved for the future (Ex. 17:33), in order that Jeremiah might use it as an object lesson in the importance of Torah. When Jeremiah rebuked his generation for neglecting the Torah, they offered the apology that they were preoccupied with the task of earning a living. Pointing to the jar, he replied to them: When your ancestors on their way from Egypt were all devoted to Torah, they did not have to worry about earning a living; God provided them with this, the manna. If your devotion to Torah were as genuine you would be similarly provided for.[137] R. Eliezer exhorted the teacher to be diligent in his work. He should repeat each lesson four times. This, R. Eliezer pointed out, was the pedagogic procedure of Moses in

---

134. Mek. *ad locum* and cf. Yalkut, *ad locum*; Mek. R. Simeon p. 82f. Perhaps the point of this homily was to counteract a popular Christian interpretation which saw in the figure of Moses, with his hands upraised, a symbol of the cross. See Justin Martyr. *Dial.* 90 and *Epistle of Barnabas,* ch. 12.

135. j Hag. II, 77b; Ecc. R. 7:18.

136. Sukka 28a.

137. Mek. Vayasa 5 (Horovitz p. 172). Cf. Tan. Beshalah 21. One of the prayers composed by R. Eliezer includes the words: "And may Thy Torah be our occupation throughout our life" (j Ber. IV, 7d). According to R. Joshua, if a man studies "two sections of the law in the morning and two in the evening and works the rest of

teaching Israel. The ordinary teacher cannot afford to do less.[133]

But the Torah which R. Eliezer idealized was limited to what had been accumulated in the past. In so far as Torah may be used to denote the thinking of contemporaries, the living contributors of the contemporary jurists and scholars of the day, R. Eliezer was opposed to it. Indeed, scholarship was to continue. But as we have already had occasion to discover in our detailed discussions on theology and ritual, that scholarship was to confine itself essentialliy to exploring and interpreting what had been achieved by tradition. Tradition was, however, to remain intact, as a great body of unchanging truths to which the present and the future must always abide. R. Eliezer warned against permitting the young to engage in the speculative study of the law and urged that they be entrusted instead to the instruction of some competent master of tradition.[139] He actually took pride in that he had never rendered a legal decision which was not based on some tradition handed down from his teachers.[140] When confronted with a question which he could not decide on the basis of tradition, he usually evaded answering.[141]

---

him of the famous eulogy of the Torah student, quoted in Ab. 6:1 in the day, he has acted as worthily as if he had observed the whole Torah" (Mek. R. Simeon p. 75; Tan. Beshalah 20).

138. Er. 54b. R. Akiba, *ibid*, likewise demanded great diligence on the part of the teacher, also deducing it from the pedagogy of Moses. For R. Eliezer's emphasis on the study of the Torah cf. also Mid. Mishle 9:12, 22:6 and P. S. E. Z., p. 15ff, which attributes to R. Eliezer the eulogy of the Talmud student that is quoted in Ab. 6:1 in the name of R. Meir.

139. This is how I interpret the maxim ומנעו בניכם מן ההגיון והושיבם בין ברכי ת"ח in Ber. 28b. Cf. Jacob Bruell, *Mebo ha-Mishnah* (Introduction to the Mishnah), Frankfort o. M. 1875, pp. 78, 80; Ginzberg, *Sekte*, p. 71.

140. Sukka 28a. There are, of course, any number of statements by R. Eliezer for which he gave hermeneutical or logical reasons. What he objected to was new regulations which could not be dervied either by logic or hermeneutics from Scripture or tradition.

141. Tos. Yoma 4:14 (p. 188); Yoma 66b; A. Z. 17a; Tos. Sukka 1:9 (p. 192); Sukka 28a.

When on one occasion his pupil R. Judah b. Batira asked for permission to solve two such problems that had been proposed to him and which he could not answer, R. Eliezer, in consenting, stipulated, ". . . provided you thereby establish the standpoint of tradition."[142]

It was entirely consistent with this that R. Eliezer went to great extremes in emphasizing the authority of the teacher. One should not teach within twelve 'mils' of his master's presence. Nadab and Abihu disregarded this rule; they were disrespectful enough to teach within the presence of Moses, and it was for this reason that they died. A pupil on one occasion taught within R. Eliezer's own presence. "He will certainly die within one year," R. Eliezer observed to his wife, and within a short time thereafter that pupil actully died. "Are you a prophet?", R. Eliezer was asked. "No," replied he ". . .but I know on the basis of a tradition that any pupil who teaches within his master's presence has merited death.[143]

---

142. M. Neg. 9:3, 11:7.

143. P. R. K. 154b. Cf. Er. 63a; Sifra, Shemini, p. 45b; Lekah on Lev., p. 53; Tan. Ahre Mot 6; j Git. I, 42c. The twelve mils represent the size of Israel's encampment in the desert. Cf. also Sifre, Deut. section 357; Mid. Tann. on Deut. 34:4; Sota 13b.

Chapter IV

R. ELIEZER THE SOCIAL CONSERVATIVE

The social doctrine of Pharisaism was likewise a development in the direction of individualism and universalism. This is manifest in the social legislation of the Pharisees which tends towards class equality, humanitarianism, and pacifism. In so far as this had already been achieved by the first century and had become part of tradition, R. Eliezer agreed with his colleagues in accepting it— even as in the case of his conception of Jewish piety which we have discussed before. Where, however, flexibility still prevailed, R. Eliezer and his colleagues generally disagreed. His colleagues endeavored to continue the development in the direction of individualism and universalism, to reach out after a greater measure of social equality, a more thoroughgoing pacifism and a more inclusive humanitarianism. He, in each instance, dissented, representing the more conservative point of view.

1. *The Family.*—We have already learnt that R. Eliezer regarded marriage and procreation as the sacred duty of every Israelite. Sex relations between men and women outside of wedlock he condemned in the severest terms.[1] He permitted marriage with a niece.[2] Where a minor girl had been given in marriage by her mother or brothers, R. Eliezer recognized her right to have the

---

1. Tos. Kid. 1:4 (p. 335).

2. Thus, R. Eliezer himself married his niece. j Jeb. XIII, 13c; I A.R.N. 16. Because R. Eliezer hesitated before going through with this marriage, Ginzberg, *Sekte,* pp. 31f, 182f, has argued that he was

marriage annulled by protesting against it before court ("miyun").[5]
These expressions of R. Eliezer were, of course, only reaffiirmations
of tradition, and the other scholars fully agreed with him.

    R. Eliezer and his colleagues differed in their attitude toward
polygamy. Pharisiac Judaism permitted polygamy, but social and

---

really opposed to it. This would put him in agreement with the
Damascan sect that also forbade marrying a niece. It is also Ginzberg's argument that the special praise of the rabbis for one who
marries his niece was only an effort to counteract the tendency that
was opposed to it. Whether there was any tendency among the
scholars of our period against marriage with a niece we cannot
decide here (Cf. Aptowitzer, "Spuren des Matriarchats im juedischen
Schrifttum," *HUCA*, IV 1927, p. 232ff). But it would be difficult
to explain R. Eliezer's hesitation in marrying his niece on such
grounds. The fact is that he did marry her in the end. It would
rather seem that R. Eliezer hesitated because she was a minor, as
is indeed the suggested explanation in the Talmud. The rabbis encouraged such marriages as an emergency measure to provide homes
for the many poor orphaned girls that were left as a result of the
war. This, it seems, was also the motive of R. Eliezer's mother when
she urged him to marry his niece. R. Eliezer, however, clung to an
older Pharisaic position which, though not fully opposed, was unsympathetic to such marriages. See below, note 3 and p. 103f.
    3. M. Jeb. 13:7, 11; Jeb. 108a; Tos. Jeb. 13:3 (p. 256); Ket.
101a. This is already assumed in the discussions of the Shammaites
and the Hillelites (M. Jeb. 13:1). Where the father gave his minor
daughter in marriage, the arrangement was binding and "miyun"
was not possible. This right should have passed on, together with
other rights, to the oldest son in the event of the father's death. The
rabbis, however, seem to have objected to a marriage without the
consent of the woman. In the case of the father the old law was
allowed to stand, but in the case where the mother or brother give
her in marriage, the girl's rights were protected through the institution of miyun. Cf. Heinemann, p. 308f. A minor boy could not marry
at all. See San. 52b and cf. Heinemannn, p. 304. For independent
marriages Roman law fixed the minimum ages at thirteen for boys
and twelve for girls. The rule was approximately the same in Jewish
law except that the formal criterion was not age but puberty. Cf.
Juster, II, p. 54.

economic conditions had limited the practice to a small minority
of well-to-do, upper class families.[4] His colleagues, therefore, looked
upon polygamy as virtually obsolete; marriage was to them essentially monogamous arrangement.   To him, however, belonging to
the upper class minority, polygamy was still a living institution;
and under certain conditions, he even recommended practicing
it.   Thus, in the case of the barren wife, his colleagues insisted
on the dissolution of the marriage so that the man might wed another woman and beget cihldren.   He, on the other hand, regarded
such a drastic step unnecessary, because one might practice polygamy and procreate through an additional wife.[5]   This difference
in attitude towards polygamy may perhaps also have been the basis
for the varying views of the scholars as to what constitutes adequate grounds for divorce.   Assuming a monogamous marriage and
granting the social outlook of the time, it is not strange that the
Hillelites should have sanctioned divorce where the wife proved de-
ficient in her culinary ability,[6] or that R. Akiba should have sanctioned it where the husband became enamored of a prettier woman.
The Shammaites—and R. Eliezer seems to have agreed with them
—objected, because they saw a practicable way out in polygamy.
Divorce was unnecessary since one might well marry the more pro-
ficient cook (or the prettier woman) as an additional wife.   They,
therefore, sanctioned divorce only for reasons of unfaithfulness.[7]

---

4.   See Krauss, *Archaeologie,* II, p. 26ff, and cf. Juster, *op. cit.,*
p. 52, note 3.   The Damascan sect was alone in prohibiting polygamy.
Cf. L. Ginzberg, *Sekte,* p. 24ff.

5.   This is clearly the implied principle of the dispute in M. Sota
4:3.   This is similarly the basis for the dispute in Ket. 52a, in the
case where a man has forsworn living with his wife.   According to
R. Eliezer's colleagues, the marriage must be dissolved.   According
to R. Eliezer, this is unnecessary, because one may fulfill the duty
of procreation by practicing polygamy.

6.   See Krauss, *ibid,* p. 50, for the great importance attached by
the ancient orientals to the wife's culinary abilities.

7.   M. Git. 9:10; j Sota I, 16b; Nu. R. 9:37. Ginzberg, *Mekomah
shel ha-Halakah,* p. 42, explains the view of the Shammaites on the

R. Eliezer and his colleagues also differed over the respective rights and obligations of husband and wife. His colleagues emphasized the rights of the wife; he, those of the husband. Tradition required that the wife perform certain domestic duties for her husband, such as grinding the flour, baking, washing clothes, cooking, nursing the children, making the bed, and spinning. The other scholars ruled that these duties were to be diminished in proportion to the number of servants she brought into the household as part of her dowry: "If she brought one servant, she is exempted from grinding the flour, baking and laundrying; if two, she is also exempted from cooking and nursing; if three, she need not even make the bed or spin; if four, she may sit leisurely in the chair—she is free of all house work." According to R. Eliezer, however, even if she brought with her a hundred maids "her husband may compel her to spin, for idleness begets unchastity."[8] A husband may, according to R. Eliezer, impose upon his wife an oath that she has not cheated him "concerning her distaff and her dough." His colleagues protested against this decision, declaring that "one could not live together with a serpent," that family life would become impossible if the husband had so little faith in his wife.[9] R. Eliezer also differed with his colleagues in extending the rights of the husband in the

---

ground that in the upper levels of society, which they represented, women enjoyed a higher status. The Hillelites and R. Akiba, in allowing divorce almost at the husband's own will, acted in accordance with the standards of a lower social level where the status of women was inferior. More research would, however, be necessary in order to determine the relative position of women in the halakah of the two schools. Cf. for example M. Jeb. 6 :6; Sifra, Mesorah, end; Shab. 64b; Mek. Mishpatim 3 where the Hillelites and R. Akiba accord a very high status to women. In the halakah of R. Eliezer which we have examined in detail the low regard for women is pronounced.

8. M. Ket. 5 :3.

9. M. Ket. 9 :4; Ket. 86b. But R. Eliezer's colleagues permitted the husband to demand such an oath where she administered his estate or commercial establishment.

the matter of annulling his wife's "vows." These rights, according to him, even precede marriage. They may be exercised by the groom twelve months after the betrothal;[10] they may likewise be exercised by the brother-in-law of a widow who is waiting for him to go through the levirate marriage with her.[11] Nor, ruled he, do these rights refer only to vows already assumed. He permitted the husband to annul in advance any vows that his wife might assume in the future.[12] His colleagues limited these rights to the husband after marriage, and to vows of past assumption only. Similarly, while R. Joshua required two witnesses to testify to a woman's unfaithfulness before submitting her to the ordeal of the "bitter water," R. Eliezer considered the testimony of one witness or the husband's mere suspicions as enough to warrant imposing the ordeal.[13]

R. Eliezer likewise minimized the rights of the woman in the matter of divorce. According to Jewish law the husband alone can grant a divorce.[14] Nevertheless, R. Eliezer's colleagues viewed the writ of divorce from the standpoint of the woman: as an instrument

---

10. Because from then on he must provide her sustenance. If the bride is a widow, the obligation of sustenance and the rights of annulling her vows begin thirty days after the betrothal. M. Ned. 10:5. Cf. A. Buechler, "Das juedische Verloebnis," in *Festschrift Israel Lewy*, p. 131.

11. M. Ned. 10:6. According to R. Eliezer, even if she has two brothers-in-law, both may annul her vows. R. Akiba prohibited it even where there is only one brother-in-law. R. Joshua prohibited it in the case where there are two brothers-in-law, but permitted it where there is only one brother-in-law.

12. M. Ned. 10:7; Ned. 75b-76a, 72b; Nazir 12b; j Ned. X, 42a.

13. There were two major steps in the process. After her first suspicious act she was warned; after the second, she would have to drink the "water of bitterness" (Nu. 5:11-24). To establish the first fact, R. Eliezer conceded that two witnesses were required; the dispute was concerning the second. M. Sota 1:1; Sifre, Deut. section 188; Nu. R. 9:37. Cf. Sifre, Nu. section 161. The whole discussion was however purely theoretic. As far as practice was concerned, the ordeal had been abolished by R. Johanan b. Zakkai (M. Sota 9:9).

14. Cf. Juster, II, pp. 58-61.

by means of which she regains her freedom to remarry. They, therefore, ruled invalid a divorce which included a condition limiting her
choice of men for remarriage, since such a divorce would not restore
to her a complete freedom. R. Eliezer, however, regarded the divorce from the standpoint of the husband, as an instrument severing
all relations with his wife. Since that would be accomplished fully
even with the condition cited, he ruled the divorce valid. His colleagues, who reckoned with the sentiments of the woman, similarly
invalidated a divorce if awarded outside of the locality where she
instructed her agent to receive it.[15] R. Eliezer ruled the divorce valid. He reasoned that since the husband can divorce his
wife even without her consent, he can likewise award the divorce
wherever he sees fit, regardless of her instructions.[16]

These decisions of R. Eliezer are entirely in consonance with
his low opinion of women in general. A woman of rank at one time
questioned him concerning some point of law. He brusquely silenced
her with the remark that a woman's wisdom is limited to the distaff.
And when his son criticized him for this uncivil reply, he exclaimed
that he would rather see the Torah destroyed than abandoned to
study by woman. He held that to teach one's daughter Torah is as
improper as to teach her obscenity. R. Eliezer regarded as immodest
any intimacies between the male guests at the marriage festivities
and the bride, such as accepting a cup of wine from her, and even
where the groom is by her side. His colleagues protested that Jewish
women possess enough moral restraint to permit a greater freedom
of behavior. His reply to this was that moral restraint is developed
only through the study of Torah, to which women have no access.[17]

---

15. According to an old law the divorce was not effective until
it reached the hands of the woman or her duly deputized agent.

16. M. Git. 9:1; Tos. Git. 9:1 (p. 333); Sifre, Deut. section 259.
Cf. Git. 83a; j Git. IX, 50a; M. Git. 6:3, 4. R. Eliezer may have allowed
the conditional divorce because he limited the grounds for divorce
to reasons of unfaithfulness. Such a condition would keep the
divorced woman from marrying her paramour. His colleagues, who
sanctioned divorce for reasons other than unfaithfulness, forbade it.

17. j Sota III, 19a. Cf. Yoma 66b; M. Sota 3:4; Kal. R. 1.

R. Eliezer likewise recognized a wide authority on the part of parents over children. Jewish law never gave the parents the right of life and death over their children, as did Roman law.[18] Nevertheless, the Bible gives the father the right to sell his minor daughter as a "maid-servant" (Ex. 21:7), adding the recommendation that either the master or the master's son take her to themselves in marriage. R. Eliezer's colleagues found it offensive to think of a father selling his daughter into slavery. They, therefore, regarded the entire arrangement, in the light of the added recommendation, as an act of giving one's daughter in marriage. Consequently, they forbade selling her to near relatives since they cannot marry her. R. Eliezer, however, continued to regard this as a case of actually selling one's daughter to slavery. He, therefore, permitted selling her even to near relatives.[19]

R. Eliezer generally placed great emphasis on the obedience

Ben Azzai but not R. Joshua (Mishnah, *ibid*) considered it a religious obligation to teach one's daughter Torah. Cf. Yalkut on Proverbs, section 940, and Sota 21b. Philo, too, is exteremely unsympathetic to women. See Heinemann, p. 239.

18. See Krauss, *Archaeologie*, II, p. 20; Juster, II, p. 55. Philo was influenced by the Roman conception. See Heinemann, p. 251.

19. Kid. 18b, 20a, 44b. The rabbis also disputed whether a master who does not arrange for the marriage of such a girl, may keep her as a maid servant. R. Jonathan b. Abtolmas and R. Ishmael ruled in the negative, while R. Eliezer and R. Akiba ruled in the affirmative. See Mek. Mishpatim 3, and cf. Buechler, *op. cit.*, p. 114. note 3. It is interesting that the actual development of the law seems, as a matter of fact, to have been in the opposite direction. Originally the maid servant was used by her master as a concubine. The legislation in Ex. 21:7f does not recommend marriage, as the rabbis understood it, but tries to protect the concubine's rights. See S. R. Driver, *The Book of Exodus*, Cambridge 1911, p. 212f. The whole institution of selling a minor daughter had, however, long become obsolete by the time of our period (Kid. 69a and cf. Ar. 12b) and the essential facts were no longer remembered. The discussion of the scholars was only Biblical exegesis, but even here R. Eliezer and his colleagues followed their respective tendencies.

owed by children to their parents. What is the extent of obedience
due to one's parents? he was once asked. According to one source
he replied: "Even if the parent throws one's purse into the sea, a
truly obedient child will not criticize him." According to another
source he replied by citing as an example of ideal obedience the con-
duct of a certain Dama b. Netina, a gentile. This Dama on one
occasion forfeited a business transaction that would have yielded him
an immense profit, because he did not want to waken his father
who had the warehouse keys under the pillow. According to a third
source, R. Eliezer took as his example another act of the same Dama.
His mother, slightly deranged, once ridiculed him and spat at him
in the presence of his peers and he was not discourteous to her.[20]
But the child's obligations to the mother were by no means equal
to those due to the father. The father ranked higher, for both
mother and child owed him obedience.[21]

2. *Economic and Social Stratification.*—R. Eliezer's thinking
remained rooted in the agricultural economy from which he had
emerged, and to which, by his vested interests, he continued to belong. He openly disapproved of the life in large cities. The ultimate redemption, he declared, will involve more than a return of
the scattered Israelites to the holy land. It will also involve a
return to the soil on the part of the urban masses, the "dwellers in
darkness and in the shadow of death" (Ps. 107:14). Universal hap-
piness and peace, as he pictured it, was entirely contingent on the
prosperity of agriculture.[22] He considered the agricultural calendar

---

20. Kid. 32a; A. Z. 24a; Kid. 31a; P. R. 123b and editor's notes.
Cf. j Pea. I, 15c, and Kid. 31a.

21. Kid. 31a. The case on which R. Eliezer expressed himself
was one where the claims of father and mother conflicted. R. Eliezer
may however have agreed with the Mishnah (Ker. 6:9) which, con-
ceding priority to the father in case of conflict, nevertheless maintains that generally father and mother should be treated as equals.
Philo explicitly demanded a greater respect for the father than for
the mother. See Heinemann, p. 251f.

22. Sem. d'R. Hiya 1:4 (in Sem. p. 214:39-40); Mid. Tehil. Ps.
72:3. Cf. Yalkut on Psalms, section 805, where the authority for this

beginning the new year in the fall as primary, and held that the first
of Tishri, not the first of Nisan (the beginning of Spring, which
started the political and religious new year) commemorates the date
of creation. [23] It was no doubt because of his interest in agriculture

---

statement is omitted. The passage in Semahot describes the four
contemporary exiles of Israel. The first is the Parthian empire; the
second, the demoralized Jewry of Palestine. The fourth is Rome
which is reached "in ships by the way of the sea." The third is the
large cities. These may refer specifically to the Jewish communities
in such large centers as Alexandria and Antioch. See also Mek. R.
Simeon p. 32, where R. Eliezer explains the praises of Palestine as
a land flowing with milk and honey to refer to agricultural products:
the "juices of fruit" and the "honey of dates." This was, of course,
also more corresponding to the facts.

    23. R. H. 8a-10b-11a, 27a. Cf. A. Z. 8a. Cf. also Mid. ha-Gadol
on Gen. p. 34; P. R. K. 134b and see Buber's note 4. R. Joshua,
considering the political and religious calendar primary, regarded the
first of Nisan as the anniversary of creation. This dispute had, of
course, important consequences in determining the chronology of the
Bible. Cf. R. H. 11b-12a. Modern scholars are generally agreed that ultimately the Jews used both calendars simultaneously. They are still
divided as to whether the original calendar began the new year in Nisan or in Tishre. They are likewise divided as to whether the civil new
year began on Nisan or Tishre. See Ginzel, *Handbuch der Chronologie,*
II, Leipzig 1911, pp. 22-26, 39f; E. Mahler, *Handbuch der juedischen
Chronologie,* Leipzig 1916, pp. 188, 217f, 243ff; Benzinger, *Hebraeische
Archaeologie,* Leipzig 1927, p. 169f; S. S. Zeitlin, *The History of the
Second Jewish Commonwealth,* Philadelphia 1933, pp. 71-76. We
cannot decide here as to which calendar the Jews used originally.
But as far as the civil new year is concerned, it would seem that in
its commercial phase it began on Tishre. Thus, Josephus, *Ant.* 1, 3, 3,
speaks of Tishre as the new year for "selling and buying and other
ordinary affairs." Since Palestine was predominantly an agricultural country, it was only natural that the economic activity of the
nation follow the rural calendar. For the political administration
of the country, however, Nisan was the new year. This is clearly
suggested in M. R. H. 1:1 which speaks of the first Nisan as "the
new year for kings." Isaac Yisraeli, *Sefer Yesod Olam* (Book concerning the Foundations of the Earth), Berlin 1777, p. 63b, quotes a
baraitha according to which R. Eliezer and his colleagues differed as

with its great need of rain, particularly in a dry country like Palestine, that R. Eliezer required the reciting of praises to God as the Giver of rain on the first, instead of the last day of the Feast of Booths. [24] R. Eliezer was likewise reckoning with rural conditions, when he decided that a public fast day, proclaimed as a special appeal to God for rain, need not be completed if rain fell before noon of that day. To the rural population such an occasion would be a great festive event, not to be marred by fasting. R. Eliezer's colleagues considered simply the formal legal question of whether a duly proclaimed public fast day may be suspended before its comple-

---

to which years of the nineteen year cycle should be intercalated in equalizing the lunar and solar years. Mahler, *op. cit.*, pp. 356, 372ff regards the baraitha as genuine, without suspecting its source. But there is no trace of it anywhere in Talmudic literature. Epstein, *M'kadmoniyot ha-Yehudim* (Contributions to Jewish Archeology), Vienna 1887 pp. 18-22, tries to relate it to a statement in the *Pirke d'R. Eliezer*. But we have already learned that the *Pirke* is a post-geonic work. Furthermore, S. Poznanski, "Calendar (Jewish)", in *Encyc. of Religion and Ethics*, III, N. Y. 1911, p. 117f, has shown that the nineteen year cycle was unknown throughout the Talmudic period. We must, therefore, dismiss this baraitha as spurious. The discussion about the calendar in P. R. E. ch. 1 is clearly apocryphal. It presents R. Akiba and R. Ishmael as contemporaries of R. Johanan b. Zakkai!

24. M. Taan. 1:1, Taan. 2b. R. Eliezer cited, in defense of his views, the custom of the Temple service where the ceremonies connected with the prayers for rain were performed on the first day of the holiday. R. Joshua demanded that these praises be recited on the last day of the holiday, because the descent of rain on the holiday itself would interfere with the dwelling in booths and would, therefore, be a mark of God's displeasure. R. Eliezer reckoned with the objection of R. Joshua by pointing out that he did not suggest pleading for rain on the first day, but merely to express gratefulness to God as the rain giver. L. Finkelstein, "The Pharisees," *HTR*, XXII 1929, pp. 193-201, assumes that it was the urban, and not the rural community, that looked to Sukkot as the festival of rain; the rural community, he claims, was satisfied with the prosperity petitions of the high priest on the Day of Atonement.

tion or not, and they ruled for completion.[25] This difference in social orientation is likewise the basis for the dispute over the status of a person who consecrated himself to the Temple. His colleagues ruled that such a person was to lose all his property to the Temple treasury except a minimum of food for thirty days, the bare necessaries of his furniture, and his tools, if he be an artisan. R. Eliezer, however, with his deeper concern for the rural population, added, that, "if a peasant, he may also retain his plow and a team of oxen."[26] R. Eliezer's rural orientation is likewise in evidence when, in fixing the minimum land from which, according to law, the corner crops were to be left as a beneficence to the poor, he made his computations in terms of the land's sowing capacity or rather area (like his colleague R. Tarfon), while R. Joshua made his in terms of the land's produce.[27] It is also to the habits of a rural environment, where people are early both in their retiring and rising habits, that we must

---

25. M. Taan. 3:9. The same Mishnah actually reports an incident in Lydda where rain descended before the fast day was over and R. Tarfon, also a rural tanna, immediately disregarded the fast and proclaimed a public holiday: "go forth and eat and drink and make a holiday"; in the evening the happy populace gathered to chant praises to God who had delivered them. The words rural and urban must be used cautiously. They describe not so much geographic as social and occupational conditions, because there were many farmers in Palestine living in towns with their lands lying outside the town areas. See Salo Baron, "Israelite Population in the Days of the Kings" (Hebrew), in *Chajes Memorial Volume*, p. 96ff.

26. M. Ar. 6:3; Tos. Ar. 4:6 (p. 547); Ar. 24a. In addition to the peasant, R. Eliezer also adds the case of a donkey driver who may retain his donkey. These are of course only further illustrations of the principle applying to the artisan.

27. M. Pea 3:6. The latter is evidently the more commercial method. Similarly R. Eliezer fixed the time of walking around a palm tree as the duration of a married woman's retirement with a man under suspicious circumstances before submitting her to the ordeal of the "bitter water." R. Joshua fixed it by the time it would take to pour a cup of wine. See Tos. Sota 1:2 (p. 293); j Sota, I, 16c; Tan. Naso 7. Cf. Sota 4a where the view of R. Eliezer is attributed to R. Ishmael and the view of R. Joshua is attributed to R. Eliezer.

attribute R. Eliezer's decision demanding the completion of the
Shema in the evening by the end of the first night watch (ten
o'clock),[28] and in the morning by sunrise. His urban colleagues
extended the time in the one case until midnight, and in the other
until nine o'clock in the morning.[29]

R. Eliezer was extremely favorable to the agricultural interests
when he resisted the efforts of his colleagues to rescind the ban
against cattle raising. The Talmud does not relate the circumstances
that were involved in the original enactment of the ban or in the
later efforts of the rabbis to rescind it. But S. Baron has made
the plausible suggestion that there was a tendency during our period
on the part of many peasants, particularly the tenant farmers, to
desert the land which was heavily burdened with Roman taxes,
priestly dues, and restrictions of the sabbatical year, in favor of the
raising of small cattle, which could be carried on under relatively
more favorable conditions. Deserted, fallow land, meant, of course,
a great loss to the landowners. Those whose soil continued to be
cultivated must also have resented the appearance of large herds of
cattle that often wandered into the fields and destroyed the crops.
Since Palestine was at the time a thickly populated country requiring for its sustenance an intensive cultivation of the soil, the rabbis
met the situation by banning the raising of small cattle. After the
war, when Palestine had suffered a great loss in population, and
when agrarian conditions must have become even more difficult as a
result of the general decline, social and economic, that the war had
spread throughout the country, the patriarch R. Gamaliel moved

---

28. R. Eliezer divided the night into three watches (Ber 3a).

29. M. Ber. 1:1, 2. R. Eliezer similarly limited the time for
eating the paschal lamb, the principal feature of the Passover feast,
until midnight. R. Akiba permitted it until daybreak. See Ber. 9a;
j Ber. I, 3a; Sifre, Deut. section 133; Mid. Tann. on Deut. 16:6; Mek.
Bo. 6. Cf. Mek. R. Simeon p. 11, where R. Elazar b. Azariah and
R. Akiba agree in fixing the time limit at midnight but differ in
their derivations. Cf. also M. Ber. 1:1, which describes the urban
R. Gamaliel's children arriving at daybreak from some festivity.

that the ban be rescinded. R. Eliezer, however, continued to champion the interests of traditional farming and oposed the change.[30] His
demand that Syrian agriculture be subjected to all the requirements
of tithing and the sabbatical year, was likewise to the advantage of
the land owning community of Palestine, because such a move was
bound to check the emigration of farmers to Syria, also a growing
phenomenon during our period, and protect the Palestine crops
from very serious competition of Syrian products.[31]

---

30. M. B. K. 7:7; B. K. 80a; Tos. Jeb. 3:3, 4 (p. 242). The
Tosefta merely quotes R. Eliezer as evading the question. Buechler,
ibid, p. 193, argues that R. Eliezer really implied a prohibition. But
even if he merely evaded, it would still show that he was out of
sympathy with the movement: he refused to sanction it, as R.
Gamaliel had done. Cf. M. Friedmann, "Four Products Prohibited
by the Rabbis" (Hebrew), *Kadimah*, N. Y. 188, p. 281f; S. Krauss,
"La defense d'elever du menu betail," p. 44f. In the Tosefta R. Eliezer
was also asked whether one may raise dogs, pigs and fowl, which he
likewise evaded answering. It seems that these too were former
prohibitions. Thus, R. Eliezer himself declared explicitly in another
connection that the raising of dogs was no better than the raising
of pigs. Tos. B. K. 8:17 (p. 362); B. K. 83a. Cf. M. Lerner, "Die
achtzehn Bestimmungen," *MWJ*, IX 1882, p. 129f, note 1. Apparently the same economic conditions had also produced a tendency
toward chicken farming, as well as dog and pig raising. Pigs could
not be used for food purposes by Jews, but they could very well have
been raised for export. The raising of dogs on a large scale may
have been a concomitant of cattle raising, since these dogs were used
to guard the flocks. The same motives that moved the rabbis to ban
the raising of cattle very likely moved them to the latter prohibitions too. In the case of the dog and the pig there were however
additional objections. The dog, at that time, was a very vicious
animal and the presence of dogs in large numbers amidst the settled
areas, proved a menace to the population. There was an innate
repugnance on the part of Jews toward pigs, perhaps heightened
by the fact that the pig was used in pagan worship and was the
symbol of the Roman empire. Cf. Buechler, *ibid*, pp. 15-24. R.
Eliezer's evasion would therefore appear here, also, to have been a
refusal to sanction change.

31. M. Hal. 4:7. Cf. Tos. Hal. 2:5 (p. 99); j Shev. VI, 36d and

But while devoted to the interests of agriculture, R. Eliezer was, nevertheless, unfriendly to the *Am ha-Ares*, the great mass of peasants and agricultural laborers who actually tilled the soil. With the Revolution no doubt as a background, during which many of these peasants and laborers had risen against the wealthy landowners, R. Eliezer remarked: "Were it nor that they are economically dependent on us, they would rise and destroy us all." The company of an *Am ha-Ares* is to be avoided because he is always to be suspected of criminal designs. As a member of the class against whom the hostility of the *Am ha-Ares* was directed, he met antagonism with antagonism. He, no doubt, exaggerated when he said: "One would violate no law in stabbing an *Am ha-Ares*, even on a Day of Atonement coinciding with the Sabbath." Such an exaggeration bespeaks, however, intense class consciousness and class conflict.[32]

R. Eliezer also betrays a decided prejudice in favor of wealth and an emphasis on the rights of private property. Thus, he explained that the generation of the flood had violated all the laws of the Torah, but what finally brought on the severe decree against them was their violation of the rights of private property: indulgence in general robbery. He was unusually severe with crimes against property. When a field, forcibly taken from its owners, was

---

cf. A. Buechler, *Am ha-Ares*, p. 259ff.

32. Pes. 49b. I am following the reading of the Munich Mss. against our text, where the latter two expressions are attributed to R. Eliezer. See Rabinowicz, *ad locum*. Buechler thinks that the animosity against the Am ha-Ares did not develop until after the Hadrianic period, and he therefore retains the reading of R. Elazar in our texts (*Am ha-Ares*, p. 183 and note 2). Cf., however, Klausner, *Historia Yisraelit*, III, Jerusalem 1924, p. 185f, and S. Zeitlin, "The Am ha-Ares," p. 57. There were of course objections to the Am ha-Ares also because he was generally ignorant of the Law and unscrupulous in his religious observances. Zeitlin, *op. cit.*, p. 55f, is, however, quite correct in pointing to social considerations as the predominating elements in this animosity. So interpreted, these expressions do not justify the deduction of Bousset, *op. cit.*, p. 188, and others, that there was a deep-seated antagonism between the scholars as such, and the common people.

flooded, R. Eliezer ruled that in making restitution another field must be returned. According to his colleagues, it was enough to return the field in its flooded state; they argued that the flood, an accident of nature, would have taken place regardless of the occupant.[33] R. Eliezer also limited the extent to which private property might be interfered with for the public interest. He permitted digging tunnels under a public thoroughfare from private premises, as long as some satisfactory test of safety be met, such as the successful paassing of a wagon with a heavy load of stones. His colleagues opposed this, apparently because they did not regard any test a sufficient guarantee of public safety. R. Eliezer similarly minimized the responsibility of a person for damages caused by a fire starting from his premises. While R. Akiba extended this responsibility to a radius of fifty ells under normal conditions and three hundred ells in the case of a strong wind, he limited it to sixteen ells in the one case and thirty, in the other.[34]

He urged meticulous care in contributing the portion of the crop required by law to be set aside for the poor.[35] Nevertheless, whenever any doubts arose, his rulings were invariably in the interests of the property owners and against the poor. He gave the proprietor the right to withdraw two-thirds of the 'poor-tithe' for distribution among his needy relatives. Others limited such withdrawals to a half; the other half was to be distributed among the general poor without any distinctions, according to the order in which they came to call for it. Similarly, R. Eliezer accorded the proprietor the right to choose the poor who are to get the corner produce of the field (Peah). According to his colleagues, the proprietor had no rights at all over this produce; it was all to belong to those poor who were first to come upon it. He also limited the law which requires relinquishing the small single branches growing

---

33. Tan., Noah 4; B. K. 117b-118a and see Rabinowicz, ad locum.

34. M. B. B. 3:8; M. B. K. 6:4; Tos. B. K. 6:22 (p. 356); Mek. on Ex. 22 :5.

35. Mek. Mishpatim, Kaspa 20.

on every vine tree for the poor; he ruled that where the vine of an entire vineyard grew in that form it was all to belong to the proprietor; R. Akiba awarded it to the poor.[36]

The respective general position of R. Eliezer and his colleagues are also betrayed in their controversy concerning the disposition of ownerless land. According to an old law, such land was "hefker," a term corresponding to the Roman conception of *res nullius,* and which made the land open to seizure by anybody. R. Eliezer considered walking or running on such land sufficient as an act of legal possession. His colleagues, probably to prevent a single individual from seizing the entire land, and to make sure that only such people would get it who would make personal use of it, confined the method of its legal acquisition to actual tilling.[31] Largely the same considerations are involved in the controversy of R. Eliezer and his colleagues concerning a tenant priest receiving tithes from the crops of his landlord. According to Biblical law, there was no objection

---

36.   Tos. Pea. 4:2 (p. 23); M. Pea 8:6; M. Pea 4:9; M. Pea 7:7; Sifra, K'doshim, p. 88a; Sifre, Deut. section 285; Mid. Tann. on Deut. 24:21. It was also, in all likelihood, the varying importance which R. Eliezer and R. Joshua respectively attached to the rights of the proprietor and the recipient, that divided them over the question of how the priests' portion of the dough, if levitically unclean, is to be separated on Passover. According to R. Eliezer, the owner's rights continue until the contribution is actually transferred to the priest. Therefore, by leaving the dough for any length of time, the owner would violate the law against keeping leaven substance in his premises. He consequently required separating the priests' portion after baking, although by baking a portion that even the priest will not be able to use (because of its uncleanness), one would be doing useless work on the holiday. According to R. Joshua, the owner's rights cease the moment the contribution is separated. Even if the dough should turn leaven, therefore, the proprietor would not violate the law, because it is no longer his property. R. Joshua accordingly required separating it before baking. M. Pes. 3:3. Cf. Tos. Pes. 2:7 (p. 158); j Pes. III, 30a; Pes. 48a; j Er. X, 26b. Cf. also M. Bek. 1:6; M. Ed. 7:1; Vehiz, p. 16.

37.   B. B. 100a; Tos. B. B. 2:11 (p. 400).

to a person giving all the tithes of his crops to one priest. During our period when the priesthood, at least in its wealthiest representatives, was not on a very high moral level, certain serious abuses set in as a result of this practice. Many of the more enterprising priests would occupy the land as tenants to receive an agreed proportion of the crop, but at the same time claim all the tithes, including those due on the proportion belonging to the landlord. This practice, apparently widespread and conducted on a large scale, proved menacing for the less enterprising priests, because it withdrew their chief source of sustenance.[38] For their protection, the rabbis ruled that a tenant priest had no right over the tithes on his landlord's share in the produce. R. Eliezer dissented, demanding all tithes for the tenant priests since "that was their original motive in going on the land."[39]

R. Eliezer's indifference to the problems of the poor is also betrayed in his attitude toward the marriage of a minor girl. We have seen that Pharisaic Judaism developed an opposition to the parents arranging for the marriage of a minor girl without her consent. Nevertheless, during our period, when innumerable orphans left by the war were suffering great poverty and distress, particularly in the lower strata of society, the rabbis reversed themselves, and encouraged such marriages as a means of providing the orphaned girls with home and shelter.[40] It would seem that such marriages were consummated by the ceremony under the canopy, living together as husband and wife being postponed until a later time when the girl would reach puberty.[41] The girl also retained the right of

---

38. Cf. Jos. *Ant.* 20:8, 8.

39. M. D'mai 6:3.

40. Cf. S. Krauss, *Archaeologie,* II, p. 26 and note 250, and see above, p.

41. Cf. M. Ed. 8:2, Tos. Ed. 3:2 (p. 459); Jeb. 89b. Zuckermandel's printed text of the Tosefta speaks of the "daughter of a priest who was married to a priest," but the variants cited support the reading in the Mishnah referring this to a "bath Yisrael," the daughter of an Israelite. See also above, p. 88, note 3.

'miyun' that she had already won previously, and could secure the dissolution of the marriage simply by registering her official protest before court. Nevertheless, the rabbis tried to accord such a marriage full legal status. They recognized the right of the husband to annul his minor wife's vows, claim her findings and the wages of her labor, as well as to inherit her property in the event of her death. If he was a priest she was permitted to eat his priestly foods. R. Eliezer, however, refused to reckon with the circumstances and disapproved of all this. A priest, he ruled, may under no circumstances marry a minor girl.[42] But even in the case of a layman, such a marriage would not be a commendable move. One who gives his minor daughter in marriage to an aged man violates, according to an interpretation of his, the injunction (Lev. 19:29): "Profane not thy daughter to make her a harlot.[43]" R. Eliezer, furthermore, sought to minimize the legal status of such a marriage where it did take place. He denied a minor wife's husband the customary rights that husbands at the time enjoyed, such as annulling her vows, claiming her findings or the wages of her labor, or inheriting her property in the event of her death. It is obvious that with such rights denied him, there would be very little to encourage a man to contract sluch a marriage.[44]

---

42. Tos. Ed. 3:2 (p. 459); Jeb. 61b. The Amoraim limit R. Eliezer's remarks to the case of a high priest. This is certainly not in the text. R. Eliezer's reason may have been the apprehension that the priest will cohabit with her, because, according to him, she was not otherwise entitled to eat priestly food. Such cohabiting would, however, be sinful since it could not possibly be for purposes of procreation.

43. San. 76a. R. Akiba (ibid) very significantly interpreted this to refer to one who waits until his daughter grows up without providing for her marriage.

44. Tos. Jeb. 13:3 (p. 256); j Jeb. XIII, 13c; Jeb. 89b, 108a; Ket. 101a. R. Eliezer's low regard for this type of marriage is further illustrated by his rulings in the case where the husband of a "minor wife" died childless. Normally he agreed that the requirement of a levirate marriage applied. But where the deceased's brother is already married to the widow's close relation, he suggested

R. Eliezer also championed the interests of the creditor as opposed to that of the debtor. Thus, he required repaying a loan where the creditor lost the pledge that was in his custody. The only protection that he offered the debtor was a ruling that the creditor must submit to an oath absolving himself from the charge of negligence. R. Akiba, in such a case, did not require repayment of the debt.[45]

As further evidence of R. Eliezer's wealthy and aristocratic orientation we may also cite his ruling that elaborate jewelry, particularly for women, and arms of war for men, were an indispensable part of a respectable outfit, and as such exempted from the prohibition against carrying on the sabbath—a stand on which his lower class colleagues opposed him sharply.[46] Undoubtedly his aristocratic

---

that the widow be encouraged to protest against the original marriage, and obtain an annulment, which would set her free without the ceremony of halisah. His colleagues were opposed to any encouragement of "miyun." The ceremony of halisah which the Bible provided where the brother-in-law wanted to evade the levirate marriage was not permitted by the rabbis with a minor widow, but they considered it valid if it had already taken place. To R. Eliezer it was invalid, and had to be repeated upon her attaining majority. See M. Jeb. 13:2, 7; Tos. Jeb. 12:12 (p. 256). Cf. M. Jeb. 13:11, Tos. Jeb. 13:7 (p. 257).

45. B. M. 81b. Cf. Sheb. 43b. Where the borrower offered a note in addition to the pledge, R. Eliezer held the creditor more responsible because of the added protection, and did not require repayment.

46. M. Shab. 6:4; Tos. Shab. 4:6 (p. 115), 4:11 (p. 116); j Shab. VI, 7d. Cf. also M. Sukka 1:11, where R. Eliezer allows the use of reed mats whether large or small as sukka coverings, except where they were specifically designed for cushion purposes. (According to an old law one was not to cover a sukka with any object used about the house.) This reflects the custom of the well-to-do who generally regarded reed mats as too hard for cushions. The other scholars, speaking from the standpoint of the masses who generally used reed mats as cushions, prohibited it, except in the case of the large mat that would prove too cumbersome for a cushion because of its size.

outlook, his detachment from the great masses of the people, was also an influence in his interpretation of the Book of Psalms as the private communication between King David and God. R. Joshua held that, though often speaking as an individual, David was in these compositions really the spokesman of Israel.[47] There is similarly the decision in which, following the standards of the rich, R. Eliezer ruled brine too humble a food for inclusion in the family feast on which second tithe funds were to be expended. His colleagues permitted it.[48]

In addition to economic status, there was another source of social stratification in the facts of pedigree. The priests, levites and lay Israelites constituted the upper layer of society and were permitted to marry among themselves. Then followed the freedmen and the proselytes who, though otherwise treated on a par with the rest of Jewry, were nevertheless barred from marriage with priests. Finally, there followed the outcasts. These included the special proselytes who were not permitted to intermarry with Jews until the third generation   (Edomites and Egyptians) and those who were not permitted to intermarry with Jews at all (Ammonites and Moabites), the descendents of the Gibeonites who served as Temple slaves ('Nethinim'), and the so-called "mamzerim" or bastards, the offspring of certain legally objectionable unions.   In addition, there were others who could not prove their paternity (foundlings, etc.), and who were given the status of doubtful bastrads.   There was also the so-called 'isah,' a class of families who had no record of their pedigree and who were barred from priestly marriages because they were suspected of disqualifying admixtures.[49]

See also M. Er. 7:10 and cf. Ginzberg, *Mekomah shel ha-Halakah*, p. 23.

47. Pes. 117a.

48. Tos. M. Sh. 1:14 (p. 87); Er. 27a. Cf. also M. Sukka 1:11, where R. Eliezer similarly follows his class standards in defining what would constitute an acceptable Sukkot booth.

49. M. Kid. 4:1 and cf. Rosenthal, "Ueber Isah," *MGWJ*, XIII 1881, pp. 113-121ff; Lewi Freund, "Ueber Genealogien und Familien-reinheit in biblischer und talmudischer Zeit," in *Festschrift Adolph*

It was inevitable that the more democratic tendencies inaugurated by Pharisaism should react against this stratification. The Pharisees decreed to qualify the 'isah' families for intermarriage with the priesthood. Some likewise qualified the children of proselytes. R. Joshua succeeded in removing all special disabilities from the Ammonite proselytes. There was also a move to raise the descendants of the Gibeonites to full Jewish citizenship.[50]

The development was somewhat different in the case of the 'mamzer'. Representing the result of a sexual irregularity, the mamzer was bound to be opposed by the rabbis, the zealous guardians of pure family life. What undoubtedly caused this opposition to be even more pointed, was the presence of large numbers of slaves and Roman soldiers, with their loose morals, in the cities of Palestine. R. Akiba sought to meet the situation through more stringent legal regulations. He extended all the disabilities of the mamzer to offspring of all unions, even if proscribed by only a simple negative commandment, as well as to offspring of Jewesses by slaves or gentiles. Some, it would seem, even suggested denying the mamzer the right to inherit property and to exclude him from the laws of the levirate marriage. R. Joshua refused to make the innocent child the target of the deterrent legislation. He, therefore, retained the traditional limitations of the 'mamzer' concept, confining it to an adulterous or incestuous union which is punishable with death.[51] But he demanded special legislation against the woman, making the slightest immodesties in her behaviour such

---

Schwartz, Berlin 1917, pp. 174-179. It would seem that the priests, levites, lay Israelites and proselytes actually kept genealogical records down into our period. See Ginzberg, Sekte, p. 124f.

50. M. Ed. 8:3; M. Kid. 4:6; Kid. 77a, 77b, 78a, 78b; M. Yad. 4:4; j Kid. IV, 65c. Cf. Jeb. 79b, where the move to raise the status of Nethinim is placed in the days of R. Judah the Patriarch.

51. M. Jeb. 4:13. Mere illegitimacy, in the sense of birth outside of wedlock, did not involve any special disabilities in Jewish law. The Mishnah finally decides against the view of R. Joshua, but Simeon b. Azai attests to its being traditional.

as being closeted with men under suspicious circumstances, enough
to convict her of sexual irregularity. The democracy of the Pharisees
asserted itself, however, when they recognized these outcasts as an
independent community, and permitted them to marry among themselves. At the same time R. Tarfon suggested a formula for alleviating the condition of the mamzer's children. By marrying a slave
girl he will have slave children who, upon emancipation, will enjoy
the improved status of freedmen.

R. Eliezer's conservatism moved him to oppose these measures.
The decree qualifying the 'isah' families for marriage with priests
was reported already by R. Joshua and R. Judah b. Batira as an
old decision, and R. Eliezer may have accepted it as traditional.
There is no expression from him concerning the status of the Ammonite converts, perhaps because the debate over this question took place after he had been banned from the academy. It is
not clear why he was silent concerning the descendants of the proselytes. It is significant, however, that R. Judah, the son of his
favorite disciple Ilai, opposed the alleviation, and continued to dis-
qualify them.[52]

He was, however, outspoken with reference to the 'mamzer'.
He opposed the deterrent measures of R. Akiba as well as those of
R. Joshua.[53] He likewise refused to sanction the barring of a
mamzer from the rights of inheritance or to exclude him from the
laws of the levirate marriage.[54] At the same time, he defended a

---

52. Cf. Buechler, "Familienreinheit und Familienmankel in
Jerusalem," in *Festschrift Adolph Schwartz,* p. 160; Rosenthal, *op. oit.,*
p. 107.

53. Kid. 75b; M. Ket. 1:6, 7, 8, 9; Tos. Ket. 1:6 (p. 261). In the
latter instance R. Eliezer was supported by the patriarch. In defining
the concept of "mamzer" R. Eliezer apparently followed the majority
view, which applied it to the offspring of an incestuous union which
is punishable by excision (M. Jeb. 4:13).

54. Yoma 66b. Cf. Tos. Jeb. 3:3, 4 (pp. 242, 243). The text,
following the version in the Munich Mss. (see Rabinowicz, *ad locum)*
reads as follows:

שאלו את ר' אליזער פלוני מהו לעולם הבא, אמר להם לא שאלתוני אלא

rigid stratification among these outcasts, and even forbade them to
marry among themselves. A union between a doubtful mamzer and
a mamzer, or between two doubtful mamzerim, might possibly link
inherently pure and 'mamzer' stock; it was, therefore, to be forbidden. Furthermore, the problem, as he saw it, was only temporary,
for he seems to have considered 'mamzer' stock as essentially sterile,
and he felt confident that it would exhaust itself within three generations. He likewise objected to the proposal of R. Tarfon with regard to legitimizing the mamzer's children, maintaining that the

---

על פלוני מהו להציל כבשה מן הארי אמר להם לא שאלתוני אלא על הכבשה
מהו להציל הרועה מן הארי אמר להם לא שאלתוני אלא על הרועה ממזר
מהו לירש מהו ליבם מהו לסוד את ביתו מהו לסוד את קברו וכו'

"They asked R. Eliezer: "What of P'loni with regard
to a share in the world to come?' He said to them (evading): 'All
you asked is about P'loni, what about saving the sheep from the
lion?'. . . He said to them: 'All you asked is about the sheep; what
about saving the shepherd himself from the lion?'. . . He said to
them: 'You have merely asked about the shepherd. What about a
'mamzers' with regard to inheritance; what about him with regard
to the laws of the levirate marriage; what about plastering one's
residence or place of burial?' " We have already learned that the
original question about P'loni referred to Solomon. See above, p. 18f.
The question about the sheep which R. Eliezer, in his evasion, proposed, and which his inquisitors apparently took up, presupposes the
ban against cattle raising: since the sheep was being raised in violation of the law, was one required to rescue it?   The same circumstances are undoubtedly presupposed in the question concerning the
shepherd: was one required to rescue him while engaged in violating
the law?   In the Tosefta the question is whether the sheep or the
shepherd may be rescued from the wolf.   For other instances of
rabbinic hostility toward the shepherd cf. Tos. San. 5:5 (p. 423); M.
Bek. 5:4; M. B. K. 10:10; Tos. B. K. 11:9 (p. 370); B. M. 84b; San.
25b.   That the cited discriminations against the "mamzer" were at
all discussed, shows that they must have been considered seriously
in some circles.   R. Eliezer refused to support them, because they
had no precedent in tradition.   Cf. Buechler, op. cit., p. 141f.   The
prohibition of plastering one's residence or place of burial, we have
already learned, was to commemorate the destruction of the Temple.
R. Eliezer refused to approve of it because it was likewise without

taint of their bastard paternity would persist even after emancipation.[55]

R. Eliezer extended the authority of the master over the slave. Thus, he subjected one who sells himself into voluntary servitude because of ecnomic need to all the laws governing an actual Jewish slave: he was to be emancipated on the Sabbatical year, and to have his ear bored if he should want to serve longer; his master could compel him to live with a slave girl so as to breed him slaves; after the expiration of his servitude, he was to receive a slave's bonus. His colleagues treated such a person as an ordinary worker who had sold his labor but who was personally free: he could serve as long as he agreed to, regardless of the Sabbatical year; his master could not compel him to live with a slave girl; nor was he to receive the slave's bonus upon leaving his work.[56]

R. Eliezer was even severer with the gentile slave. He ruled that a gentile slave may not be kept in a Jewish home, unless he is circumcised.[57] When one of his maid servants died, his disciples, considering the slave a regular member of the family, assumed that he was in mourning, and came to offer him condolence. R. Eliezer, however, rebuked them: "Did I not teach you that no mourning is practiced for the death of a slave, as slaves are like animals? The loss of a slave calls for no more sympathy than such as is offered one who lost an ox or an ass, and which is sufficiently well expressed in the formula, 'May God restore your loss' ".[58] R. Eliezer also opposed the tendency, apparently pronounced during our period,

---

support in tradition. See above, p. 76f, note 166.

55. M. Kid. 4 :3; j Jeb. VIII, 9c; Jeb. 78b; M. Kid. 3 :13.

56. Kid. 14b. The reading, however, is doubtful as some texts have Eleazar. See Tosafot Veidokh, *ibid,* p. 15a. Judged in the light of his general position, R. Eliezer would very well fit here. The whole discussion was, of course, largely theoretical as Jewish slaves were extremely rare in our period. See Krauss, *Archaeologie,* II, p. 83.

57. Mek. Bo 15. R. Ishmael merely suggested that the master may circumcise the slave if he wants him to eat of the paschal lamb. He may, however, keep him without circumcision. Cf. above, p. 63.

58. j Ber. II, 5b. Cf. Ber. 16b; Sem. 1:25.

of emancipating gentile slaves.[59]   These freedmen were generally absorbed into the Jewish community, and R. Eliezer was very likely apprehensive lest the continued absorption of an inferior stock produce an ethnic deterioration in Jewry.[60]   Nevertheless, he himself, on one occasion, emancipated one of his gentile slaves in order to add him to the required quorum of ten for a religious service.[61]

R. Eliezer was also very severe with the criminal. His colleagues, continuing the general tendency of the Pharisees who had always been lenient "in punishment,"[62] reinterpreted the *lex talionis* of the Bible (Deut. 21:22) to require monetary compensation for injuries inflicted. They limited the exposure of the criminal after execution to cases of idolatry and blasphemy. Women were not to be exposed at all. A male criminal was stoned with his garments stripped; a woman was to be stoned with her garments on. It was likewise because of humanitarian reasons that R. Akiba excluded the children from the destruction that was to be visited upon an 'idolatrous city' (Deut. 13:13-19). In all these instances R. Eliezer defended the severer view. He retained the *lex talionis* of the Bible in its literal form. He required the exposure of all criminals executed through stoning; nor did he draw any alleviating distinction in favor of female criminals or of children in an idolatrous city [63]   Capital

---

59. Git. 38b.

60. The same circumstances produced a reaction against the emancipation of slaves in Rome. See H. Wallon, *Histoire de l'esclavage dans l'antiquite,* III, Paris 1879, p. 412f. This would explain why R. Akiba also opposed emancipation. R. Ishmael alone sanctioned it.

61. Git. *l. c.* The Talmud draws the distinction that where it was to help in the fulfillment of a religious obligation, R. Eliezer did not object to emancipation.

62. Jos. *Ant.* 20, 9, 1. Cf. Finkelstein, "The Pharisees", p. 222f. and note 87.

63. B. K. 84a, Lekah on Ex. 21:24. Cf. Mek., ed. Horovitz, *ad locum* and editor's notes; M. San. 6:4, San. 45b; Sifre, Nu. section 114, Sifre, Deut. section 221; Mid. Tann. on Deut. 21:22. Cf. below, p. 153 Tos. San. 9:6 (p. 429), 14:3 (p. 436). Philo's criminal code was like-

punishment could, of course, no longer be administered by Jewish courts in the Palestine of R. Eliezer's day. R. Eliezer would probably have been more careful, had he been confronted with practical questions affecting the administration of justice. Nevertheless, these discussions betray the general attitude of R. Eliezer and his colleagues toward the criminal: they are inclined to an increased humanitarianism; he, to a greater severity.

R. Eliezer's colleagues also extended their general humanitarianism to the treatment of animals. They required a formal trial before executing wild animals that escaped from the trainer or circus and committed damage. R. Joshua, for humanitarian reasons, permitted the raising of an animal from a pit on a festival, even where the animal could not possibly be slaughtered for food purposes that day. R. Eliezer took the harsher view in both instances. He did not require a trial for the wild animals but ruled instead that "whoever is first to kill them has done a noble thing." He permitted raising an animal from a pit, provided that it could be slaughtered for food purposes the same day; raising it otherwise, however, would involve, he declared, a desecration of the festival.[64]

---

wise severe, and was much closer in fact to the outlook of R. Eliezer than to that of his colleagues. See Heinemann, p. 217f. According to the *Scholiast* on Megillat Taanit, the reinterpretation of the *lex talionis* was already debated by the Pharisees and the Sadducees. R. Eliezer's literalism must, therefore, appear strange, since it contradicts what must at this time have been regarded as Pharisaic tradition, which he generally followed. I consequently accept the suggestion of Finkelstein, *op. cit.,* p. 217, note 81, who, following Wellhausen, *Die Pharisaer und Sadduzaer,* p. 61, regards the statement in the *Scholiast* as a later gloss. Cf. Ginzberg's note on Geiger *Kebusat Maamarim,* ed. Poznanski, Warsaw 1910, p. 390ff, maintaining that R. Eliezer's interpretation was only Biblical exegesis but that, as far as practice was concerned, he accepted compensation instead of talio as a rabbinic ordinance.

64. M. San. 1 :4; Tos. San. 3 :1 (p. 418); Shab. 117b, 124a; Tos. Besa 3 :2 (p. 205); Besa 37a; j Besa III, 62a, and cf. Maimonides, *Mishneh Torah,* Laws of Festivals 2 :4. The Mishnah does not specify that these were animals used in connection with circuses. But what

3. *Political Attitudes.*—R. Eliezer realized the indispensability of peaceful relationship between the different sections and classes within the national life. But he never extended this into a vision of general world peace, when war and the instruments of war would be done away with. Thus, we learnt that he regarded arms, such as "swords, spears, bows, shields, and lances" as ornaments, and as such permitted carrying them on the Sabbath. His colleagues prohibited them with the indignant retort, that such objects were only instruments of shame and degradation; and, to support their argument, they quoted from the peace visions of Isaiah: "They shall beat their swords into ploughshares. . ." Indeed, the Talmud knows of a tradition according to which R. Eliezer maintained that arms would remain an indispensable adornment to a gentleman's outfit even in the messianic age.[65] We should also recall, in this connection, R. Eliezer's extremely hostile view concerning the non-Jewish world, in contrast to the broader outlook of his colleagues—a subject that we have already treated in a previous connection.

R. Eliezer was bitterly opposed to Rome, although throughout the crisis in Jerusalem he remained attached to his pacifist teacher R. Johanan b. Zakkai, and was one of the prime movers in the stratagem by which the latter was smuggled out of the besieged city to surrender and make independent terms with Vespasian.[66] He re-referred to Rome as "wicked," as Israel's "enemy" par excellence.[67] In the days of the hereafter, Amalek or Rome will, like many other

---

else would a "wolf, a lion, a bear, a tiger, a leopard, etc." be doing in the city? Circuses at which such animals "performed" were a popular amusement in the Palestine of our period. Cf. Jos. *Ant.* 15, 8, 1. It is significant that where such damage or injury was committed by an ox, an animal used in the field, R. Eliezer agreed with his colleagues in requiring a trial before a court of twenty-three juror-judges (Tos. *l. c.*)

65. I Yir'at Het 5 and II Yir'at Het, end (in Masektot Zeirot ed. Higger, pp. 80:17, 84:4); M. Shab. 6:4, Shab. 63a.

66. See above, p. 13.

67. P. R. 90a.

people, come volutarily to seek incorporation with Israel, but while the others will be accepted, Amalek will not.[68] He took particular delight in picturing the great destruction that God will in those days inflict on Rome in retaliation for her harsh treatment of Israel.[69]

R. Eliezer likewise opposed the Samaritans. Eating their bread, he declared, was like eating of swine's flesh.[70] He took particular pains to argue that Mount Gerizim which was sacred to the Samaritans did not correspond to the sacred mountain by that name mentioned in the Bible (Deut. 11:30).[71] He suspected Samaritans of wilfully deceiving Jews into a violation of the Law.[72] He regarded all Samaritans as doubtful bastards, because they did not observe the Pharisaic regulations concerning marriage and divorce. Marriage between Jews and Samaritans was, of course, to be prohibited. Indeed, if Samaritans should want to observe the Law they must not even marry among themselves. Like all doubtful bastards, they

---

68. P. R. 28b; Mek. on Ex. 17:16; A. Z. 24a. R. Eliezer speaks only of Amalek, but Amalek was understood during this period to refer to Rome. See Ginzberg, *Legends,* V, p. 272, note 19 and cf. above, p. 42, note 16.

69. See above, p. 42.

70. M. Shev. 8:10. When this opinion of R. Eliezer was quoted by R. Akiba's pupils, he silenced them with the remark: "I shall not tell you R. Eliezer's real views with regard to this." In j Shev. VIII, 38b, the Amoraim differ as to what R. Akiba meant to suggest by his remark. According to R. Jose, he meant to suggest that R. Eliezer was more severe; according to R. Hezekiah, that he was more lenient. The fact, however, that R. Akiba himself was extremely lenient with regard to the Samaritans (Kid. 75b) would tend to support the interpretation of R. Jose: R. Akiba was unwilling to quote R. Eliezer's real views, which were even more severe, because he did not sympathize with them. Otherwise how account for R. Akiba's unwillingness to clarify the point? Cf. Ginzberg's article on Akiba in *J. E.,* I, p. 307. Cf. also below, p. 149, note 65.

71. Sifre, Deut. section 56; Mid. Tann. on Deut. 11:30; j Sota VII, 21c.

72. M. Demai 5:9; Tos. Demai 5:22 (p. 55).

would have to confine choosing their mates for marriage from the ranks of the liberated slaves.[73]   According to R. Dimi in the Talmud,[74] R. Eliezer did not even include the Samaritans within the category of Jews; he regarded them instead as descendents of the Cuthean settlers, whose conversion to Judaism was not genuine but the result of the fear inflicted on them by the lions that ravaged their settlements (II Kings 17:24-34). Ginzberg, however, argues that since he measured them by the standard of compliance to Jewish law, he must have considered them as heretical Jews.

R. Eliezer championed the interests of the community against the individual.   He ruled that land used as a public thoroughfare without the owner's protest within a reasonable time, has been forfeited, and becomes part of the public domain.   His colleagues considered such land semi-public: the owner was to retain title to it, but he could no longer interfere with its public use.[75]   As far as government was concerned, he was a monarchist.   He explained that the elders in Israel requested very properly when they petitioned the prophet Samuel: 'Give us a king to judge us' (I Sam. 8:5, 6). It was to the added comment of the ignorant among the people: 'that we may be like other nations' (I Sam. 8:20; cf. I Sam. 8:5), that the prophet objected.   He made a special exception in favor of the king from certain of the restrictions on the Day of Atonement.[76]

R. Eliezer, like the rest of the scholars,[77] looked back with particular delight on the royal house of David.   Among the six precious things that God gave to Israel he listed the kingdom of the

---

73. M. Kid. 4:3; Kid. 75a. Cf. Tos. Kid. 5:1 (p. 341). Cf. also above, p. 109.

74. Kid. 75a.

75. M. Er. 9:2; Er. 94a.

76. San. 20b; M. Yoma 8:1. There are no anti-monarchical sentiments in Midrashic or apocryphal writings. See Aptowitzer, "Bemerkungen zur Liturgie und Geschichte der Liturgie," MGWJ, LXXIV 1930, p. 117f, and Heinemann, p. 184f

77. Cf. Moore, Judaism, II, 325ff, 347,

House of David. He, ruled R. Eliezer, who does not include in his grace after a meal thanks to God for the kingdom of the House of David, has not satisfied his religious obligations. Temporarily the Davidic kingdom may have fallen, but ultimately it will be restored. Then it will endure forever—as long as Israel itself will endure.[78] In this connection we should also recall the great extent to which R. Eliezer emphasized the authority of the high priest.

In the limited autonomy that the Jews of Palestine enjoyed under Rome, the great source of authority resided with the patriarch. R. Eliezer emphasized this authority. When at the feast in honor of his son's marriage, the patriarch Gamaliel II served a cup of wine to R. Eliezer, he refused it. When R. Joshua accepted it, he rebuked him: 'Is it right that we sit and R. Gamaliel stand and wait on us?' R. Joshua's retort was that a greater man than Gamaliel, the patriarch Abraham, once stood and waited on his guests [79]

---

78.   Mek. Jethro, Amalek 1; R. Simeon p. 88; Ber. 48b; Tan., Buber, Tesaveh 9. Cf. Tan. Tesaveh 13 and Vehiz p. 199f. Cf. also above, p. 18f.

79.   Kid. 32b; Sifre, Deut. section 38; Mid. Tann. on Deut. 11:10. Cf. Mek. Jethro, Amalek 1 (ed. Horovitz p. 195) and Vehiz. p. 69.

Chapter V

R. ELIEZER THE LEGAL FORMALIST

The operations of any legal system involve the excercise of logic. A principle that unifies and rationalizes a mass of particulars tends inevitably to project itself to new cases. To some extent, then, the task of the jurist is that of the logician. He must treat law as any logical proposition—discover its implications and apply them to new situations. Tapering down from the syllogism at the one end to mere anology at the other, this method is used in every system of jurisprudence.

The achievement of this method is legal uniformity, which has its advantages—it makes for a jurisprudence that is impartial, certain, and equal. But it also presents certain very serious limitations. For the particular cases to which law must be applied are not uniform. Great injustice often results when an abstract law is imposed uniformly on situations that present many variations of circumstances. To overcome the limitations of uniformity, individualization or equity is resorted to.[1]

The striving for legal uniformity as well as for individualization is present in all legal systems. What, however, determines the relative importance attached to each? Current thought[2] is in

---

1. M. R. Cohen, *Reason and Nature*, N. Y. 1929, p. 425ff.

2. Pound, *An Introduction to the Philosophy of Law*, New Haven 1922, ch. 1-4; "Mechanical Jurisprudence, *Columbia Law Review*, VIII 1908, pp. 605-623; "Administrative Application of Legal Standards," in *Reports*, American Bar Association, 1919, p. 447; B. N. Cardozo, *The Nature of the Judicial Process*, New Haven 1921, pp.

agreement that the social, economic and political objectives of a jurist are the determining factors. A jurist who is not satisfied with the status quo and wants social change, will, particularly where it is difficult to bring about a formal modification in the existing law, emphasize individualization. He will rely to a lesser degree on formal logic. Law to him will be more personal and subjective; it will be more flexible. Uniformity will be at a minimum. A jurist, on the other hand, who represents the attitude of a stable community and wants that community to continue with all its institutions in their existing form, will generally emphasize legal uniformity. His interpretations will be analytical, formal, logical. He will look upon the law as impersonal and objective. Individualization will be at a minimum.

R. Eliezer's colleagues represented the forces of social change. They, consequently, adopted an attitude toward the law which was free and flexible, which facilitated change—which emphasized individualization. R. Eliezer, on the other hand, opposed change. His halakah, in terms of religious and social objectives, was a defense of the status quo. In his attitude toward the law itself, therefore, he reflects a similar spirit—an emphasis on uniformity and stability. The law is to him a great impersonal fact, a body of eternal and immutable formulae. The applications of the law are mechanical, in accordance with the dictates of a rigorous logic. Conditions under which the law has to be carried out are disregarded. Individualization is minimized.

This difference in legal atitude between R. Eliezer and his colleagues will emerge clearly upon a detailed analysis of their respective halakic systems. We must, however, precede that with a more

---

9-13, 53; *The Growth of the Law*, New Haven 1924, pp. 59, 101. These writers explain in terms of this principle the different forms of legal reasoning current in different ages. This principle may, however, also be applied to account for the different legal interpretations among different interpreters within the same age. Social and economic objectives may vary from time to time. They also vary within the different social and economic classes at any given time.

adequate presentation of what we mean by legal uniformity and legal individualization.

The Method of Uniformity and the Methods of Individualization.

Legal uniformity, we learnt, was the achievement of the logical approach to the law—what Cardozo calls "the method of philosophy."[3] How is individualization achieved? The principal media for securing individualization may be summarized as follows:

1. *The method of subjectivity.*—According to this conception, the law is not to regard all facts of equal significance. The law is to take into consideration the mental processes, the intentions preceding each act. The law ceases to deal with objective facts alone. The personal and subjective elements are introduced.

2. *The method of pragmatism.*—This assumes that all law is to be regarded as a means to an end. To discover the rule that shall apply in any given situation the law must not be treated as a logical proposition whose implications are to be followed inevitably. The important thing is to understand what ends that law was originally intended to achieve. It is only in the light of these ends that decisions ought to be made.

3. *The method of history.*—This method is two-fold. On the one hand it insists that in applying the law we take into consideration the actual history of its origin. "The tendency of a principle to expound itself to the limits of its logic may be counteracted by the tendency to confine itself within the limits of its history."[4] Every law came into being in response to certain conditions. To apply a law after its originating conditions have changed, is unreasonable and arbitrary. On the other hand, it also insists that in the application of law we take into consideration the history of each case as presented. In extending a law from one case to another, we must make sure that the histories of the two cases are the

---

3. *Judicial Process*, p. 31.
4. Cardozo, *ibid*, p. 51.

same, that the conditions prevailing in the one situation are paralleled in the other.

4. *The Method of Socialogy.*—This method assumes that the final end of all law is the welfare of society. When the application of any law would clearly harm social welfare, no matter how explicit that law is, it is to be discarded. "When social needs demand. . . there are times when we must bend symmetry, ignore history, and sacrifice custom in the pursuit of larger ends."[5]

We shall now survey some of the important controversies between R. Eliezer and his colleagues in the different branches of Jewish law—ritual law, agricultural law, the law of the Sabbath and of the Holidays, as well as civil and criminal law. This will demonstrate that while they employed all the methods of legal individualization, he practically disregarded them, emphasizing legal uniformity.

R. ELIEZER AND THE METHODS OF INDIVIDUALIZATION

I.   THE METHOD OF SUBJECTIVITY[6]

1. *Laws of Levitical Impurity.*

(a)   According to an ancient practice, a person who contracted any manner of levitical uncleanliness that lasted till evening was required, for regaining purity, to immerse himself in a ritual bath. But suppose that he took such a bath without having in mind its ritual purpose? R. Eliezer's colleagues regarded it inadequate. To R. Eliezer, however, the lack of original intent did not matter. He

---

5.   Cardozo, *ibid*, p. 65.

6.   For a general treatment of the problem of Intention (subjectivity) in Jewish law, see L. Ginzberg, *Mekomah shel ha-Halakah*, and S. Zeitlin, "Studies in Tannaitic Jurisprudence," in *Journal of Jewish Lore and Philosophy*, I, 1919, pp. 298-311. These writers emphasize the problem of intention as affecting the halakah of the schools of Shammai and Hillel. Cf. also M. Higger, *Intention in Talmudic Law*, N. Y. 1927.

suggested that "a person may on coming out define the object for which he has bathed."[7]

(b) The Bible provides (Lev. 15:20, 26), that if a person afflicted with an issue comes in contact with an object by stepping, lying, or sitting on it, that object will receive an impurity of the first degree known as *midras*. The halakah draws this distinction, however. To transmit the impurity, the person must be in contact with that object in the course of its intended use. Thus, if he steps on a leather rug that rug will receive the impurity of *midras*. Suppose, however, that he wore a leather apron and that by accident he sat or stepped on it. That leather will remain levitically pure, because stepping or sitting on it does not represent a use for which it was intended. R. Eliezer, however, refused to draw such distinctions. As long as he stepped or sat on it, the impurity is transmitted, though such use was without intention.[8]

(c) The law also provides that objects, to be susceptible to impurity, must represent something of value. As a general rule, the Mishnah suggests that once an object is discarded, it becomes free from possibilities of impurity. Should anyone, however, recover it, it is again invested with value, and may once more become impure. But the Mishnah excepts the case of a purple or crimson colored garment,—to which R. Eliezer added, even a piece of that material, if new—that, because of intrinsic worth, must be considered valuable even when discarded. But Rabbi Simeon disagreed. To him value was not intrinsic but subjective. When discarded, any object, no matter what its intrinsic worth, must be declared valueless and, therefore, free from the possibilities of becoming unclean.[9]

---

7. Hag. 19a. The rabbis likewise required the one who prepared the red heifer to intend that his work fill its ritual purpose. According to R. Eliezer, such intending was unnecessary. M. Para 4:1, 3. Cf. M. Para 8:4.

8. M. Kel. 26:5. Cf. M. Nidda 6:3.

9. M. Kel. 27:12. It must not be assumed, of course, that R. Eliezer actually disputed with R. Simeon. The latter was not a con-

(d)   The law also provides that an object may lose its suscept-
ibility to uncleanliness, upon being sufficiently altered. Thus, a piece
of cloth that is converted into a wick will no longer be capable of
becoming levitically unclean.   Suppose, however, the change from
cloth to wick was not complete: the cloth was twisted into the form
of a wick, but was not singed over the flame. To R. Akiba the
twisted form indicated intention to convert it into a wick. That was
to him sufficient, and he exempted it from impurity. To R. Eliezer,
however, evidence of intent was not enough; in spite of its twisted
form, the piece of cloth maintained its original status—it might,
upon exposure, receive levitical impurity.[10]

(e)   An object to receive impurity, the law likewise provides,
must be a finished product.   But what is a finished product?   Is
a shoe, while still on the shoemaker's last, to be considered a finished

---

temporary of R. Eliezer.   R. Simeon represents an even further
development of the Hillelite position. See Zeitlin, *ibid,* p. 303f.   At
a later date, R. Simeon, in reviewing the older law, expressed dissent.
The compiler of the Mishnah put these views in juxtaposition.   Cf.
also M. Kel. 28:2, Tos. Kel. 6:8 (p. 596), where R. Eliezer, R. Joshua
and R. Akiba disagree concerning a piece of cloth smaller than three
by three inches which is used in scrubbing the bath or cleaning the
pots.   R. Joshua considers the esteem of the owner which in this case
is negligible, and pronounces the cloth free from all susceptibilities
to uncleanliness.   R. Akiba draws a distinction.   If the owner specifically prepared the cloth for that purpose, he apparently considers it
more or less important; it is therefore susceptible to levitical uncleanliness.   If, however, the cloth was applied to its new use only after
it had been discarded, the owner obviously considered it worthless,
and it is therefore free from uncleanliness.   R. Eliezer disregarded
these considerations.   He reckoned only with the objective fact that
the cloth is in use.   Refusing to distinguish between one use and
another, he ruled the cloth in both cases capable of becoming unclean.
In the Tos. there are two different versions of this dispute.   R. Meir
attributes our view of R. Akiba to R. Eliezer and R. Akiba is not
mentioned.   R. Judah transmits the version as we have quoted it
from the Mishnah.   In the light of the respective general positions
of these scholars, the version of R. Judah appears more plausible.

10.   M. Shab. 2:3.

product? Undoubtedly, the owner considers it as such; the act of removing it from the last he does not consider significant. The Rabbis, moved by the subjective consideration of the owner, declared such a shoe a finished product, and therefore susceptible to uncleanliness. R. Eliezer, however, dissented. As long as it has not been removed from the last, it cannot be considered finished, and until then it is not susceptible to uncleanliness.[11]

2. Agricultural Law.

(a) The Bible (Deut. 22:9), prohibits the growth of diverse seeds in a vineyard. What, however, if one permits thorns to grow therein? It is obvious that such growth represents negligence; no one grows thorns with intention. The Rabbis consequently declared that in such a case the prohibtion against diverse seeds did not apply. R. Eliezer ruled that it did apply.[12]

---

11. M. Kel. 26:4; Tos. Kel. 4:7 (p. 594); Tos. Ed. 2:1 (p. 457); San. 68a. A different version of the controversy between R. Eliezer and his colleagues is transmitted by R. Simeon Sh'zuri in Tos. Kel. 4:7 (p. 594). Cf. the somewhat similar dispute concerning a baker's ranging boards in M. Ed. 7:/, Tos. Ed. 2:] (p 457). R. Eliezer colleagues, reckoning with the baker's intentions in using them, regarded these boards as regular vessels and as such capable of becoming unclean (M. Kel. 10:1). R. Eliezer disregarded the baker's use, and since these boards per se are not vessels, they cannot become unclean. Cf. also the discussion in M. Kel. 10:1, Tos. Kel. 7:6 (p. 577), whether inverting a vessel with its mouth down and bottom up can give the bottom the status of a cover so as to render all over which it is superimposed immune from uncleanliness. R. Eliezer's colleagues, following the intention of the owner, ruled in the affirmative, while R. Eliezer ruled in the negative.

12. M. Kil. 5:8; Sifre, Deut. section 230. The Bible similarly prohibited the wearing of a garment of "two kinds of stuff mingled together." (Lev. 19:19.) R. Eliezer included within the scope of this prohibition hand towels and bath towels, because their uses at times correspond to those of garments: a person may receive warmth from the use of a hand towel in drying his hands or from enwrapping himself in a bath towel in drying his body. His colleagues exempted them from the prohibition because they regarded such uses as unin-

(b)   The law of tithes was interpreted by the Rabbis to refer only to the seasonal harvest. Crops ripening earlier or later were exempted, because the owner does not regard them as valuable. An exception was made in the case of a field adjacent to the farmer's home, where each crop had to be tithed, because such crops were gathered as they ripened. R. Eliezer's ruling was that, regardless of the land's location, all grain ripening before the seasonal harvest must be tithed, because it is guarded. True, the guard which is exercised over it is only, so far as it is concerned, accidental; the principal objective is to watch the seasonal, later-ripening crop. But an act need not be intentional, and as long as the crop is watched, the law of tithes applies.[13]

(c)   Tithes offered by a deaf-mute were declared by the Rabbis invalid, since tithing to them was an act requiring intention, of which a deaf-mute was not considered fully capable. According to a tradition quoted by R. Isaac, R. Eliezer agreed that tithing must not be a mechanical act, but he maintained that the limited intention of which a deaf-mute is capable ought to be adequate. As a regular practice he recommended that the tithing of a deaf-mute should be confirmed by a legal guardian; but he considered the tithing valid even without such confirmation.[14]

(d)   The Biblical law does not fix the portion of the crop that

---

tentional.   See M. Kil. 9:3 and cf. Tos. Kil. 5:17 (p. 80).   In the Tosefta there is a difference of opinion as to the respective views of R. Eliezer and his colleagues. The tradition of R. Meir agrees with the Mishnah. R. Judah reverses their views. In the light of R. Eliezer's general position on intention, the tradition of R. Meir appears correct. Possibly R. Eliezer followed his class orientation when he applied the prohibition to thorns. As a great landowner he may have raised camels which feed on thorns. He would consequently regard thorns as a food, which his colleagues would deny.

13.   Tos. D'mai 1:3 (p. 45). Cf. M. Maas. 1:1.

14.   Tos. Ter. 1:1 (p. 25). It is significant that in the passage cited, R. Judah, the son of R. Eliezer's ardent disciple Ilai, is quoted as validating the tithes of a deaf-mute without any reservations whatever.

must be contributed as *terumah* to the priest. The Mishnah esti-
mated that an acceptable minimum would vary between one-fortieth
and one-sixtieth of the crop, depending on the liberality of the
contributor. What, however, of a maximum? According to R.
Tarfon and R. Akiba no maximum was to be fixed; that was to be
left entirely to the individual. R. Eliezer, however, insisted on an
objective standard. Modelling the *terumah* after the tithe, he fixed
the maximum at one-tenth of the crop.[15]

(e) The benedictions to be recited before enjoying any article
of food are recorded in the Mishnah. That to be recited over fruit
expresses thanks to "the Creator of the fruit of the tree." An exception is made in the case of wine, over which He is praised as
"the Creator of vine." [16] But what is meant by the term 'wine'?
Ought that be taken to include the liquid in its undiluted state,
fresh from the winepress? According to R. Eliezer's colleagues, we
follow the intention of the owner. If he regards it as wine, and so
intends to use it, it has the status of wine, with its appropriate
benedictions. R. Eliezer, on the other hand, demanded that the

---

15. R. Ishmael allowed terumah contributions up to fifty per
cent of the total crop. M. Ter. 4:3, 5. Cf. M. Ar. 3:2 where R. Eliezer
prescribes a fixed amount to be contributed by one who consecrated
a purchased field to the Temple (fifty silver shekels per unit
on which an *omer* of barley may be sown). His colleagues suggest
estimating the field in the open market, and then contributing its
value to the Temple. Cf. also the discussion in Tos. Nidda 2:3 (p. 642)
and Ket. 60a concerning the fixing of a terminus *ad quem* after which
a child was no longer to suck at his mother's breasts. R. Joshua
refused to set any definite time, leaving the matter entirely with
the family. R. Eliezer fixed two years as the limit. Cf. S. Krauss,
Archaeologie, II, p. 9f, who points out that even longer "sucking"
periods were not unusual in the ancient Orient. Cf. also the controversy between the Shammaites and the Hillelites concerning the time
of obligatory sucking (Ket. 60a, b). The Shammaites fix it at two
years and the Hillelites at eighteen months. R. Eliezer probably
followed the Shammaite view and left no room at all for any family
discretion in the matter.

16. M. Ber. 6:1.

wine's status be determined by its intrinsic character, and not by the intention of the owner. Until it is mixed with the proper proportion of water, it cannot yet be regarded as a food; the same benediction was to be pronounced over it as for any other fruit in ts raw state.[17]

3. Laws of Holidays and Vows

(a)   Food, to be used on the Sabbath or a holiday, had to be prepared on the previous day.[18] What was meant by the word 'prepared'? May an egg laid on the holiday be eaten the same day? It was certainly prepared the day before, but without the knowledge of the owner. May a person pick up on a holiday pieces of wood lying about the yard, in order to use them for the fire? These were certainly prepared before the holiday, but without the express intention of the owner. In these instances, R. Eliezer was lenient. To him intention was not the principal factor; as long as these objects were prepared before the Sabbath or holiday their use was permitted. His colleagues, however, objected, insisting that preparation without intention was inadequate.[19]

(b)   R. Eliezer and his colleagues discussed the problem of intention in its relation to Sabbath observance from still another point of view. If a man intended to perform an act which is prohibited on the Sabbath, but actually did something entirely different, but also involving a Sabbath violation; for instance, he intended

---

17.   M. Ber. 7:5; Tos. Ber. 4:3 (p. 8); Ber. 50b. Cf. also Tos. Maas. 2:2 (p. 82).

18.   Besa 2b; Pes. 49b.

19.   Tos. Y. T. 1:1 (p. 200); Besa 4a; M. Besa 4:6; Tos. Y. T. 3:18 (p. 206). Cf. Besa 81b. The question about the egg was already disputed by the Shammaites and the Hillelites. See M. Besa 1:1 and cf. Ginzberg, ibid, p. 32, and Zeitlin, ibid, p. 305. R. Eliezer and his colleagues also differed as to whether this "preparation" need be specific or may be general. Thus, R. Eliezer considered it adequate if one set aside a larger stock of food products from which he expects to select a smaller amount for his Sabbath needs. According to his colleague, one must actually "prepare" the specific amount he wishes to use on the Sabbath (M. Besa 4:7).

to pluck figs and actually plucked grapes. R. Joshua maintained
that such an act, not representing the doer's specific intention, was
not included within the Biblical prohibition; hence, its commission
did not involve the sacrifice of a sin-offering. R. Eliezer regarded
such an act a genuine violation of the Sabbath, and accordingly
required the sacrifice of a sin-offering.[20]

(c) If the animal to be offered as a Passover sacrifice was
lost, the law provided that another should be substituted. What,
however, if the lost one were recovered? A distinction was then
drawn depending on whether the recovery preceded or followed the
slaughter of the substitute. Since the substitute animal might be
slaughtered at any hour between noon of the 4th day of Nisan and
the evening thereafter, depending on the pleasure of the owner, the
time involved in these regulations was obviously subjective. R.
Eliezer objected to this, refusing to consent to a subjective time. He,
therefore, ruled that the fate of the recovered animal was to depend
on the time when the sacrifice might begin—which was fixed at the
hour of noon.[21]

(d) Where a person consecrated his animals and beasts of
chase to the Temple, the Rabbis ruled that the *koy*, a kind of
bearded deer or antelope , was likewise to be included. They were
not certain whether the *koy* belonged to the one genus or the other,

---

20. M. Ker. 4:3; Ker. 19b; Sifra, Vayikra, p. 20b; Tos. Ker. 2:4
(p. 564).

21. Tos. Pes. 9:15 (p. 171), Pes. 96b. If the recovery preceded
the sacrifice of the substitute, the original one was to be kept until
it acquired a blemish, when it was to be sold, and the purchase price
used to buy a peace offering; if the recovery followed the slaughter
of the substitute, then the original one was to be sacrificed as an
ordinary peace offering.   For R. Eliezer's insistence on objective
standards see also M. Sukka 2:6 and Sukka 29a where he makes it
mandatory to eat fourteen meals in the booth during the seven day
period of the feast of Tabernacles (two regular meals for each day,
which was then the custom with the average person).   The other
scholars merely required eating in the booth throughout the festival,
but did not prescribe the number of meals.

but they followed the apparent intentions of the owner who had consecrated both. R. Eliezer, disregarding the fact of intention, excluded the *koy* from the consecration.[22]

4. *Civil and Criminal Law.*

(a)   In the determination of the status of the first born,[23] the midwife's testimony was accepted as to which one of two twin boys emerged first. To guard against mistakes on the part of the midwife, the Rabbis laid down the condition that she must have stayed in the room throughout the time of the birth process. R. Eliezer, however, considered even that as staking too much on the subjective impressions of an individual. He required the added condition that she must have remained constantly fixed in her position: if she merely turned aside, although not leaving the room until the children were actually born, her testimony may not be believed.[24]

(b)   In certain criminal cases the factor of intention had already become well recognized traditionally, and R. Eliezer accepted it.   Thus, he absolved a stone thrower from all responsibility for injuries inflicted by him upon a person who appeared on the scene after the stone had actually been thrown.   He similarly absolved from murder charges one who, intending to kill an animal, accidentlly killed a human being.   Where, however, a persona intending to kill a human being, missed his target, and accidentally killed another human being, R. Eliezer regarded the act as murder. R. Simeon did not, because as far as the person actually murdered was concerned, the killing was accidental and without intention.[25]

---

22.   Ned. 18b.

23.   For the preferences of the first-born in Jewish law, see *J. E. s. v.* "Primogeniture".

24.   Kid. 73b.

25.   B. K. 41b; j B. K. 4b; M. San. 9:2; Ket. 33a. Cf., however, San. 74a and 89a where the same statement is quoted in the name of R. Elazar. Cf. above, p. 121f, note 9.

II. THE METHOD OF PRAGMATISM.

1. Laws of Levitical Purity.

(a) If a person has a stock of levitically clean and another stock of levitically unclean food products, he need not, according to law, remove the priestly share from each separately; he is permitted to remove the total share from the stock of that which is levitically clean, provided that the two stocks are close together. Apprehensive, however, lest such a person keep the two stocks too far apart so as to avoid the danger of actual contact, which will communicate the uncleanliness of the one stock to the other, the Rabbis enacted a precautionary measure, demanding that the priestly share be removed from each stock separately. R. Eliezer, on the other hand, followed the strict law and permitted removing a common share for both stocks.[26]

(b) The water that was to be used in connection with the ashes of the 'red heifer' had to be levitically pure. But may such water be entrusted to the care of a levitically unclean person, if the owner is not occupied and can occasionally watch him? R. Eliezer again decided on the basis of strict law and permitted it. His col-

---

26. M. Ter. 2:1; Tos. Ter. 3:18 (p. 30) and cf. variants; j Ter. II, 41a. The same controversy occurs concerning the method of removing the priest's share from the dough. M. Hal. 2:8; Tos. Hal. 1:10 (p. 98); Sota 30a. Cf. Tos. Ter. 9:9 (p. 41) (according to the version of R. Jacob). Cf. also M. Shab. 22:1 where R. Eliezer's colleagues prohibit on the Sabbath the honey flowing out of the honeycombs crushed prior to the Sabbath, as a deterrent against crushing them on the Sabbath itself. He permitted it. His colleagues also prohibited kneading dough on Passover with oil or honey; they feared that with the great leavening effects of these liquids, the bread might rise before being put into the oven. He permitted it (Pes. 36a). Cf., however, j Pes. II, 29c, where it seems that R. Eliezer's permission was extended while aboard a ship, when no other liquids may have been available.

leagues, following a more pragmatic outlook, were apprehensive of contact, and declared it prohibited.[27]

2. *Laws of the Sabbath and Holidays.*

(a) The Bible prohibits all manner of work on the Sabbath. At an early date the Rabbis tried to define the meaning of the term "work" and through an ingenious method of exegesis included in it thirty-nine distinct categories of labor.[28] But in formulating these categories, the Rabbis did not indicate their limitations. For instance, dyeing was forbidden on the Sabbath—did the use of rouge on a woman's face constitute such a violation? Paring one's nails was likewise interdicted—did that include biting or tearing them off? Did writing on the Sabbath, also forbidden, include the scratching of a mark on the skin? These and many other illustrations of minutiae of labor were cited—what was to be their status? R. Eli. ezer's colleagues analyzed the Sabbath laws pragmatically. Since the purpose of the law was obviously to prevent over-exertion on the day devoted to one's spiritual interests, such acts, though admittedly out of harmony with a very meticulous observance of the Sabbath, could not be considered violations. Their commission, acordingly did not involve the sacrifice of sin-offering. R. Eliezer, on the other hand, disregarded the law's objectives. He emphasized the simil-

---

27. M. Para 7:10. Cf. M. Neg. 7:4, 5; Sifra, Tazria, p. 68a; Tos. Neg. 3:5 (p. 621) where R. Eliezer's colleagues are much more severe than he with one who deliberately removed a symptom of leprosy from his skin before submitting to an examination by the priest. This severity was intended to act as a deterrent for the future. R. Eliezer followed the strict law. Cf. also M. Nidda 1:3, 5, Tos. Nidda 1:5 (p. 641), 1:9 (p. 642), 9:13 (p. 651), Nidda 7b, 9b, where the rabbis regarded a woman who does not menstruate regularly as unclean for some time before she became aware that her period had begun, because of the apprehension that the menses may have started before she perceived it. R. Eliezer was again lenient. A similar controversy is repeated concerning the uncleanliness of men and women because of "discharge" in M. Nidda 10:3, Sifra, Mesora, p. 77a, Nidda 7b, 68b.

28. M. Shab. 7:2; Mek. Vayakhel 1; Shab. 49b; B. K. 2a.

arity between the principal and the derivative types of work, and refused to draw a legal distinction between them. The ommission
of either one, according to him, constituted a violation of the Sabbath, and therefore called for a sin-offering.[29]

(b) While the Bible prohibits all manner of work on the
Sabbath, certain types of work of a religious nature were exempted
from that prohibition: circumcision on the eighth day; the offering
of the daily sacrifices; the sacrifice of the paschal lamb; the presentation of the two loaves of bread on the Feast of Weeks. All
these were to take place at their usual time, even on Sabbath. But
the problem arose of defining the limits of that exemption—was
all manner of work included therein, even if such work could have
been done before the Sabbath? Might, for instance, a man make
a knife on the Sabbath, if he desired to use it that day in circum-

---

29. M. Shab. 10:6, 12:4; Shab. 95a; Tos. Shab. 9:13 (p. 122),
11:15 (p. 126); Tos. Y. T. 4:4 (p. 207); j Shab. III, 10c, XII, 13d.
Cf. M. Shab. 17:7; Tos. Shab. 11:15 (p. 126), 12:14 (p. 127); Tos.
Y. T. 4:4 (p. 207); Shab. 12a, 75b, 94b, 95a, 107b, 137b; Ker. 17a.
Cf. also Tos. Shab. 14:17 (p. 132), where R. Eliezer seems to prohibit
even the making of the bed, presumably because it resembles construction. He permits it only where it was once made up on Friday
at sundown. The complete statement reads as follows: מוללין את
המלול ומציעין את המוצע ואופין את האפוי ומבשלין את המבושל
"One may husk wheat that has been husked; make up beds that
have been made up; bake what has been baked and cook what has
been cooked." Cf. note of Elijah Gaon on Orah Hayim 318:15 who
takes our passage literally as applying to a Sabbath, when one is
allowed to keep food on the fire provided its real preparation preceded the day before. A number of other sources quote this passage,
omitting the first two cases cited; and they interpret it to apply to
a holiday preceding a Sabbath when one may prepare food for the
Sabbath provided an *erub tabshilin,* a fictional preparation, began on
the weekday before. See Mek. B'shalah 4; R. Simeon p. 78; Besa
15b; j Besa II, 61a. There is, however, no way of applying this interpretation to include the case dealing with the making of the bed
or the husking of wheat. Cf. also Mek. R. Simeon p. 108, where the
general view of the rabbis derives a permission to make beds on
the Sabbath.

cision or sacrifice? R. Akiba decided in the negative. Since the purpose of the law was, obviously, that the Sabbath shall not interfere with the continuity of certain religious observances, it was enough that these observances themselves were permitted. Why, then, include work not inherently necessary for the maintenance of that continuity? R. Eliezer, on the other hand, carried the law to the limits of its logic. He ruled that the prohibition applied only to work done for a secular purpose. For a religious purpose, all work was permissible, even where it could have been done prior to the Sabbath.[30]

(c) The Bible considers a deliberate violation of the Sabbath a capital crime (Ex. 31:14). A man, however, who violated the Sabbath in error or through ignorance, was required merely to sacrifice a sin-offering. But suppose a person committed in one span of forgetfulness a number of acts, either on the same Sabbath or spread over a number of Sabbaths. How many sin-offerings were required of him? R. Eliezer's colleagues decided on the basis of what they conceived to be the purpose of the law. Why is a sin-offering required at all? Surely not to atone for the acts performed. These were not forbidden per se, but only on the Sabbath; in the case cited, the person who committed them was not aware that it was the Sabbath. Obviously the sin-offering was to atone for his forgetfulness. But only one span of forgetfulness was involved; therefore, only one sin-offering was required. R. Eliezer, however, disregarded these considerations. Normally, for every such act performed a sin-offering was required; as the law must be made uniform, the number of sin-offerings must correspond to the number of such acts performed.[31]

---

30. M. Pes. 6:1, 2; Pes. 69a; Tos. Pes. 5:1 (p. 163); A. Z. 46b; M. Shab. 19:1; j Shab XIX, 16d; Shab. 131a-b.

31. M. Ker. 3:10; Ker. 17a; j Shab. VII, 9a-b; Sifra, Vayikra, p. 16b. The same principle is involved in the case where a husband, in one span of forgetfulness, cohabits a number of times with his menstruant wife. R. Eliezer's colleagues require only one sin-offering, while he requires an equivalent number. See Ker. 15a, 17a. Cf. also

(d)   The Passover laws as formulated in the Bible (Nu. 9:10, 11), permit a person who found himself on the fourteenth day of Nisan "in a journey afar off" from Jerusalem to offer the paschal lamb and celebrate the festival on the fourteenth day of the following month.   The problem arose of defining the expression "in a journey afar off." The other scholars decided in the light of what was obviously   the law's purpose—to ease the situation for a man who could not reach Jerusalem in time for the regular Passover celebration.   They therefore fixed the distance at a radius of fifteen miles from the city.   R. Akiba even laid down the rule that no matter where a person is, if he is unable to offer his paschal sacrifice in the regular time, he falls into the category of one who is "in a journey afar off," and may postpone his celebration for the following month. R. Eliezer, on the other hand, disregarded the objectives of the law. He found that in connection with the law of tithes the same expression "in a journey afar off" was used, meaning outside the area   where the   tithe   may   be   eaten. He,   therefore, concluded, that in our case, too, the expression must have a similar meaning—outside the area where the paschal lamb might be eaten.   He accordingly fixed that distance as anywhere outside the city limits of Jerusalem.[32]

(c)   The dwelling in booths required on the festival of Sukkot was obviously to constitute a symbolic act of recalling the experience of the Israelites while on their way from Egypt.   But will the law be fulfilled if a person, instead of building his own booth, arrange to share the booth of his neighbor? R. Eliezer's colleagues

---

Tos. Jeb. 11:4 (p. 252; Cf. also Tos. Nazir 4:8 (p. 289) and Nazir 18b, Tos. Ker. 1:14 (p. 562).

32.   Sifre, Nu. section 69; Pes. 92b-93a and cf. Tosefot, ad locum; Pes. 94b.   Cf. M. Pes. 9:2 where the anonymous view is attributed to R. Akiba and the view of R. Akiba is omitted, and Tos. Pes. 8:2 (p. 169) where the anonymous view is omitted.   Our sources do not fix the radius of fifteen miles explicitly but describe it as the distance between Jerusalem and Modein "and a similar measure from every side."   That distance was, according to the Talmud, fifteen miles. See Pes. 93b and cf. Neubauer, La Geographie du Talmud, p. 99;

permitted it, since the purpose of the law is achieved by the mere act of dwelling in the booth, regardless of who built it. R. Eliezer, however, demanded that each person erect his own booth, for it is written: "And ye shall keep unto *yourselves* the feast of booths seven days" (Deut. 16:13).[33]

3. Civil and Criminal Law.

(a) A woman taken as a war captive is permitted to become the wife of her captor under certain conditions, one of which is that prior to her marriage, she must shave her head and "do" her nails (Deut. 21:10-13). What is meant by the word "do"? R. Akiba tried to determine this in the light of the purpose of the law. She is told to shave her head—why? Obviously, to make herself appear less beautiful; perhaps when her captor sees her in that state, his infatuation may pass. The instruction concerning her nails must, therefore, be also directed to the same end; that must mean that she is required to grow her nails. R. Eliezer, however, disregarded the purposes of the law. In a very formal way, he compared the regulations concerning the hair with those concerning the nails; the one means, to shave—the other must have a similar meaning: to cut. The verse must therefore be translated, according to him: "And she shall pare her nails."[34]

(b) Was a person permitted to accept the retailer's customary addition to the exact measure of a purchase, if he forswore deriving any benefit from him? In giving him this addition, the retailer was obviously not extending him any benefit; he was merely treating him as any other customer. R. Eliezer's colleagues, for this

---

P. Thomsen, *Loca Sancta,* Halle 1907, p. 90.

33. Sukka 27b. The controversy may go back to the social differences between R. Eliezer and his colleagues. In the upper classes each one could afford to build his own booth.

34. Jeb. 48a; Mid. Tann. on Deut. 21:12; Sifre, Deut. sections 212, 213; Lekah, Deut. 21:12 (p. 69f); Sem. 6:13.

reason, permitted it.   He, with his more formalistic thinking, forbade it.[35]

(c)   Custom demanded that the beds be lowered as a sign of mourning after the death of a near relative.   A pragmatic conception of the custom would obviously demand that it begin when the family actually settles down to mourning—after burial.   This was the ruling of R. Joshua.   R. Eliezer, on the other hand, demanded that it begin immediately after the corpse has been removed from the house, even before the funeral was over.[36]

(d)   The custom of lowering the beds was not to be observed during a period of mourning coinciding with a festival.   But was it to be observed after the festival was over?   All agreed that if the custom had been carried out for three days prior to the arrival of the festival, it was not to be repeated afterward. But suppose it had been carried out for less than three days?   R. Eliezer's colleagues looked at the facts pragmatically.   The lowering of the beds was a genuine expression of grief when coming at the proper time. But to enforce it after eight festive days have already passed would be trying to stimulate artificial grieving. They, therefore, decided the question in the negative; R. Eliezer, in the affirmative.[37]

(e)   A Jew was obviously not permitted to offer any gifts to idols.   But may he construct an idol's decorations if he is to be compensated for it? The other scholars were apprehensive lest this lead to a closer approach to idolatry, and enacted a precautionary

---

35.   Meg. 8a, Ned. 32b, B. B. 57b.

36.   j Ber. III, 5d; j M.K. III, 83a; M. K. 27a; Sem. 11:19. Krauss, *Archaeologie*, II, p. 70f, explains this custom as a survival from the time when all the objects used by the dead were destroyed as polluted with evil spirits.

37.   M. K. 20a.   Cf. Tos. M. K. 2:9 (p. 230) and Sem. 7:2 where the views of R. Eliezer and his colleagues are reversed.   In the light of their respective general positions the version as reported in Moed Katan seems correct.   Our sources cite a parallel dispute between the Shammaites and the Hillelites.   Accepting the version in Moed Katan, R. Eliezer will agree with the former and his colleagues with the latter.

measure forbidding it. R. Eliezer decided on the basis of strict law, and permitted it.[38]

(f) One who, in the excitement of a quarrel, accidentally struck a pregnant woman passing by, with the result that she miscarried, was required by Biblical law (Ex. 21:22) to pay damages.

---

38. M. A. Z. 1:8. This opinion of R. Eliezer is deleted from a number of Mishnah editions, and Yom Tob Lippman Heller (Commentary on the Mishnah, *ad locum*. Cf. also Rabinowicz, *ad locum*) insists that it is not genuine. It would, however, be difficult to explain how it came into the text. Its omission from some of the texts may well be attributed to a copyist who found R. Eliezer's view offensively lenient. Perhaps the abbreviation לע"ג in our Mishnah is equivalent to לעובד י דר י גל ו לין, instead of לעבודת גלולין although in such a case the abbreviation should have been לעו"ג. This would mean that R. Eliezer's colleagues forbade selling jewelry to a pagan because they were apprehensive that he might donate it to idols. R. Eliezer permitted it. If this interpretation is correct, R. Eliezer would, however, agree in banning the sale of decorations for the immediate purpose of idolatry. Cf. also M. A. Z. 3:9 where the colleagues of R. Eliezer are unusually severe with a Jew who uses wood that had been part of an idol as a deterrent for the future. R. Eliezer applies the simple penalty of strict law: the Jew must forfeit an amount of money equivalent in value to the benefit derived from the wood. Cf. also A. Z. 31a where R. Eliezer permits keeping wine in a Jewish home that is located in the court of a gentile, provided that the wine barrels are sealed or the Jew retains the keys to the house. This was generally prohibited because of the apprehension that the gentile might forge the seal or get into the house through duplicate keys; he might then touch the wine, thereby possibly consecrating it for idolatrous purposes. For other instances where R. Eliezer is lenient while his colleagues enact deterrent or precautionary measures see M. Demai 4:3 and cf. Ned. 84a; Makot 16b; Tos. M. Sh. 4:6,7 (p. 93); j D'mai V, 24c and cf. Tos. D'mai 3:16 (p. 92), and see variants cited; M. Kil. 2:10, 3:4, 5:3, 6:2, Tos., *ibid,* 3:10 (p. 77), 4:5 (p. 78); M. Nazir 3:3, 4, 5, Tos. Nazir 2:12 (p. 285), Nazir 16b, 39b, 47a, 63b; M. Hul. 2:6, Tos. Hul. 2:11 (p. 502); Tos. M. Sh. 4:6 (p. 93); B. M. 54a; M. Para 9:1; M. Er. 7:11 and cf. Maimonides, Commentary on Mishnah, *ad locum;* M. Bik. 2:10; Hul. 79b, 132a; M. Seb. 8:7, Tos. Seb. 8:19 (p. 492).

But did it make any difference where he struck her? The colleagues of R. Eliezer looked at the law pragmatically. The payment of damages was obviously to afford some measure of compensation to the injured family, as well as to penalize the culprit for carelessness. The damages were consequently to be paid even when the blow struck the woman on the arm or foot, and the miscarriage was the result of her fright. According to R. Eliezer, the fine was to be paid only if the blow struck her at the womb, so that the embryo received the injury directly.[39]

III. The Method of History

1. Laws of Levitical Uncleanliness.

(a) A levitically unclean person was permitted to postpone his celebration of the Passover to a later date (Nu. 9:10-11). The Rabbis interpreted this law to refer only to the case of an individual. Should the community as a whole, because of some emer-

---

39. Mek. Mishpatim 8. Cf. B. K. 49a, j B. K. V, 5a. Aptowitzer, "Observations on the Criminal Law of the Jews," *JQR*, N. S., XV 1924-5, p. 106f, thinks that R. Eliezer presupposes the opinion that the embryo has individuality even before birth; otherwise, it should not make any difference where the blow was struck. Since the Talmud explains a number of R. Eliezer's statements on the basis of the view that the embryo is only part of the mother's womb (*ubar yerek imo*), and since our opinion of R. Eliezer as transmitted in the Mekilta by Aba Hanin is also quoted elsewhere in the name of other authorities (in B. K. 49a in the name of R. Eliezer b. Jacob and in j B. K. V, 5a, in the name of Aba Jose b. Hanin), he concludes that R. Eliezer is not really the author of our statement; he attributes it instead to R. Eliezer b. Jacob. It is, however, impossible to decide on this basis, because one may very well explain the position of R. Eliezer in the Mekilta without presupposing an attitude towards the status of the embryo. Cf. Geiger, *Kebusat Maamarim*, p. 119ff. who argues that R. Eliezer, following the view of the Bet Shammai, considered the embryo an independent individuality. Cf., however, Ginzberg's notes, *ad locum*. See also M. Pea 5:2, Tos. Er. 1:2 (p. 138), j Er. I, 18b, Er. 11b-12a and cf. M. Er. 1:2, which may likewise be explained on the basis of our principle.

gency, be levitically impure, then the disabilities of that impurity might be disregarded, and the paschal lamb was to be sacrificed at the usual time.[40] But this interpretation raised the following question: "Shall people whose impurity was not caused in the public emergency, such as lepers, etc., be included in the general exemption"? The colleagues of R. Eliezer decided in the negative— the exemption being clearly a device to overcome an emergency, it must not be applied to cases which do not fall into such a category. R. Eliezer, however, generalized the exemption and included all cases therein.[41]

(b) There were certain forms of levitical impurity that could be communicated by a dead body. What, however, if the body was "burnt to ashes"? R. Eliezer's colleagues reckoned with the change in circumstances, and ruled that the ashes could not communicate any impurity. R. Eliezer, however, continued to regard the ashes as a "dead body," and held that they could cmmunicate the impurity.[42]

(c) The ploughed area of one hundred ells within which a grave was located communicated impurity like the grave itself because of the apprehension that bits of bone might be scattered through it. What is the law, however, if an additional contiguous area of one hundred ells was ploughed? The other Rabbis distinguished between a factual grave and a legal "grave", and declared that the additional area would not receive the impurity. R. Eliezer equated the two, and pronounced the new area similarly unclean.[43]

(d) A bed standing as a complete whole was to receive

---

40. In case of war, for example, the mere contact with a weapon was enough to communicate impurity. Cf. Hul. 3a; Pes. 67a.

41. M. Pes. 9:4, Pes. 67b, Men. 95b, Sifra, Sav, p. 37b.

42. M. Ohol. 2:2, Nidda 28a. The assumption in the Mishnah is that the ashes of the corpse are unmixed with the ashes of any other burnt material, which may mean that we are dealing here with a case of cremation. Cf. Higger, "On the Cremation of the Dead" (Hebrew), in *Halakot v'Agadot*, N. Y. 1933, p. 170.

43. M. Ohol. 17:2. Cf. M. Tem. 1:5, Tem. 12b-13a.

levitical impurity as a unit: an impurity coming in contact with one part of the bed would make the whole bed unclean. Suppose, however, that the bed be separated into its parts, but two of the parts remained attached to each other; are the two parts to be treated as a unit? R. Eliezer's colleagues decided the question in the negative, because, unlike the situation presented by the bed standing as a complete whole, the two attached parts are not a functional unit. He disregarded the difference, and ruled in the affirmative.[44]

2. Laws of the Sabbath, Holidays, and Interdictions.

(a) We have learnt that to extend the two thousand ells which a person was permitted to walk outside of the city limits on the Sabbath or a holiday, the legal fiction of the *erub* was developed. It was agreed that one could not break up the Sabbath or holiday and establish two *erubim,* one for each half day, so as to extend his locomotion in two directions. But suppose that a Sabbath and holiday came ocnsecutively—might two *erubim* in two different directions be established then, one for each day? R. Eliezer followed the precedent of the law involved where the Sabbath and the holidays came apart in time, and decided the question in the affirmative. To the others, the consecutive occurrence of these two days linked them into one spiritual occasion, which, like any Sabbath, or festival day, could not be broken up through two *erubim.* They, therefore decided the question in the negative.[45]

(b) Circumcision, as above noted, could take place even on the Sabbath. If, however, the circumcision took place on the Sab-

---

44. M. Kel. 18:9. Cf., however, the interpretation of the Gaon (Elijah), *ad locum,* according to which R. Eliezer held that a bed may receive impurity only as a unit, but his colleagues maintained that the parts of the bed may also become unclean. Cf. also Tos. Kel. 8:8 (p. 587). Cf. also M. Ohol. 2:4, 9:15, 12:8, 14:4, M. Ed. 6:3; Tos. Ohol. 2:7 (p. 599), 3:7 (p. 600), 9:7 (p. 606), 10:8 (p. 607), 13:10, 12 (p. 611); Tos. Ed. 2:10 (p. 458).

45. M. Er. 3:6, Tos. Er. 5:1 (p. 143). Cf. M. Men. 7:3; Tos. Men. 8:19 (p.524); Tos. Nazir 4:11 (p. 290).

bath prior to the eighth day of the child's life, all agreed that a genuine violation of the Sabbath was committed, and a sin-offering was required. But what if the circumcision took place on a Sabbath *after* the eighth day of the child's life? R. Eliezer equated the two cases and required a sin-offering in the latter instance as well. R. Joshua insisted, however, that the two cases presented different histories, and must not be regarded as analogous. The Biblical obligation of circumcision commences only on the eighth day of the child's life. Where it was advanced one day, the circumcision is not a fulfillment of a Biblical command. Where, on the other hand, the circumcision was delayed one day, a command was carried out. Such an act cannot, therefore, be considered a genuine violation of the Sabbath, and a sin-offering is consequently not required.[46]

(c) The Bible describes in great detail (Ex. 12:5-12) the rites of the paschal sacrifice. One problem, however, is entirely omitted. Can a "second tithe" animal be offered as such a sacrifice? R. Eliezer decided in the negative, following the precedent of the paschal sacrifice offered by the Israelites in Egypt, which could not have been of the 'second tithe', since tithes were not as yet contributed then. He cited in support of his decision the fact that the same term 'Pesah' is used for both paschal sacrifices (Ex. 12:11, 43). R. Akiba objected to such formalism and decided the question in the affirmative.[47]

(d) Where priestly grain was lost in a stock of secular grain the mixture was prohibited for lay use, unless the secular grain contained one hundred and one times the amount of the admixture, in which case the latter was declared neutralized and the total stock permitted. What, however, if the secular grain was contained in a barrel and the priestly grain dropped on top of it? In that case

---

46. M. Shab. 19:7; Tos. Shab. 15:10 (p. 133); Shab. 137a, j Shab. XIX, 17b. I am accepting R. Simeon's version of the dispute. Cf. M. Pes. 6:5; Tos. Pes. 5:4 (p. 163).

47. Men. 82a; Jeb. 46a. Cf. also his reasoning in Mek. Mishpatim, Nezikin 16, Sifra, Vayikra, p. 12b, Mid. Tann. on Deut. 25:9, Men. 68b. According to Deut. 14:22-27, the so-called "second tithe,"

R. Joshua did not require neutralization through one hundred and one times the amount; it would be sufficient, he declared, if the owner removed from the top a measure equivalent to the amount dropped. R. Eliezer, on the other hand, refused to draw any distinctions, and required neutralization in the latter case as well.[48]

(e) The raven "after its kinds" was included among the unclean birds that one was not permitted to eat (Lev. 11:15 and Deut. 14:14). R. Eliezer's colleagues, however, permitted two members of the raven family, the starling and the white-bellied swallow, because they do not have all of the raven characteristics; the former, possessing a crop and the latter, an easily pealing crow. R. Eliezer disregarded the differences in characteristics and prohibited both.[49]

---

in kind or in the proceeds of redemption, was to be consumed in a family feast in Jerusalem.

48. M. Ter. 4:11, Tos. Ter. 5:11 (p. 34), j Ter. IV, 43a. In the Tosefta there is a tradition by R. Judah reversing the positions of R. Eliezer and R. Joshua. R. Meir supports the version in our Mishnah. In the light of their respective general positions the latter appears correct. In the Palestinian Talmud the traditions of R. Meir and R. Judah are reversed. The version in the Tosefta is probably more accurate, because R. Meir would rather have recorded his own opinion in the Mishnah than that of his opponent R. Judah. Where, however, one does not know which barrel the *terumah* fell on, R. Joshua agreed that neutralization was required. But he differed with R. Eliezer in that the latter required the neutralization of the barrel in the total stock, while he required the neutralization of the dropped amount. Cf. M. Ter. 4:10.

49. Hul. 62a. Cf. *ibid* 65a; B. K. 92b; M. Seb. 1:1, 8:11; M. Ter. 3:3; M. Yad. 4:2; Tos. Seb. 1:1 (p. 479), 8:24 (p. 493); Sifra, Vayikra, pp. 25b, 33a-b; Pes. 73a; Tem. 18b, where R. Eliezer demands a uniform law for the guilt-offering and the sin-offering because they are both "the means of expiating sins," disregarding their unique element. His colleagues worked out a separate code of regulations for each. Cf. also M. Bik. 2:6, j R. H. I, 57a, where R. Eliezer treats the *etrog* plant as a tree with reference to all details of agricultural law, although in some respects it partakes of the nature of the herb (it requires constant watering, the rain not suffic-

3. Civil Law and Criminal Law.

(a) Normally two competent witnesses were required to establish a legal fact. But the Rabbis made a concession to a woman claiming personal knowledge of her husband's death, and permitted her to remarry on the basis of her own testimony. They took due precautions against fraud, however, by prescribing severe penalties in case her testimony is later proven to have been false. But suppose the husband were married to an additional wife: may the same testimony liberate her also for marriage? R. Eliezer's colleagues, limiting the original concession to the circumstances of its origin, decided the question in the negative. R. Eliezer decided it in the affirmative.[50]

(b) The gleanings, forgotten sheaves, and the corner of each field, in addition to a tithe on the produce of the soil, were to be given as a beneficence to the poor (Lev. 23:22; Deut. 24:19, 26:12). A man of means who found himself in need while away from home was permitted by an old law to share in this beneficence. But was he required, on returning home, to make any restitution to charity? R. Eliezer's colleagues decided in the negative. They reckoned with the man's circumstances. If his means are, for the time being, not available to him, he becomes, for all intents and purposes, a poor man. He enjoys an inherent right to charity, and is, therefore, under no legal compulsion to make any restitution. R. Eliezer's ruling, not reckoning with the circumstances, denied him a right to charity. He might temporarily draw upon charity, because that was provided for in the old law; but on returning home, he must make full restitution.[51]

(c) Jewish law, as all law, draws a distinction between movable and immovable property, but this distinction was not well

---

ing as in the case of the tree). His colleagues reckoned with this difference and treated it in some respects like a tree and in others, like a herb.

50. Tos. Jeb. 14:3 (p. 258). Cf. M. Jeb. 16:2.
51. M. Pea 5:4.

defined. How were fixtures to be regarded? In the light of their temporary appearance, they should be considered immovable, but judging from their inherent nature, they should be regarded as movable. R. Eliezer considered only their temporary status, and generalized: "All that is attached to the soil is like the soil itself"— immovable property. His colleagues emphasized their inherent nature, and pronounced them movable.[52]

(d)   In describing the ceremony of strangling a heifer near the spot where a man was murdered by an unknown hand (Deut. 21:1), the Bible speaks of "one found slain... lying in the field...". The whole ceremony is obviously a survival of a more primitive custom,[53] and R. Eliezer's colleagues insisted that it be applied only to such cases that would satisfy the Biblical description completely. It was not to be applied if the corpse betrayed signs of death by strangulation ("slain" was understood to imply death through an iron weapon); if the body, upon discovery, was still convulsing; if it was found beneath a mound or suspended from a tree, or in a river. R. Eliezer refused to draw any distinctions, and extended the practice to the latter cases as well.[54]

---

52. M. Shev. 10:7; Tos. B. B. 3:1 (p. 401); B.B. 65b; M. Ok. 3:10; Tos. Ok. 3:16 (p. 690). It depends, of course, on the object to which the fixtres are attached. In M. Kel. 15:2 a case is cited where the fixtures are attached to a house, and R. Eliezer regards them as part of the house.

53. H. P. Smith, *The Religion of Israel*, New York 1928, pp. 32f, 192, traces this practice back to a sacrifice placating the ghost of the slain man.

54. Sifre, Deut. section 205. In j Sota IX, 23c, the respective views of R. Eliezer and his colleagues are reversed. Cf. M. Sota 9:2 where the view of the colleagues of R. Eliezer, according to the version of the Sifre, is recorded as the anonymous law. This, as well as their respective general positions, support the reading in the Sifre Cf. also Sota 45b where the reading R. Elazar is substituted for R. Eliezer. Cf. also Tos. Neg. 1:13 (p. 619); Bek. 17b, 18a. Somewhat similarly R. Eliezer's colleagues limited the law of the bird's nest (Deut. 22:6) to the female bird. R. Eliezer also included the male partridge (since it joins the female in brooding). See M. Hul. 12:2;

(e)   We are told in Scriptures (Deut. 21:22), "And if a man
have committed a sin worthy of death, and he be put to death,
and thou hang him on a tree; his body shall not remain all night
upon the tree, but thou shalt surely bury his body upon the same
day." The Bible speaks in general of "a sin worthy of death," but
R. Eliezer and his colleagues seem to have regarded the practice
of exposure as referring to a particular sin—that of blasphemy.
They arrived at this interpretation by translating the phrase
כי קללת אלהים תלוי,   "for he who is hanged is a reproach unto
God", which continues the quotation, as "for one who cursed God
is hanging." The question was then raised as to what extent the
practice of exposure after execution should be limited. R. Eliezer
was willing to apply it to all forms of capital punishment. He
recognized, however, the qualifying nature of כי קללת אלהים תלוי,
and, therefore, limited it to those cases which resembled blasphemy.
But he considered the resemblance adequate if it touched the most
general features of blasphemy—the form of punishment. All capital
crimes which, like blasphemy, were punishable by stoning (סקילה),
therefore, involved exposure after execution. The other Rabbis were
willing to extend the injunction concerning exposure to cases re-
sembling blasphemy, but they insisted that the resemblance must
embrace those features in which blasphemy is most unique—the
nature of the crime. Only idolatry presents a complete resemblance
to blasphemy; they both constitute a denial of the very essence of
religion—God. The extension of the Deuteronomic injunction was,
therefore, to be limited to idolatry alone.[55]

Tos. Hul. 10:9 (p. 512); Sifre, Deut. section 228; Mid. Tann. on Deut.
22:7.

55.   M. San. 6:4; San. 45b; Sifre, Nu. section 114; Sifre, Deut.
section 221; Mid. Tann. on Deut. 21:22. The Amoraim attribute this
dispute to a varying use of the rules of hermeneutics. R. Eliezer
is said to have used the principle of   ריבוי ומיעוט, while the other
scholars used the principle of   כלל ופרט (San. 46a). They account

IV. The Method of Sociology.

1. *Ritual Law.*

(a) The ritual law for the purification of a person who has recovered from leprosy provides the following (Lev. 14:28): "And the priest shall put of the oil that is in his hand upon the tip of the right ear of him that is to be cleansed, and upon the thumb of of his right hand, and upon the great toe of his right foot." But suppose the person "to be cleansed" lacked "the thumb of his right hand" or "the great toe of his right foot?"[56]   R. Eliezer's colleagues, realizing that it would be a great injustice to bar the re-entrance of a person into a community for such a reason, suggested that the oil be placed on the thumb of his left hand or the large toe of his left foot.[57] Though departing somewhat from the Scriptural injunction, they nevertheless felt that such a ceremony would be adequate. R. Eliezer insisted that the law must be carried out literally. Where a person lacked the "thumb of his right hand" or the "great toe of his right foot" the ceremony of purification could not

---

similarly for the disputes between R. Eliezer and his colleagues in B. K. 117b (according to the reading recommended by Rabinowicz, *ad locum*) and Nazir 34b. Cf. Sifre. Nu. section 24, and j Nazir VI, 53c, which show that the correct reading is R. Eliezer and not R. Elazar, as is the reading in our Nazir text. This explanation of the Amoraim seems, however, unjustified since R. Eliezer makes explicit use of the principle of כלל ופרט in Mek. Nezikin, Mishpatim ם (ed. Horovitz, p. 277). Cf. also j Nazir VI, 55a, where he is said to have followed the principle of כלל ופרט but according to R. Ishmael's version of it.

56. Leprosy often results in the decay of toes and fingers. See the article on leprosy by Sir Leonard Rogers, in *Encyc. Brittanica*, 14th ed. XIII, p. 957f.

57. R. Simeon suggested putting the oil on the spot where the thumb of the right hand or the great toe of the right foot normally is.

take place, and the individual was consequently not readmissable into the community.[58]

(b)   If a priest married a divorcee or a childless widow who had been released from the levirate marriage by the ceremony of *halisah*,[59] the sons of the union were debarred from the priesthood: they were not permitted to eat terumah or to officiate at Temple sacrifices.   Suppose, however, a priest discovers that he is the son of such a marriage after he had for some time, unaware of his true status, exercised the usual priestly functions.   For the future he

-----

58.   Nazir 46b.   This is, however, problematic since a totally different version of the dispute is given in M. Neg. 14:9, San. 45b, 88a, and Yoma 61b.   The view of R. Simeon, as recorded in the baraitha, is there attributed to R. Eliezer and the latter's view is quoted anonymously, while the view of the *Hakamin* is attributed to R. Simeon. The version of the baraitha is much more in accordance with the respective general positions of these scholars in the halakah.   There is a somewhat similar dispute between the Bet Shammai and the Bet Hillel concerning a bald-headed nazarite.   According to the Bet Shammai, "he is not required to have a razor passed over his head." According to the Hillelites, he is.   The Amoraim offer two different interpretations for this dispute.   According to one, the Shammaites do not require passing the razor, because they hold it would be ineffective; the Hillelites, on the other hand, require it, because they accept it as equivalent to the generally required shaving of the hair. According to the other interpretation, the Shammaites allow such a nazarite's return to normal life without any hair shaving, while the Hillelites object, maintaining that, being unable to shave his hair, the bald-headed nazarite may never return to normal life.   See Nazir *l. c.* The former interpretation would support the reading in the baraitha because it brings R. Eliezer in consonance with the Shammaite view. Supporting this interpretation is also the fact that it presents the Shammaites and the Hillelites in greater harmony with their respective general positions in the halakah, and that, moreover, the Shammaite R. Eliezer considered the shaving of a nazarite's hair mandatory, while his colleagues did not.   See Nazir 14b, 28a, 46a.

59.   The Biblical verse mentions only a divorcee, but according to a Rabbinic interpretation the same prohibition also applied to a *halusah*.   See Sifra, Emor, p. 94a.

was, of course, to be debarred, but what of the past? The Rabbis were generally lenient, realizing that when that priest ate terumah he acted in complete good faith, and that serious disturbances would ensue if the sacrifices at which he had officiated were invalidated. They, therefore, legitimatized what he had done in the past. R. Eliezer, however, took the severer course: he demanded due payment for all the terumah which that priest consumed, and invalidated his sacrifices.[60]

(c) When the New Year coincided with the Sabbath, the blowing of the ram's horn was prohibited, except at the Temple services in Jerusalem. When after the destruction of Jerusalem, the focus of Judaism was moved to Jabneh, R. Johanan b. Zakkai, in order to make the change more authoritative, decided to invest the new center with the old privilege enjoyed by Jerusalem, and decreed that there, too, the ram's horn be blown on the New Year falling on the Sabbath. R. Eliezer submitted to this decision of his teacher. After the death of R. Johanan, when it became apparent that Jabneh might also have to be abandoned, and the center of Judaism located elsewhere, the colleagues of R. Eliezer declared themselves ready to extend the old privilege of Jerusalem to the new center. This

---

60. M. Ter. 8:1; Mid. Tann. on Deut. 26:3. Cf. Kid. 66b. The Mishnah cites another difference between R. Eliezer and his colleagues which was based on the same principle. Suppose a priest dies while on a journey, and after some time the news of his death reaches his home—must his wife or slave make restitution for the terumah they ate between the time that the husband and master died and the time that the news reached them? R. Eliezer's colleagues again felt it unfair to tax a person who acted in good faith, and did not require restitution. He demanded restitution for the full value of the terumah consumed, plus a fine of an additional fifth. Restitution plus a fine were required of one who ate terumah as a שׁוֹגֵג. But this concept of שׁגּג describes not complete good faith, but a lack of deliberate intent to violate the law. One who, for example, does not know the law or the fact that the food before him is terumah is a שׁוֹגֵג. He is nevertheless guilty of negligence.

time, however, R. Eliezer dissented and opposed the suggestion of change.[61]

(d) We have previously learnt that reckoning with the new conditions prevailing after the war of 70 C.E., R. Eliezer's colleagues introduced certain modifications in the ritual of Judaism. The Eighteen Benedictions were introduced into the ritual of private prayer. The old custom of carrying the fruit of neighborhood vineyards in the fourth year for consumption to Jerusalem was declared abolished. Similarly, the ritual of admitting a proselyte to Judaism was reorganized with the omission of the customary sacrificial offering. R. Joshua, possibly to meet the challenge of Christian propaganda, was even willing to modify the ritual still further, by omitting the requirement of circumcision, so unwelcome to the would-be convert. In all these instances, R. Eliezer defended the old order and opposed change.[62]

(e) There were a number of primitive customs which survived in the Bible, and which the more developed point of view of the Rabbis no longer regarded as mandatory. Thus, they permitted a *nazarite* to return to normal life and drink wine, even if he did not shave his hair. Similarly, they validated a *halisah* ceremony even if it took place in the evening, or if the widow did not spit in her brother-in-law's face (Deut. 25:9). R. Eliezer, defending the older practice, took the negative view in both instances.[63]

---

61. M. R. H. 4:1; R. H. 29b. Cf. above, p. 56f.

62. See above, pp. 57, 58, 61, 69.

63.   Nazir 14b, 28a, 46a. M. Jeb. 12:2, 3. Nevertheless, where the widow removed the shoe of the left foot, instead of the right foot, as custom required, R. Eliezer declared the halisah ceremony valid, while his colleagues ruled it invalid. Already the Amoraim felt that this was out of harmony with R. Eliezer's general position, and they sought to affect a reconciliation. Among the suggestions proposed is one of R. Isaac b. Joseph in the name of R. Johanan, correcting the reading in the Mishnah by reversing the positions of R. Eliezer and his colleagues.

2. Agricultural Law.

(a)   The regulations concerning the Sabbatical year as provided for in the Bible involved the complete cessation from agricultural work for a full year in every cycle of seven years. This proved
a great burden upon the rural population of Palestine, particularly
during our period, when distress and poverty were widespread. As
a result the tendency appeared among the Rabbis to interpret these
laws in a more lenient spirit, with the exception of R. Eliezer who,
unresponsive to these conditions, demanded the full continuity of
the law in its complete rigor. Thus, vegetation and fruit grown
spontaneously during the Sabbatical year were permitted for immediate and direct personal use, but the owner was to renounce title
and share them with the general public. R. Eliezer, against the
objections of his colleagues, nevertheless forbade using such fruit
when presented with them as a gift. He reasoned that the recipient
might thereby become obligated to the donor, and one was not to
enter into any obligations in using Sabbatical year products.[64]

Similarly, he demanded burning all leather to which oil made
of Sabbatical year products was applied. He argued that such application of the oil was not a direct, personal use. His colleagues
merely required setting aside and eating in lieu of Sabbatical year
products, any other quantity of food equivalent in value to the mis-
used oil.[65] Where the spontaneous growths had all been removed

---

64.   In this R. Eliezer apparently followed a ruling of the Bet
Shammai. See M. Shev. 9:9 and cf. j Shev. IX, 39a. (The reading
in the Palestinian Talmud is corrupt; it misquotes the respective views
of the Bet Shammai and Bet Hillel. Cf. M. Shev. 4:2). R. Eliezer
permitted these fruits provided the recipient now renounced title
and invited outsiders to share them with him. Cf. the note of Elijah
Gaon, ad locum.

65.   M. Shev. 8:9. The Mishnah reports that when this opinion
of R. Eliezer was cited to R. Akiba by his pupils, he silenced them
with the comment: "I will not tell you R. Eliezer's real opinion with
reference to this." Two Palestinian scholars R. Jose and R. Hezekiah
in the name of R. Aba discuss what this "real opinion" of R. Eliezer
was (j Shev. VIII, 38b). According to the tradition of R. Jose, it

from the field, one was no longer permitted to use any portions of it that had previously been gathered into the house. However, if a person pressed three kinds of vegetables, R. Joshua permitted eating the sauce as long as at least one of the ingredients still remained on the field. R. Eliezer again showed his severer attitude by forbidding it even where only one of the ingredients had been exhausted from the field.[66] At the conclusion of the Sabbatical year, R. Joshua permitted the owner to reclaim for personal use such spontaneously grown vegetation as was still in the field. R. Eliezer denied the owner this right, and awarded such vegetation to the poor.[67] We have already learnt that R. Eliezer, opposing R. Gamaliel, demanded the subjection of Syrian agriculture to all the same Sabbatical year regulations that were in force in Palestine.[68]

(b) We recall that R. Eliezer, not reckoning with the newer conditions, opposed all modification of the prohibition of cattle raising.

---

was: "may the bones of such a man be burnt." According to tradition of Hezekiah, R. Eliezer was even more lenient than his colleagues, permitting the leather without any restrictions. No definite decision is possible as to which of the two traditions is correct, but the probability is in favor of the traditions of R. Jose. For one thing, as a disciple of R. Akiba and R. Johannan b. Nuri, two of Eliezer's leading pupils (See *J. E.*, VII, p. 240), he had access to accurate sources of information about R. Eliezer's views. The harshness and crudeness of the expression, not unusual, we learnt, for R. Eliezer, would explain why the more tender R. Akiba refused to quote it. It would also explain how the confusion occurred between R. Eliezer's real view and the view as recorded in the Mishnah: R. Akiba's pupils may not have heard accurately, and they referred the "may be burnt" to the leather, instead of to "the bones of that man." This would also put R. Eliezer's view into greater harmony with his general attitude toward the laws of the sabbatical year.

66. M. Shev. 9:5, Sifra, Behar, p. 107b. R. Gamaliel required removing each ingredient as it was exhausted from the field.

67. M. Shev. 5:3, Tos. Shev. 4:3 (p. 65).

68. See above, p. 99.

3. Civil and Criminal Law.

(a)   R. Eliezer forbade a husband to live with his wife for seven days after the first night of marriage. He reasoned that the bride certainly menstruated on the first coition, and she must therefore be treated like any other menstruant woman (Lev. 15:19). R. Joshua objected to marring the marriage festivities, and suspended the prohibition until after the third day of marriage.[69]

(b)   If a court, after due investigation, established the widowhood of a woman and declared her free to remarry, and later the judgment of the court proved to have been erroneous, the Mishnah ruled that the woman may neither live with her new husband nor return to her former husband. Yet the Mishnah conceded that no manner of guilt can be attached to the woman, since she followed the advice of court and acted in complete good faith; she was, therefore, exempted from sacrificing a sin-offering. R. Eliezer, on the other hand, refused to extend such an exemption. "Though the mountains fall, yet the law must prevail," was his maxim. He held that the woman must seek atonement through the sacrifice of a sin-offering.[70]

(c)   During the great political and social unrest that followed the fall of Jerusalem (70 C.E.), it became apparent that the prevailing law of evidence was working great hardship on Jewish women. Many of them lost their husbands in the then frequent riots, massacres, and raids of hostile soldiery, but could not find two competent witnesses to testify to that effect, and thereby be per-

---

69. Kal.; j Ber. II, 5b. Cf. Kal. R. 1. I am following for the view of R. Joshua the reading in four of the six manuscripts in the possession of Dr. M. Higger, against the version in our printed texts. M. Nidda 10:1 cites a parallel dispute between the Shammaites and the Hillelites. R. Eliezer agrees with the Shammaites; R. Joshua (according to our accepted reading), with the Hillelites. While officially the wedding celebration lasted for a week the essential festivities were confirmed to the first three days (Ket. 7a).

70. M. Jeb. 10:1; Jeb. 92a. Cf. Jeb. 36b and see the interpretation of Rashi, ad locum.

mitted to remarry. After some deliberation, the scholars, led by R. Gamaliel, took the bold step and proclaimed a general leniency with regard to the testimony required to free a woman for remarriage. Even indirect evidence, the testimony of a woman, a slave, or a maid-servant was declared acceptable. But R. Eliezer disregarded the emergency, and continued to cling to the old law.[71]

(d) The Mishnah[72] lists the methods by which title to property may be acquired. Title to immovable property was acquired upon the paymet of money, the writing of a deed, or actual occupation. The title to movable property was acquired upon the symbolic act of "pulling," something like the *traditio* in Roman law. At an early date, however, it was realized that in some instances this law worked great hardships. A person on his death bed, for example, may want to dispose of his property, but there may not be enough time left for the writing of a deed. An exemption was, therefore, declared in the case of one making bequests "mortis causa," whose mere words were to be considered as a duly executed legal document. R. Eliezer again refused to be moved by such considerations, and opposed the change.[73]

(e) A mourner was required to abstain from his regular occupation for the first seven days of his mourning period; others were, however, permitted to do this work for him where it was a matter of warding off acute financial loss. With this concession as a precedent, R. Eliezer's colleagues permitted a mourner's friends to do his regular flax sowing, because by delaying he might miss

---

71. M. Jeb. 16:7, R. Akiba was unwilling to extend this leniency to include the testimony of a woman, a slave or a near relative of the parties concerned; but he regarded the testimony of one competent witness sufficient. It is interesting that the otherwise progressive R. Joshua agreed with R. Eliezer and also opposed the change, although he was, no doubt, motivated by a different reason. He was probably true to his great solicitousness about the purity of family life and apprehended fraud on the part of the woman. Cf. above, p. 107f.

72. M. Kid. 1:3.

73. M. B. B. 9:7; Tos. B. B. 10:12 (p. 412). Cf. j Kid I, 60c, d.

the seasonal rainfall, after which flax sowing would no longer be profitable. R. Eliezer forbade it, arguing that if the required seasonal harvest should be missed, it would still be possible to raise another crop.[74]

(f) We have already learned[75] that, moved by humanitarian considerations, the Rabbis modified a number of the more primitive procedures in the criminal law of the Bible. They reintepreted the *lex talionis* to require monetary compensation for the inflicted injuries. They exempted female criminals from exposure after execution, and excluded children from the destruction of the in-

---

74. Sem. 5:6. Cf. M. K. 11b where our view of R. Eliezer is quoted anonymously, and the view of R. Eliezer's colleagues is quoted in the name of R. Judah. Elijah Gaon corrects our reading in Sem. to agree with the corresponding reading in Moed Katan. See his note in Semahot, *ad locum*. This is, however, entirely unwarranted by the text.

75. See above, p. 111f. In these, as well as in a number of other instances we have met, R. Eliezer was obviously closer to the plain meaning of the Biblical text. His colleagues, who were defending a deviation from the older law, were forced to interpret the texts more freely. This cleavage extended itself to their respective exegeses of the Bible in general. Thus, R. Akiba interpreted the "booths" in which the Israelites dwelt in the desert (Lev. 23:43) as protecting wings of divine glory. R. Eliezer followed the literal meaning. See Mek. Bo 14; Tan. Bo 9; Sifra, Emor, p. 103a. Cf., however, Sukka 11a and Mek. R. Simeon p. 26, where the positions of R. Eliezer and R. Akiba are reversed. Similarly R. Joshua interpreted Shittim (Nu. 26:1) and Refidim (Ex. 17:1) as being the respective symbols for the fact that there the Israelites committed foolishness (*sh'tus*) and weakened (*ripu*) themselves by neglecting the Torah. R. Eliezer regarded them as actual place names. See San. 106a; Bek. 5b. Cf. Mek. Amalek, Beshalah 1; R. Simeon, p. 82. R. Akiba interpreted "her father and mother" in Deut. 21:13 as meaning allegorically her past idolatry; and "a full month" (lit. "a month of days"), as really meaning three months. R. Eliezer retained the literal meaning. See Mid. Tann. on Deut. 21:13; Sifre, Deut. section 213; Jeb. 48b; Sem. 6:13; Lekah, *ad locum*. R. Joshua turned Ecc. 11:6 ("In the morning

habitants of an idolatrous city. R. Eliezer opposed each of these modifications.

---

sow thy seed, and in the evening withhold not thy hand") into a moral dictum, that people shall seize every opportunity to do good, morning and evening. R. Akiba took it, in a similarly moral sense, as an exhortation to scholars that they continue raising disciples, in youth as well as later on in life. R. Eliezer interpreted it literally as advice to farmers that they sow in the spring as well as in the late summer, since one cannot know which harvest will succeed. See Tan. Haye Sarah 6. Cf. Ecc. R. 11:10; Gen. R. 61:3. This interpretation may, of course, also be related to R. Eliezer's rural orientation. Cf. above, pp. 94-98. For R. Eliezer's interest in the plain meaning of the Biblical text, cf. also Makot 12a; Mek. Bo 14 (ed. Horovitz, p. 51); Sifre, Nu. section 84; j Sukka IV, 54c; Mid. Tann. on Deut. 11:23, 14:29, 16:5, 19:13, 21:16, 24:4.

Chapter VI

R. ELIEZER IN THE HISTORY OF THE HALAKAH

We have now traced R. Eliezer's halakah in detail. It betrays a marked affinity to the halakah of the Sadducees and to the halakah of the Shammaites. This may well be explained by a recognition of the social interests which the Sadducees, the Shammaites, and R. Eliezer had in common.

Scholars have not as yet reconstructed fully the background, the philosophy, and the history of the Sadducees. The facts hitherto known, however, indicate clearly that the Sadducees represented the upper layer of Jewish society, the nobility, the priesthood, the landed interests; while the Pharisees represented the urban middle and lower classes. In the light of their social orientation, it was only natural that the Sadducees should oppose Pharisaic individualism and universalism. Rooted in the soil of Palestine, identified with Palestine's political destiny, with a great following among the high priestly families, it was inevitable that they teach a piety which centered in the Temple and the nation. In defending the propertied classes and the priesthood, in their unsympathetic attitude toward the slave and the criminal, the Sadducees were only championing their own immediate class interests. Conservative in their conception of Jewish piety and social doctrine, the Sadducees also, very naturally, developed a system of jurisprudence which emphasized tradition and opposed change.

The Shammaites, represented within Pharisaism the same basic social interests that had been defended by the Sadducees. The genesis of Shammaism goes back to the reign of Herod. It was dur-

155

ing the reign of Herod that Sadduceeism suffered a great decline.
As the partisans of the deposed Hasmoneans, the Sadducees were
considered by Herod the enemies of the throne, and felt the
brunt of his persecutions. In addition, Herod very likely favored the Pharisees, because their devotion to and propagation of
Torah distracted the attention of the people from the affairs of state,
which he wanted to retain in his own hands. Finally, Herod's active
encouragement of trade and commerce was a great impetus to the
growth of hte middle class, the party identified with Pharisaism. But
now that the Pharisees were in the ascendency, they were very
naturally joined by many of the former Sadducees. Many Sadducees,
wealthy landowners with surplus capital, undoubtedly entered the
now vastly expanded field of business, and thereby moved closer to
the social and economic interests of the middle class. Furthermore,
with the greater development of trade and commerce, the middle
class itself was divided into an upper and lower layer. The upper
layer constituted a new aristocracy—the aristocracy of wealth. Without doubt many of these "nouveaux riches" now acquired land, the
continued mark of high social status. In the very nature of things,
this upper layer of the middle class moved closer to the old aristocracy of the land—the Sadducees. A cleavage now occurred within
Pharisaism; the party split into two well defined factions. Representing the upper middle class as well as the ex-Sadducees, were
the conservative Shammaites; while the lower middle class was
represented by the progressive Hillelites. Such specific tenets of
Pharisaism as the beginning of the Shabuot celebration on the fiftieth
day after the first day of Passover; the Sukkot ritual of the water
libations on the altar on each of the seven days of the festival, and
the procession of the congregation about the altar, willow branch
in hand, on the last day; the beliefs in angelology, the resurrection
of the dead and the immortality of the soul—all these were by now
regarded as the sine qua non of Pharisaic orthodoxy. As such, they
were, of course accepted by the Shammaites as well as the Hillelites.
But on the broader questions of Jewish piety and social doctrine they
clashed. The Hillelites tried to continue the main trend of Pharisa-

ism in the direction of individualism and universalism. The Shammaites resisted, defending the more conservative point of view.

We have already noted that after the close of the war, the Pharisees resolved their difference by formally repudiating Shammaism. But while it is possible to vanquish a political party, such victory does not in itself eliminate the class interests which that party represents. R. Eliezer was the disciple of an ardent Hillelite, R. Johanan b. Zakkai. He apparently accepted the formal repudiation of Shammaism. But we know that he was a great landowner, a member of the upper class. It was consequently inevitable that, wherever Pharisaism was still flexible, he reassert the point of view related to his class interests—the old point of view of the Sadducees and the Shammaites. It was the common rural background which made him, like the Sadducees "boorish in behaviour" (Jos. *Wars* II 8,4). It was fully in consonance with his class traditions that he taught a theology in which there was very little concern for the individual; that he was hostile to the non-Jewish world and unfriendly to proselytizing propaganda; that he emphasized the Temple, the cult of sacrifices, and the priesthood; that he championed the interests of agriculture and defended the rights of property; that he was unsympathetic to the women, the poor, the lowly born, the slave, and the criminal. Conservative in his attitude toward piety and social doctrine he, like the Sadducees and the Shammaites, was very naturally moved to develop a system of jurisprudence which emphasized stability, uniformity, and opposed change. That, like the Sadducees and the Shammaites, R. Eliezer too was finally repudiated, is only an indication of the extent and the direction of the class struggle—a struggle of which the combatants may not have been fully conscious, but which every utterance of theirs betrays.

ABBREVIATIONS

Ab.—Abot
A. R. N.—Abot de R. Nathan
A. Z.—Abodah Zarah
Ant.—Antiquities
Ar.—Arakin
B. B.—Baba Eatra
B. K.—Baba Kama
B. M.—Baba Mesia
Bek.—Bekorot
Ber.—Berakot
B. H.—Bet ha-Midrash
Chajes Memorial Volume—
    Abhandlungen zur Erinner-
    ung an H. P. Chajes
Cat. Bod.—Catalogous Libror-
    um Hebraeorum in Biblio-
    theca Bodliana, by M. Stein-
    schneider
D. E. R.—Derek Eres Rabba
D. E. Z.—Derek Eres Zuta
Deut. R.—Deutoronomy Rabba
Ecc. R.—Ecclesiastes Rabba
Ed.—Eduyot
Er.—Erubin
Ex. R.—Exodus Rabba
Gen. R.—Genesis Rabba
Git.—Gittin
Hag.—Hagigah
Hal.—Hallah
Hor.—Horayot
HTR—Harvard Theological
    Review

Kid.—Kiddushin
Lam. R.—Lamentations Rabba
Lekah—Midrash Lekah Tob
Lehnw.—Griechische und latein-
    ische Lehnwoerter, by S.
    Krauss
Lev. R.—Leviticus Rabba
M.—Mishnah
Mak.—Makshirin
Maas.—Maaser or Massrot or
    Maaser Rishon
M. K.—Moed Katan
M. Sh.—Maaser Sheni
Matt.—Matthew
Meg.—Megillah
Meil.—Meilah
Mek.—Mekilta
Men.—Menahot
MGWJ—Monatschrift fuer Ge-
    schichte und Wissenschaft
    des Judentums
Mid. Tann.—Midrash Tannaim
Mid. Tehil.—Midrash Tehillim
MWJ—Magazin fuer die Wis-
    senschaft des Judentums
Ned.—Nedarim
Nu. R.—Numbers Rabba
Ohol.—Oholot
Ok.—Okzin
o. M.—on-the-Main
O. Y.—Osar Yisrael
P. R.—Pesikta Rabbati

158

HUCA—Hebrew Union College
   Annual
Hul.—Hullin
Is.—Isaiah
j—Palestinian Talmud
JBL—Journal of Biblical Lit-
   erature
J. E.—Jewish Encyclopedia
Jeb.—Jebamot
Jos.—Josephus
JQR, N. S.—Jewish Quarterly
   Review, New Series
Kal.—Kallah
Kal. R.—Kallah Rabbati
Kel.—Kelim
Ket.—Ketubot

P. S. E. Z.—Pseudo Seder
   Eliahu Zuta
REJ—Revue des Etudes Juives
R. H.—Rosh Hashanah
San.—Sanhedrin
Sem.—Semahot
Shab.—Shabbat
Sheb.—Shebuot
Shek.—Shekalim
Shev.—Shebiit
Taan.—Taanit
Tan.—Tanhuma
Tem.—Temurah
Ter.—Terumah
Tos.—Tosefta
Y. T.—Yom Tob
Zab.—Zabim

BIBLIOGRAPHY

A — Sources

Abot de R. Nathan, ed. Schechter, Vienna 1887.

Agadat B'reshit, ed. Buber, Cracow 1903.

Apocrypha and Pseudepigrapha, ed. Charles, Oxford 1915.

Bible

Epistle of Barnabas (in *The Ante-Nicene Fathers*, I, N. Y. 1896).

P. Eusebius, *Ecclesiastical History* (Eng. by C. F. Cruse), N. Y. 1856.

Genesis Rabba, ed. Theodor, Berlin 1903-12.

Jerome (Hieronimus), *Opera Omnia*, Paris 1845-6.

Josephus, *Works* (English by W. Whiston), London 1906.

Justin Martyr, *The Dialogues with Tryphon* (English by A. L. Williams), London 1930.

Masektot Zeirot, ed. M. Higger, New York 1929.

Mekilta on Exodus, ed. Friedmann, Vienna 1870.

Mekilta, ed. Horovitz—Rabin, Frankfort o. M. 1928-1931.

Mekilta, R. Simeon b. Johai, on Exodus, ed. D. Hoffmann, Frankfort o. M. 1905.

Midrash ha-Gadol on Genesis, ed. Schechter, Cambridge 1902.

Midrash ha-Gadol on Leviticus, ed. Rabinowitz, New York 1932.

Midrash Lekah Tob, or Pesikta Zutarta, on the Pentateuch, Vilna 1884.

Midrash Tanhuma, ed. Horeb, 1924.

Midrash Tanhuma, ed. Buber, Vilna 1885.

Midrash Rabba on the Pentateuch and the Five Scrolls, ed. Horeb, 1924.

Midrash Tannaim, ed. Hoffman, Berlin 1908-1909.

Midrash Vehizhir, ed. Freimann, Warsaw 1880.

Midrash Tehillim, ed. Buber, Vilna 1891.

Mishnah, ed. Horeb, 1924; ed. W. H. Lowe, Cambridge 1883.

New Testament.

Origen, *Contra Celsum* (in *The Ante-Nicene Fathers*, IV, N. Y. 1890).

Pesikta Rabbati, ed. Friedmann, Vienna 1860.

160

Pirke de R. Eliezer (English by Friedlander), London 1916.
Pesikta de R. Kahana, ed. Buber, Vilna 1925.
Seder Eliahu Rabba and Zuta, ed. Friedmann, Vienna 1902.
Seder Eliahu Zuta (Pseudo), or Nispahim l'Seder Eliahu Zuta, ed. Friedmann, Vienna 1904.
Semahot, ed. Higger, New York 1931.
Sheba Masektot Ketanot, ed. Higger, New York 1930.
Sheiltot of R. Aha of Shabha, ed. Vilna 1861.
Sifre on Numbers and Deuteronomy, ed. Friedmann, Vienna 1864.
Sifre Zuta, ed. Horovitz, Breslau 1910.
Sifra, ed. Weiss, Vienna 1862.
Taanit, ed. Malter, Philadelphia 1928.
Talmud, Babylonian, Montreal 1919.
Talmud, Palestinian, Krotoshin 1865.
Tosefta, ed. Zuckermandel, Pasewalk 1881.
Yalkut Shim'oni, ed. Horeb, 1924.

B — Encyclopedia

Encyclopaedia Britannica, s. v. "Leprosy."
Eshkol, s. v. "Eliezer ha-Gadol b. Isaac."
Hasting's *Encyclopaedia of Religion and Ethics,* s. v. "Calendar" (Jewish), "Evil Eye," "Knots."
Jewish Encyclopaedia, s. v. "R. Akiba," "Aquila," "R. Johanan b. Zakkai," "R. Jose the Galilean," "Midrash Haggadda," "Pirke d' R. Eliezer," "Primogeniture".

C — Literature

Aptowitzer, V.—"Observations on the Criminal Law of the Jews," *JQR,* N. S., XV 1924, pp. 55-119.
Aptowitzer, V.—"Spuren des Matriarchats im juedischen Schrifttum," *HUCA,* IV 1927, pp. 207-241.
Aptowitzer, V.—"Zur Kosmologie in der Agada," *MGWJ,* LXXII 1928, pp. 363-370.
Aptowitzer, V.—"Aufhebung des Brauches des taeglichen Dekaloglesens im oeffentlichen Gottesdienst," *MGWJ,* LXXIV 1930, pp. 104-126.
Aptowitzer, V.—"Bemerkungen zur Liturgie und Geschichte der Lit-

urgie", *MGWJ*, LXXIV, 1930, pp. 104-126.

Bacher, W.—*Die Agada der Tannaiten*, Strassburg 1903.

Baron, S.—"Israelite Population in the Days of the Kings" (Hebrew), *Abhandlungen zur Erinnerung an H. P. Chajes*, Vienna 1933, pp. 76-136.

Benzinger, I.—*Hebraeische Archaeologie*, Leipzig 1927.

Blau, L.—"Die aelteste Eheform," *Abhandlungen zur Erinnerung an H. P. Chajes*, pp. 6-22.

Blau, L.—*Das altjuedische Zauberwesen*, Strassburg 1898.

Bousset, W.—*Die Religion des Judentums im neutestamentlichen Zeit-alter*, 3d ed. Tuebingen 1926.

Bruell, J.—*Mebo ha-Mishnah*, Frankfort o. M. 1875.

Buechler, A.—*Die Priester und der Cultus*, Vienna 1895.

Buechler, A.—*Rer galilaeische Am ha-Ares des zweiten Jahrhunderts*, Vienna 1906.

Buechler, A.—*Political and Social Leaders of the Jewish Community in Sepphoris*, Oxford 1909.

Buechler, A.—"Das juedische Verloebnis und die Stellung der Ver-lobten eines Priesters im ersten und zweiten Jahrhundert," *Festschrift Israel Lewy*, Breslau 1911, pp. 110-144.

Buechler, A.—*The Economic Conditions of Judea after the Destruc-tion of the Second Temple*, London 1912.

Buechler, A.—"La purete levitique de Jerusalem," *REJ*, LXII 1911, pp. 201-215; LIII 1912, pp. 30-50.

Buechler, A.—"Familienreinheit und Familienmakel in Jerusalem vor dem Jahre 70," *Festschrift Adolph Schwartz*, Berlin 1917.

Buechler, A.—*Types of Palestinian Piety*, London 1922.

Buechler, A. — "The Origin of the Benediction Hatob v'Hametib" (Hebrew), *Abhandlungen zur Erinnerung am H. P. Chajes*, pp. 137-168.

Cardozo, B. N.—*The Growth of the Law*, New Haven 1924.

Cardozo, B. N.—*The Nature of the Judicial Process*, New Haven 1921.

Chajes, H. P.—"Ben Stada," *ha-Goren*, IV 1903, pp. 33-37.

Cohen, M. R.—*Reason and Nature*, New York 1929.

Conder, F. R. & C. R.—*A Handbook of the Bible*, New York S. A.

Cassel, P.—"Anmerkungen zu Megillat Taanit", in his *Messianische Stellen des alten Testaments*, Berlin 1865.

Driver, S. R.—Notes in his edition of *The Book of Exodus*, Cam-bridge 1911.

Derenbourg, H.—*Essai sur l'histoire et la geographie le la Palestine*, Paris 1867.

Dæhne, A. F.—*Geschichtliche Darstellung der alexandrinische Religionsphilosophie,* I, Halle 1834.

Edersheim, A.—*Life and Times of Jesus the Messiah,* New York 1910.

Elbogen, C. I.—*Der juedische Gottesdienst,* Frankfort o. M. 1924.

Elijah Gaon Vilna.—*Biur Ha-GRA* (Commentary on Shulhan Aruk, Orah Hayim, ed. Lemberg 1904).

Elijah Gaon Vilna.—*Elijahu Rabba* (Commentary on Mishnah, Order Taharot, in ed. Vilna 1910, vol. VI).

Elijah Gaon Vilna.—*Nushat Ha-GRA* (Critical notes to tractate Semahot, ed. Montreal 1919).

Epstein, A.—*m'Kadmoniyot ha-Yehudim,* Vienna 1887.

Finkelstein, L.—"The Development of the Amidah," *JQR,* N. S., XVI 1925, pp. 1-43, 127-170.

Finkelstein, L.—"The Birkat ha-Mazon," *JQR,* N. S., XIX 1928, pp. 211-262.

Finkelstein, L.—"The Pharisees: Their Origin and Their Philosophy," LIII 1934, pp. 142-149.

Finkelstein, L.—"Is Philo mentioned in Rabbinic Literature," *JBL, HTR,* XXII 1929, pp. 185-261.

Friedlaender, G.—Introduction to his edition of the *Pirke de R. Eliezer,* London 1916.

Friedmann, M.—"Four Products Prohibited by the Rabbis" (Hebrew), *Kadimah,* I 1899, pp. 187-192, 277-282.

Freund, L.—Ueber Genealogien und Familienreinheit in biblischer und talmudischer Zeit, *Festschrift Adolph Schwartz,* pp. 163-193.

Gandz, S.—"The Knot in Hebrew Literature," *Isis,* XIV 1930, pp. 189-214.

Gaster, M.—*Exempla of the Rabbis,* London 1924.

Gaster, M.—"Araber und Samaritaner", *MGWJ,* LXXVII 1933, pp. 304-306.

Geiger, A.—*Urschrift und Uebersetzungen der Bibel in ihrer Abhaengigkeit von der inneren Entwicklung des Judentums,* Breslau 1857.

Geiger, A. — *Juedische Zeitschrift fuer Wissenschaft und Leben,* 1862-1875.

Geiger, A.—*Kebusat Ma'amarim,* Berlin 1877.

Geiger, A.—*Nachgelassene Schriften,* 1875-78.

Ginzberg, L.—*Geonica,* II, New York 1909.

Ginzberg, L.—*Eine unbekannte juedische Sekte,* New York 1922.

Ginzberg, L.—*Legends of the Jews,* 6 vols., Philadelphia 1909-1928.

Ginzberg, L.—*Genizah Studies,* I, New York 1928.

Ginzberg, L.—*Mekomah shel ha-Halakah b'Hokmat Yisrael,* Jerusalem 1931.

Ginzberg, L.—"Die Hagada bei den Kirchenvaetern," *Abhandlungen zur Erinnerung an H. P. Chajes,* pp. 22-50.

Ginzel, F. K.—*Handbuch der Chrnologie,* II, Leipzig 1911.

Graetz, H.—"Die Reise der vier Tannaiten nach Rom," *MGWJ,* 1 1851, pp. 192-202.

Graetz, H.—"Agrippa II und der Zustand Judaeas nach dem Untergang Jerusalems," *MGWJ,* XII 1881, pp. 481-500.

Graetz, H.—"Eine Strafmassregel gegen die Leviten," *MGWJ,* XXXV 1886, pp. 97-108.

Graetz, H.—*Geschichte der Juden,* Leipzig 1891-1909.

Gressman, H.—*Die Aufgaben der Wissenschaft des nachbiblischen Judentums,* Giessen 1926.

Gressman, H.—*The Tower of Babel,* New York 1928.

Halevi, I.—*Dorot ha-Rishonim,* Pressburg and Frankfort o. M., 1897-1918.

Halper, B. Z.—"Recent Hebraica and Judaica," *JQR,* N. S., VIII 1917-18, pp. 477-488.

Heinemann, I.—*Philons Griechische und juedische Bildung,* Breslau 1929.

Herford, R. T.—*Christianity in Talmud and Midrash,* London 1903.

Higger, M.—*Intention in Talmudic Law,* New York 1927.

Higger, M.—"On the Cremation of the Dead" (Hebrew), in his *Halakot v'Agadot,* New York 1933.

Hirsch, S. R.—*Gesammelte Schriften,* Frankfort o. M. 1902-1912.

Horowitz, H. M.—"Maaseh m'de R. Eliezer b. Hyrcanus," in *Bet Eked ha-Agadoth,* I 1881, pp,. 1-16.

Jawitz, Z. W.—*Sefer Toldot Yisrael,* Berlin, Cracow and Vilna 1905-1910.

Jhering, R.—*The Law as a Means to an End* (English by I. Husik), Boston 1913.

Joel, M.—*Blicke in die Religionsgeschichte zu Anfang des zweiten christlichen Jahrhunderts,* Breslau 1880-1883.

Jellinek, A.—*Bet ha-Midrash,* Leipzig and Vienna 1841-1878.

Juster, J.—*Les Juifs dans l'empire romain,* 2 vols., Paris 1914.

Kadushin, M.—*The Theology of the Seder Eliahu,* New York 1932. New York 1927.

Klausner, J.—*Historia Yisraelit,* Jerusalem 1924-25.

Klausner, J.—*Jesus of Nazareth* (from the Hebrew by Danby),

Klein, S.—"La מותבא רבא de Lydda," *REJ,* IX 1910, p. 107ff.

Kohler, K.—*Origin of the Synagogue and the Church,* New York 1929.

Kohut, A.—*Ueber die juedishce Angelologie und Daemonologie in ihrer Abhaengigkeit von Parsismus,* Leipzig 1866.

Kohut, A.—*Aruk ha-Shalem,* Vienna 1926.

Krauss, S.—*Griechische und lateinische Lehnwoerter im Talmud, Midrash und Targum,* Berlin 1898-9

Krauss, S.—"La defense d'elever du menu betail en Palestine et questionnes connexes," *REJ,* LIII 1907, pp. 14-56.

Krauss, S.—*Talmudische Archaeologie,* Leipzig 1910-12.

Krauss, S.—"Die Versammlungstaetten der Talmudgelehrten," *Festschrift Israel Lewy,* pp. 17-35.

Krauss, S.—*Monumenta Talmudica,* V, Vienna and Leipzig 1914.

Krauss, S.—*Kadmoniot ha-Talmud,* Odessa 1914.

Krauss, S.—"Conception of Wind, Rain and Dew in the Talmud" (Hebrew), *ha-Sofeh l'Hokmat Yisrael,* X 1926, pp. 306-317.

Lonsano, M. Di.—*Shte Yadot,* Venice 1618.

Lerner, M.—"Die achtzehn Bestimmungen," *MWJ,* IX 1882, pp. 113-144; 1883, pp. 121-156.

Levi, Is.—"The Attitude of the Talmud and Midrash toward Proselytism" (Hebrew), *ha-Goren,* IX 1923, pp. 5-30.

Levy, J.—*Neuhebraeisches und chaldaeisches Woerterbuch ueber die Talmudim und Midrashim,* Leipzig 1876-89.

Lichtenstein, H.—"Die Fastenrolle," *HUCA,* VIII-IX 1931-1932, pp. 251-353.

Mahler, E.—*Handbuch der juedischen Chronologie,* Leipzig 1916.

Maimonides, M.—*Commentary on the Mishnah,* included in Babylonian Talmud.

Maimonides, H.—*Mishneh Torah,* ed. Horeb, 1926.

Malter, H.—Life and Works of Saadia Gaon, Philadelphia 1921.

Mann, J.—"Changes in the Divine Religious Service of the Synagogue due to Persecutions," *HUCA,* IV 1927, pp. 241-311.

Marmorstein, A.—*The Old Rabbinic Doctrine of God,* London 1927.

Montgomery, J. A.—"The 'Place' as an Appellation of Deity," *JBL,* XXIV 1905, pp. 17-27.

Montgomery, J. A.—*The Samaritans,* Philadelphia 1907.

Moore, G. F.—"Intermediaries in Jewish Theology," *HTR,* XV 1922, pp. 41-85.

Moore, G. F.—"Fate and Free Will in the Jewish Philosophies according to Josephus," *HTR,* XXII 1929, pp. 371-389.

Moore, G. F.—*Judaism in the First Centuries of the Christian Era,* Cambridge 1927-1930.

Neubauer, A. *La Geographie du Talmud,* Paris 1868.

Pound, R.—"Mechanical Jurisprudence," *Columbia Law Review, VIII* 1908, pp. 605-23.

Pound, R.—"Administrative Application of Legal Standards," *Reports* American Bar Association, 1919.

Pound, R.—*An Introduction to the Philosophy of Law*, New Haven 1922.

Rabinowitz, S. P.—Notes to Graetz, *Dibre Yeme Yisrael*, Warʻw 1890-99.

Rabinowitz, R. N.—*Dikduke Soferim*, Munich 1868-97.

Rappaport, S. J.—*Erek Millin*, Prague 1852.

Rosenthal, F.—"Ueber Isah," *MGWJ*, XIII 1881, pp. 38-48, 113-140, 207-217.

Rosenthal, F.—*Vier apokryphische Buecher*, Leipzig 1885.

Scheurer, E.—*Geschichte des juedischen Volkes*, 3 vols., 4th ed., Leipzig 1901-1911.

Siegfried, K.—*Philo von Alexandria*, Jena 1875.

Smith, H. P.—*The Religion of Israel*, New York 1928.

Smith, W. R.—*The Prophets of Israel*, London 1919.

Steinschneider, M.—*Catalogus Librorum Hebraeorum in Bibliotheca Bodleiana*, Berlin 1933.

Strathman, H.—*Geschichte der fruechristlichen Askese*, I, Leipzig 1914.

Tarn, W.—*Hellenistic Civilization*, London 1927.

Thomsen, P.—*Loca Sancta*, Halle 1907.

Toetterman, C. A.—*R. Eliezer b. Hyrcanus* (Latin), Leipzig 1877.

Vogelstein, H., and Rieger, P.—*Geschichte der Juden in Rom*, I, Berlin 1896.

Wallon, H.—*Histoire de l'esclavage dans l'antiquite*, Paris 1877.

Weil, J.—"Gen agathen Kai pollen", *REJ*, LXXXII 1926, pp. 129-131.

Weiss, I. H.—*Dor Dor v'Dorshav*, N. Y. and Berlin 1924.

Wohlgemuth, J.—"Zur Charakteristik des Suendenbewustseins im Talmudischen Judentum," *Jeshurun*, XI 1924, pp. 97-112.

Wellhausen, J.—*Die Pharisaer und die Sadducaer*, Hanover 1924.

Yisraeli, I.—*Sefer Yesod Olam*, Berlin 1777.

Zeitlin, S.—"Les 'Dix-huit Mesures'," *REJ*, LXVIII 1914, pp. 22-36.

Zeitlin, S.—"Studies in Tannaitic Jurisprudence," *Journal of Jewish Lore and Philosophy*, I 1919, pp. 297-311.

Zeitlin, S.—*Megillat Taanit as a Source for Jewish Chronology and History in the Hellenistic and Roman Periods*, Philadelphia 1922.

Zeitlin, S.—"The Am ha-Ares," *JQR*, N. S., XXIII 1932, pp. 45-63.

Zeitlin, S.—*The History of the Second Jewish Commonwealth*, Philadelphia 1933.

Zeitlin, S.—"Jesus in the Early Tannaitic Literature," *Abhandlungen zur Erinnerung an H. P. Chajes*, pp. 295-308.

Lang; 5, Leipzig I

Zeller, E.—*Die Philosophie der Griechen*, ed. 5, Leipzig I, 1892; ed.
  3, II, 1879.
Zuckermandl, M. S.—*Gesammelte Aufsaetze*, Frankfort o. M. 1912.
Zunz, L.—*Gottesdienstliche Vortraege*, Berlin 1832.
Zunz, L.—*Zur Geschichte und Literatur*, Berlin 1845.
Zunz, L.—*Die synagogale Poesie des Mitelalters*, Berlin 1855.
Zunz, L.—*Literaturgeschichte der synagogalen Poesie*, Berlin 1865-67.

INDEX OF NAMES

THE JEWISH PEOPLE

HISTORY • RELIGION • LITERATURE

AN ARNO PRESS COLLECTION

Agus, Jacob B. **The Evolution of Jewish Thought:** From Biblical Times to the Opening of the Modern Era. 1959

Ber of Bolechow. **The Memoirs of Ber of Bolechow (1723-1805).** Translated from the Original Hebrew MS. with an Introduction, Notes and a Map by M[ark] Vishnitzer. 1922

Berachya. **The Ethical Treatises of Berachya, Son of Rabbi Natronai Ha-Nakdan:** Being the Compendium and the Masref. Now edited for the First Time from MSS. at Parma and Munich with an English Translation, Introduction, Notes, etc. by Hermann Gollancz. 1902

Bloch, Joseph S. **My Reminiscences.** 1923

Bokser, Ben Zion, **Pharisaic Judaism in Transition:** R. Eliezer the Great and Jewish Reconstruction After the War with Rome. 1935

Dalman, Gustaf. **Jesus Christ in the Talmud, Midrash, Zohar, and the Liturgy of the Synagogue.** Together with an Introductory Essay by Heinrich Laible. Translated and Edited by A. W. Streane. 1893

Daube, David. **The New Testament and Rabbinic Judaism.** 1956

Davies, W. D. **Christian Origins and Judaism.** 1962

Engelman, Uriah Zevi. **The Rise of the Jew in the Western World:** A Social and Economic History of the Jewish People of Europe. Foreword by Niles Carpenter. 1944

Epstein, Louis M. **The Jewish Marriage Contract:** A Study in the Status of the Woman in Jewish Law. 1927

Facets of Medieval Judaism. 1973. New Introduction by Seymour Siegel

The Foundations of Jewish Life: Three Studies. 1973

Franck, Adolph. **The Kabbalah, or, The Religious Philosophy of the Hebrews.** Revised and Enlarged Translation [from the French] by Dr. I. Sossnitz. 1926

Goldman, Solomon. **The Jew and The Universe.** 1936

Gordon, A. D. **Selected Essays.** Translated by Frances Burnce from the Hebrew Edition by N. Teradyon and A. Shohat, with a Biographical Sketch by E. Silberschlag. 1938

Ha-Am, Achad (Asher Ginzberg). **Ten Essays on Zionism and Judaism.** Translated from the Hebrew by Leon Simon. 1922. New Introduction by Louis Jacobs

Halevi, Jehudah. **Selected Poems of Jehudah Halevi.** Translated into English by Nina Salaman, Chiefly from the Critical Text Edited by Heinrich Brody. 1924

Heine, Heinrich. **Heinrich Heine's Memoir:** From His Works, Letters, and Conversations. Edited by Gustav Karpeles; English Translation by Gilbert Cannan. 1910. Two volumes in one

Heine, Heinrich. **The Prose Writings of Heinrich Heine.**
Edited, with an Introduction, by Havelock Ellis. 1887

Hirsch, Emil G[ustav]. **My Religion.** Compilation and
Biographical Introduction by Gerson B. Levi. **Including
The Crucifixion Viewed from a Jewish Standpoint:** A Lecture
Delivered by Invitation Before the "Chicago Institute for
Morals, Religion and Letters." 1925/1908

Hirsch, W. **Rabbinic Psychology:** Beliefs about the Soul
in Rabbinic Literature of the Talmudic Period. 1947

Historical Views of Judaism: Four Selections. 1973

Ibn Gabirol, Solomon. **Selected Religious Poems of Solomon Ibn
Gabirol.** Translated into English Verse by Israel Zangwill
from a Critical Text Edited by Israel Davidson. 1923

Jacobs, Joseph. **Jesus as Others Saw Him:** A Retrospect
A. D. 54. Preface by Israel Abrahams; Introductory Essay by
Harry A. Wolfson. 1925

Judaism and Christianity: Selected Accounts, 1892-1962.
1973. New Preface and Introduction by Jacob B. Agus

Kohler, Kaufmann. **The Origins of the Synagogue and
The Church.** Edited, with a Biographical Essay by H. G. Enelow.
1929

Maimonides Octocentennial Series, Numbers I-IV. 1935

Mann, Jacob. **The Responsa of the Babylonian Geonim as a
Source of Jewish History.** 1917-1921

Maritain, Jacques. **A Christian Looks at the Jewish Question.** 1939

Marx, Alexander. **Essays in Jewish Biography.** 1947

Mendelssohn, Moses. **Phaedon; or, The Death of Socrates.**
Translated from the German [by Charles Cullen]. 1789

Modern Jewish Thought: Selected Issues, 1889-1966. 1973.
New Introduction by Louis Jacobs

Montefiore, C[laude] G. **Judaism and St. Paul:** Two Essays. 1914

Montefiore, C[laude] G. **Some Elements of the Religious
Teaching of Jesus According to the Synoptic Gospels.** Being
the Jowett Lectures for 1910. 1910

Radin, Max. **The Jews Amongs the Greeks and Romans.** 1915

Ruppin, Arthur. **The Jews in the Modern World.** With an
Introduction by L. B. Namier. 1934

Smith, Henry Preserved. **The Bible and Islam;** or, The Influence
of the Old and New Testaments on the Religion of Mohammed.
Being the Ely Lectures for 1897. 1897

Stern, Nathan. **The Jewish Historico-Critical School of the
Nineteenth Century.** 1901

Walker, Thomas [T.] **Jewish Views of Jesus:** An Introduction
and an Appreciation. 1931. New Introduction by Seymour Siegel

Walter, H. **Moses Mendelssohn:** Critic and Philosopher. 1930

Wiener, Leo. **The History of Yiddish Literature in the
Nineteenth Century.** 1899

Wise, Isaac M. **Reminiscences.** Translated from the German and
Edited, with an Introduction by David Philipson. 1901